# WHAT IS THE OLD TESTAMENT?

BOOKS BY THE SAME AUTHOR:

*The Christian Experience*

*The Sacramental Society*

*The Bible Doctrine of Society*

*The Bible Doctrine of Wealth and Work*

*The Bible Doctrine of Womanhood*

# WHAT IS THE OLD TESTAMENT?

*AN INTRODUCTORY STUDY*

*By*

**C. RYDER SMITH, B.A., D.D.**

*PRINCIPAL OF RICHMOND COLLEGE, SURREY*

LONDON
THE EPWORTH PRESS
EDGAR C. BARTON

*First edition* - 1931
*Second edition* - 1933
*Third edition* - 1936

MADE AND PRINTED BY
THE DEVONSHIRE PRESS, HIGHER FLEET STREET, TORQUAY,
ENGLAND.

# TABLE OF CONTENTS

# FOREWORD

To-day there are so many branches of knowledge, and the amount of study needed to master any one of them is so great, that no one can hope to be an expert in more than a few. For his knowledge of other subjects he must rely upon the findings of other men. In consequence, to-day the number of introductory manuals is legion. Their purpose is to pass on the results of expert study to people who are not themselves experts in the subject treated.

There is room for books of this kind about the Old Testament. A number have been written, but none perhaps that follows quite the same method as this one.

It was undertaken at the request of the Connexional Local Preachers' Committee of the Wesleyan Methodist Church, and written particularly for the use of lay preachers, but it is hoped that it will meet the needs of many other lovers of the Bible.

In such a book it is neither possible nor desirable for the writer to quote authorities for every statement. To adapt a phrase of Charles Reade's, I have filled my bucket from many taps, and I am unable to say which particular drops in it have come from any particular tap. I have, however, ventured sometimes to refer to one or other of my earlier books when I express an opinion of my own that seems to need further elucidation.

It goes without saying that the experts are not always agreed, but I have tried to summarize the findings of the great majority. When, therefore, I use such a phrase as 'the experts,' I mean this majority.

A few experts take what is called the Fundamentalist or

Traditionalist position ; this book does not represent their distinctive convictions. Yet the reader will perceive that it does not seem to me that the differences between their position on the one hand and that of the ' Higher Critics ' on the other, involve anything that is vital to Christianity. It is not unlikely that the Christian reader, to whom the subject is quite new, will find considerable difficulty in admitting this claim as he reads some of the earlier chapters of the book. I hope, however, that by the time he reaches the end he will see that his fears are groundless.

While the responsibility for what I have written is wholly my own, I desire very heartily to thank both my wife and my friends and colleagues, the Revs. Christopher R. North, M.A., and A. Marcus Ward, B.A., for reading the proofs and making a number of valuable suggestions. I have also had the advantage of consulting with Dr. Maldwyn Hughes. Mr. Ward has been good enough to draw up the index.

C. R. S.

June, 1931.

# PREPARATORY CHAPTERS

## CHAPTER I

# THE POINT OF VIEW

IN one of his letters Paul uses the phrase 'a purpose of God according to election.'[1] He seems to use it of nations as well as of individuals. Among the races to whom it clearly applies, Greece and Israel are foremost.

It is through Greece that men have learnt what beauty is. There is evidence in every picture gallery, for at its entrance there are copies of Greek statues—of famous figures of Venus, Apollo, Laocoon and so on. All books on the history of aesthetics give pre-eminence to Greece.

It is through Israel that men have learnt what religion is. The account of this is in the Bible. 'Salvation is of the Jews.' The New Testament, like the Old, could not, 'speaking humanly,' have arisen anywhere except among the Jews. Jesus is 'the Israelite indeed.' He is more than this, but He is this.

As the line of the evolution of true art lay through Greece, so the line of the evolution of true religion lay through Israel. This was not accident, but the will of God. It is worth while to compare Greece and Israel in more detail.

Thousands of years before Christ, the men of two races, the Phœnician and the Greek, sailed the Mediterranean Sea. The immediate purpose of both was trade.[2] But there was something else that the one race gleaned from the sea, and the other left ungarnered. This was Beauty. Before them both 'the rosy-fingered dawn' sprang, on

[1] Rom. ix. 11.

[2] Here I have used some sentences from an article printed in *The Methodist Recorder* on January 22, 1925.

multitudinous mornings, from the rim of the wave; both gazed on the same dappled sea; both watched the white wake of the lengthening foam. To both the same revelation —note the word—of beauty was given. But the one race used its eyes, and the other race, on the whole, shut its eyes. To vary the phrase, the one responded to the appeal of beauty century by century, and the other did not so respond. And the race that used its eyes came to see better than the one that neglected its opportunity. After a great while, there was a Greek poet called Homer, of whom I have quoted a phrase, a Greek dramatist called Aeschylus, and a Greek sculptor called Pheidias; but where are the immortal artists of the Phœnicians? There are none. After the millenniums all the world still goes to school to Greece to learn what beauty is.

Did Greece learn beauty by revelation or by discovery? By both, for revelation and discovery are just the Godward and manward sides of the same process. Our Lord has the saying, 'He that hath ears to hear, let him hear.' In this story the race that had eyes to see, saw more and more and more.

Again, in the same far-away days, there were two races,[1] Israel and Edom, that dwelt in the hills about the deep cleft that we call the 'Jordan Valley,' but which of old time was called the Arabah. The two began at much the same level. Does not the Old Testament say that their fathers were twins? In all the ways that gather under the modern doctrine of immanence—through nature, and conscience, and history, and what later times called 'miracle'—God began to speak to both, as He does to the other races of the world. The one race did not listen much, and, when it did, listened very inattentively; and after a while, it had ears but it heard not; it had conscience, but it did not understand. The other race was slow too, but not so slow; reluctant, but not altogether unwilling. It listened, and,

[1] I take two for simplicity's sake, though I should have to vary the metaphor somewhat if I took other instances.

and in due time it needed to be discarded, as our Lord Himself said.[1]

Or, to take an example of the immature, the command 'Thou shalt not kill,' while true, is quite incomplete. It is not complete until Someone said 'Thou shalt not hate.' This is what Jesus in effect said when he 'fulfilled' or 'completed' the 'Law and the Prophets'—that is, the Old Testament.[2]

An important consequence follows—the art of Greece is not to be judged by any of its products, but by its final products, and similarly with Hebrew religion. By 'final' here we do not necessarily mean latest in time, but most nearly perfect. The Venus of Milo is normative—that is, it sets the standard—for all later art, and not the ugly image of Artemis at Ephesus that 'fell down from Jupiter.' It is not because of its origin, or its incomplete or mistaken products, that Greece is hailed by all the world as the teacher of art, but because of its consummate work—the Venus of Milo or the Parthenon of Athens.

Similarly, the Old Testament is not to be judged by the polygamy of Abraham or the ferocity of Samson, but by the teaching of the fifty-third chapter of Isaiah. Or, to take the ultimate instance, the Bible is not to be judged as the Book of Religion by any other test than the perfection of Jesus. It is the final product, not the process, that makes art or religion, or anything else, normative for mankind.

Another point may be mentioned. In Greece, of course, art did not emerge and develop *in vacuo*. It was part and parcel of the national life. Therefore, it arose and developed and reached its consummation in a given environment of history, and commerce, and government and religion; and, to understand it thoroughly, all these things, and others too, need to be studied. The Parthenon, for instance, was a temple; that is, it was meant to serve

[1] John iv. 21 ff.
[2] Matt. v. 21 ff.

the purposes of a given religion, and it cannot be fully understood except when so considered. Yet, in practice, it is not difficult to take Greek art by itself and present it as normative for later art, without presenting its accompaniments in Greek life as normative too.

Similarly, Hebrew religion arose and developed and reached its Christian zenith, in a given environment of history and government and so on; and, fully to understand it, these things must be known. Yet, in practice, it is not difficult to isolate Biblical religion, and to represent this as ultimately normative for the religion of mankind, without thereby presenting the accompanying elements in the national life of the Hebrew race as normative too.

This is easier because all the great men of Israel were great in religion; and all the writers of the books of the Bible were men whose primary interest and passion was religious. David was a soldier of merit, but no one would include him in a list of the twelve greatest soldiers of the world. Solomon was a patron of the arts, but no one would pretend that his masterpiece, the Temple of Jerusalem, considered merely as an example of architecture, was as wonderful as the Great Pyramid or the Taj Mahal or St. Peter's at Rome. The Psalms are poetry—some of them poetry of rare value—but no one would say that any one of them, examined merely as literature, is the equal of the Iliad or King Lear.

Again, there is history in the Bible, but the chief interest of its historians is not history but religion; there is law, but, for the lawgivers of Israel, law is just a part of religion; there is song, but it is religion that is sung. It seems to me that this religious passion dominates even those parts of the Bible that seem to some to be exceptions—such books as Proverbs, Esther and the Song of Songs—and I shall illustrate this later.

If the Bible be taken as a whole, all men agree that its one masterful claim upon the attention of men is because it is a book of religion. It is not difficult, in practice, to consider and study this separately, even though, if the study is to be anything like complete, something must be known of other things in Israel besides its religion.

The word 'evolution' has sometimes been used above as a synonym for 'development.' Perhaps a *caveat* ought to be added about it. When we speak of evolution in such a realm as biology, some still think of a regular, uninterrupted, inevitable growth. I understand that even in biology this concept is giving way, and it is claimed that the development is neither regular nor uninterrupted. However this may be, when the word is used of any kind of human development—development in government, or science, or art, or religion—none of the adjectives used above is in place. In the realm of man evolution may not be regular and uninterrupted, for sometimes it proceeds by strides and sometimes it hardly proceeds at all. It is not inevitable, for the element of human freedom enters; and a race, like an individual, may refuse progress, as indeed has already been illustrated in the cases of Phœnicia and Edom.

In human development much depends upon the emergence of great men. Who can say when, or whence, they will come? It is easy to show that Shakespeare would not have been just the same Shakespeare if he had not been born in Elizabethan England. But who can show that his birth was inevitable then? Similarly, Isaiah would not have been the same Isaiah if he had not been born in Israel in the Assyrian period. But who can prove that there must needs have been such an one as Isaiah born there and then?

The history of any human achievement is largely the history of the creativeness of great men, and great men are phenomena of which there is no science. This is preeminently true of the religion of Israel. Moses, Elijah, Amos, Isaiah and Jeremiah, were its makers, and not the multitude of ordinary Hebrews who learnt from them. Of course this is true in quite a unique way of Jesus.

And now we must say, what has already been hinted once

or twice, that there is a point where the comparison between Greek art and Hebrew religion fails. No one thinks that Homer or Pheidias was God Incarnate. Multitudes believe this of Jesus. This means that for them Christianity is the final religion in a way in which Greek art is not final. Some may say that at some future day there may be an art that will surpass and supersede that of the Greeks; and that Greek art, therefore, is only the best so far, normative or authoritative so far. But for those who believe that Jesus was God 'made manifest in the flesh,' the religion that He taught must be for ever normative—must be perfect in the absolute sense of that word. For what can supersede God?

It follows too, as has already been pointed out, that, for Christians, religion, and not art, or science or anything else, is the fundamental thing in life. To use an uncommon word, it follows that religion is architectonic for the life of men. If once religion is right, all else—art, and science, and commerce and so on—will 'come right' too. For when God became man, it was not to be a sculptor, or a king, or a man of science, but to be a man of religion. Much else follows on this, but it would be out of place to pursue it here. In the ultimate sense of the word, Jesus is unique, for He alone is God.

Someone may ask, however, 'Does it not follow that there is no need of the Old Testament?' Or, at least, 'What place has it in the Book of Religion? Can we not do without it?' There are several answers. One is that it is just as possible, and just as impossible, to take Jesus without the Old Testament, as it is possible to take a rose without the plant on which it grew or the soil from which it sprang. Another is that in the teaching of Jesus the Old Testament is constantly taken for granted, and that it is therefore impossible fully to understand what He means, without the Old Testament. A third is that Jesus appears in a given historical context, so to speak, and that it is impossible properly to understand Him without that context.

Perhaps all these reasons really resolve into one. Between the Old Testament and the New there is an organic connexion. The Bible is, in the last resort, not two books but one. Some small attempt is made to show this below. 'Think not,' said our Lord, 'that I came to destroy the Old Testament; I came not to destroy but to complete.' There is abundant evidence that He brooded over the Old Testament; what was good for Him, is not unlikely to be good for other men.

It is possible now, perhaps, to put the account of the Bible given here into a kind of definition. The Bible is the record of the gradual revelation or discovery of the final religion.

## Chapter II

# THE GEOGRAPHY OF PALESTINE

If any one were to 'go to Jericho,' he would be standing nearly thirteen hundred feet *below* the level of the sea. If he were to look north, he would look up the deepest valley in the world. Away above it he would see the heights of Lebanon clad in snow. The bottom of the long valley is a narrow sloping strip. This is called in the Hebrew tongue the 'Arabah,' and translated in the English versions 'The plain,' a very misleading word. Down the middle of the valley the Jordan twists and rushes in a deep bed. Behind the traveller there lie the waters of doom called the Dead Sea. In the whole Bible no one ever crosses it.

Hidden away on the west lies the coast of Syria, at an average distance of some seventy miles. If the traveller passes west from Jericho, he begins to climb a limestone range of hills. When he has climbed about as high as Snowdon, he comes to Jerusalem. Roughly, a third of his climb will have been below sea-level and two-thirds above it. The range of limestone hills now lies north and south of him. In the north it drops at length into the Kishon Valley, to rise again in the less regular hills of Galilee. South of him the hills broaden and grow more and more barren, until they sink, through the Negeb—'the south,' in the English versions—into the sheer desert. There is a plain between the broad ridge and the Mediterranean, except where a spur of the hills cuts across it in Carmel.[1]

[1] In the southern part of this plain a range of foot-hills, called in Hebrew the 'Shephelah' (English 'the lowland') runs parallel to the main 'hill country.'

This 'hill country,' and especially the longer and larger part of it south of the Kishon Valley, was the stronghold of Israel.

The northern hills of Galilee are very important for a few years of New Testament history, and there was a part of 'the Land' east of Jordan; but the unbroken range between Kishon and the Negeb is the arena of almost all the chief events of Hebrew history during more than a thousand years. So the Hebrew was a man of the hills. He hated the strange and unknown horror of the sea. He knew something of the deserts at his doors. But on the hills he was at home.

At all periods the great majority of the folk lived by the land. They were chiefly peasant farmers. Their cities were few, though one of them, Jerusalem, was of pivotal importance during much of their story. Competent writers guess that in the heyday of Solomon's glory there may have been a million Hebrews. Israel was a small people inhabiting a small land. Palestine west of Jordan is only about the size of Wales. A friend of mine and his wife walked at a leisurely pace from Jerusalem to Nazareth, and it took them three days.

Almost all the principal places in Hebrew history—Hebron, Bethlehem, Jerusalem, Bethel, Shechem, Samaria, Shiloh—lie on the range of hills whose limits are the Arabah, the Kishon Valley, the Mediterranean and the Negeb. The two great tribes of Old Testament times, Judah and Ephraim, each of which gave its name to a kingdom, lay on this range, the one on its southern, and the other on its northern part. Little Benjamin was tucked in between them, but there were no natural barriers.

Apart from the Jordan, there was no river, for the Kishon is only a stream, and the other 'rivers' marked on maps are dry water-courses as often as not. Men of the plain, of the sea, of the desert, have all played great parts in history; but the Israelites, like the Welsh, the Swiss and the Afghans, were men of the hills. And most of them lived in hill-villages, each dependent in the main on the produce of its own bit of tilled land.

If any one would understand the history of Israel, he will do well first to pore for an hour over a map, and over the right kind of map—a map that does not trouble much with tribal boundaries, but shows the physical features, and most of all, the 'hill country.' Some examples of the way in which the geography of Palestine illuminates its history, will be given below.

Again and again in the story of Israel it is necessary to remember her relation to other nations, and this means that a larger map must be studied. It must be big enough to show the Nile and the twin rivers, Tigris and Euphrates. For Egypt and Mesopotamia were the two wealthiest, strongest, most thickly populated and most powerful realms of the Bible world through many of its centuries.

The best beginning is to pick out the Nile and the twin rivers of 'Mespot' and ask how people would pass from one to the other. The direct route, 'as the crow flies,' was desert, and so was rarely taken. *The* way was round by what is now called 'the fertile crescent.' A glance at the map will show that if any one started from the Persian Gulf and wanted to reach Egypt, he would travel at first north-west, up the Tigris-Euphrates plain; then, he would bear west for a little towards the Mediterranean; soon, however, he would bend south, parallel to the Lebanon ridge, and make for Damascus; thence he would reach Jordan somewhere near the Sea of Galilee, and pass along Esdraelon[1] to the level strip by the sea; when he had threaded this, a bit of desert would bring him to the Nile.

Egypt and Mesopotamia were two centres of empire, civilization and wealth. The inevitable way from one to the other, whether for armies, traders or any others, lay across and past Palestine. But this world path did not

[1] That is, the Kishon Valley.

touch 'the hill country' at all. So it appears that Israel was both isolated and not isolated. She was at once the bridge of the world and secluded from it. Here is the key to much in her history. There are many illustrations of this given below.

## CHAPTER III

# THE HISTORY OF ISRAEL[1]

OUR chief subject is the religion of Israel, but in order to understand this it is necessary to make a rapid survey of Hebrew history.

### *A. The Conquest of Canaan*

Arabia is the motherland of the Semitic peoples. It stretches from Aden to Damascus, and is as large as India. Almost all of it is desert. From time to time during the third and second millenniums before the Christian Era floods of Semitic peoples poured from Arabia into different parts of the fertile crescent. They had been nomads, but now they settled; that is, they became agricultural in their habits. Several such waves of Semitic invaders streamed, one after another, into Palestine. Among them there came the Phœnician people, and the Amorite and the Canaanite.[2] The last of these invaders were the Israelites. They poured into Palestine somewhere between 1600 and 1200 B.C., conquered and settled.

At present we know next to nothing about the origins of these people except what their own records tell us.[3] These

[1] For Table of Dates, see pp. 236 ff.

[2] Not the Hittites, who had an empire in the north about B.C. 1250, and who may not have been Semitic.

[3] In the tablets found at a place in Egypt called Tel-el-Amarna, there are records which show that about 1350 B.C. a people called 'Habiri' were threatening Palestine from the East; they *may* have been Hebrews. Again, in an inscription of a Pharaoh called Mernephthah, about 1230 B.C. we find a few words, 'Israel is spoiled; its seed is not.'

records have Abraham and Moses for their heroes. They connect the Semitic tribe, or set of tribes, called the Hebrews, with both the great centres of civilization named in the last chapter. Abraham comes from Babylonia; Moses delivers Israel from servitude in Egypt. But, while they are connected in these ways with the old, old areas of civilization, they refuse to be absorbed in either. Abraham leaves Babylon, and Moses forsakes Egypt. Already the Israelites are a distinct race of people.

The Hebrew records have two accounts of their conquest of Palestine.[1] It is not very easy to piece the two together. One is sometimes called the 'wholesale account' and the other the 'piece-meal.' In the Book of Joshua twelve tribes act together in a common and swift conquest; in the first chapter of the Book of Judges we see three groups of tribes each carrying on its own campaign in its own part of the country, with varying and slow success. Elsewhere we learn that a fourth group had already received its 'inheritance' on the east of Jordan.

The best way to understand the situation of Israel at the time of the Conquest, is not to think of her as divided into twelve tribes, but as falling into four groups of tribes, three being west of the Jordan and one east. Of the western groups one, whose chief tribe was Judah, settled in the southern part of the main mass of the 'hill country'; another, whose chief tribe was Ephraim, settled in the northern part of the same range—that is, its villages lay right in the middle of Palestine; the third group settled further north, beyond Esdraelon, in the 'hill country' that was later called Galilee. The fourth group occupied a large area east of Jordan, whose southern border was a river called the Arnon that runs into the Dead Sea, but whose northern and eastern boundaries are somewhat indeterminate.

Until the time of Saul it is best to think of the Hebrews as a rather loose confederacy of tribes, which fell geographic-

[1] In Joshua Ch. i.-xii. and Judges Ch. i. respectively.

ally into these four groups, the connexion of the southern or 'Judah' group with the rest being loosest of all. Between the times of Joshua and Saul the four groups rarely all acted together; yet they recognized a kind of common loyalty, for they worshipped the same God. They had a traditional alliance with one of the nomadic tribes, the Kenites, who also worshipped Jehovah.[1] To-day political unity is the most commonly accepted mark and means of a people's common life, but this has not always been so. Among many peoples, especially in early times, religious unity, the worship of the same god, was the chief tie that bound peoples together. From first to last this was the great element in the unity of Israel.

In the 'wholesale account' of the Conquest, we find that Joshua wins first a great victory right in the middle of the 'hill country,' and then turns, first south and then north, to complete his work. He belonged to the tribe of Ephraim, and he may really have been the leader of the group of tribes whose greatest name was 'Ephraim.' In this way the two accounts of the Conquest might be more or less reconciled. At any rate the story of his great victory in the Battle of Beth-horon bears many marks of historicity. It is the culminating point of a campaign that began with the capture of Jericho.[2] It is worth while tracing it a little in detail.

[1] Though the vowels of the name 'Jehovah' are certainly wrong, this form of the word will be used in this book as being current English for the 'proper name' of the God of Israel. Originally, in Hebrew manuscripts, consonants only were written, the vowels of each word being supplied in reading aloud, from daily use. The consonants of the Divine name were JHVH. There came a time, however, when it was never pronounced, through reverence; another term was used instead. In the unbroken silence of centuries, the vowels that went with JHVH were forgotten. It was only four hundred years ago that the vowels of the form 'Jehovah' were supplied. They were borrowed from the Hebrew word that was used instead of JHVH in reading. Wherever the Revised Version prints 'LORD' or 'GOD' in capitals, the Hebrew word is JHVH.

[2] Joshua v. 10—x. 27.

The Israelites had crossed the Jordan at a time when the 'inhabitants of the land' would rely upon the flooded river to foil their quick advance. The Hebrews captured Jericho, the only place of strength in the deep trench of the Jordan. They made their headquarters at Gilgal, where they set the Ark. This place lies close to the river, and was for a long time one of the chief shrines of Israel.

The 'hill country' lay right before the invaders, and their next task was to attack an enemy that lay three thousand feet above them. At the end of one of the defiles that led into the 'hill country' there was a 'city' called Ai. After a first repulse, they captured this place by stratagem. A city near it, called Gibeon, now made haste to come to terms.

Meanwhile, however, the other 'kings' of the Amorites in the 'hill country' had taken alarm, and a number of them banded themselves together to punish Gibeon, and, no doubt, to thrust Israel back into the Arabah. This put the Hebrews into imminent peril. For, so far, to set off the disadvantage that they had to fight uphill in the literal sense of the word, they had had the advantage that their foes were divided. The whole story, both in Joshua and Judges, represents the Canaanites[1] as divided into many little states, each consisting of a single settlement or 'city' with the land that lay around it. The foes of Israel, therefore, were divided among themselves, and their kinglets were each other's rivals. Israel was likely to prevail if it could take them one by one. If any number of them combined, it would be hard indeed to climb the three thousand feet of steep slope and beat them.

The moment of danger came with the alliance of the kings

[1] This name is here used for all the old inhabitants. It may also be used for one of the sets of tribes that had settled in Palestine. Of the rest the most important are the Amorites and the Jebusites. The last will be named later. There is some evidence that, when Israel burst into the land, the Amorite settlements lay chiefly on the hills, and the Canaanites in the lower lying lands, particularly in Esdraelon.

against Gibeon, and Joshua's generalship was on its trial. With the help of Jehovah it proved equal to the occasion. Joshua made a forced and secret march by night up the slope; when his men reached the tableland, they found a ridge to lurk behind; they attacked suddenly, but for a while the day seems to have been doubtful; then a storm of thunder and hail swept up behind them, the hail beating into the faces of the foe. As a Hebrew would put it—Jehovah came to their help, 'riding upon the wings of the wind.' I suppose that we should say, in our tamer speech, that, in the light of the sequel of history, there was Providence in the storm.[1]

When the Amorites broke, however, the darkness of the storm-cloud helped them in turn for they were fleeing down the west side of the 'hill country,' and Israel needed light to complete the victory. The storm cleared away, and out shone the sun. When the sun began to decline, up rose the full moon in the east. And so the Hebrews were able to make a full end of the foe. The day was decisive, for Joshua was now astride the 'hill country.' This is the one clear story of the process of conquest.

*B. The Exploits of the 'Judges'*

When the Hebrews had won their 'inheritance' in Palestine, their troubles were by no means at an end. Four dangers remained.

There were other Semitic tribes in the east and south-east—Ammon, and Edom, and Moab—which might covet and attack the wealthier land of Palestine. These were fewer in numbers than the Hebrews, but under a strong leader, they might threaten conquest. There are instances in the stories of Ehud and Jephthah. The one slew a Moabite conqueror and the latter repelled an Ammonite invasion. The peril of the Ammonites was not fully met till Saul defeated Nahash.[2]

[1] See Ch. ix.
[2] 1 Sam. xi.

Next, there was constant danger of raids from the desert. This peril reached its height in the days of Gideon. The nomads, chiefly under the name of 'Midianites,' swept annually into Esdraelon in the time of harvest, and carried away the Hebrew crops. Gideon, noticing that their unity was very loose and their vigilance relaxing through the success of years, devised a panic at midnight. His victory was so complete that centuries afterwards 'the day of Midian' was a synonym for a triumphant slaughter.[1] Later on, Saul slaughtered the Amalekites in the south.[2] This danger seems to have passed finally with these victories. No doubt there were often border raids by the nomads, but these were on a small and comparatively harmless scale.

The third risk lay in the Canaanites, for, as the first chapter of Judges especially shows, the incoming Israelites were very far from exterminating them. It was not the will that failed them, but the power. The story of Abimelech gives a typical picture of the consequent mixture of peoples.[3] Probably there were Canaanite villages in most parts, alongside Hebrew villages.[4] But in two areas in particular the Canaanites were strong. One of their tribes, the Jebusites, held Jerusalem and the land around, till the days of David.[5] And in Esdraelon and further north, the Canaanites were specially numerous and strong. The story of Deborah and Barak shows how their political power here was finally broken. But, while they were not again politically a menace, there remained many Canaanites in the land, and ultimately the Hebrews coalesced with them, with very serious religious results, as will appear below.

[1] Isa. ix. 4.
[2] 1 Sam. xv.
[3] Judges ix.
[4] e.g. Judges xix. 11-14.
[5] There are various accounts of the fate of Jerusalem—Josh. xv. 63; Judges i. 8, 21—but it seems clear from 2 Sam. v. 6ff, that it was not finally subdued till David's time. Gezer, a Canaanite 'city' in the same latitude, but lying on a hill well out on the plain towards the sea, held out till the days of Solomon, 1 Kings ix. 15ff.

The fourth danger was from the Philistines. These were not a Semitic, but a European people, and in their struggle with Israel we see an early instance of the conflict of West and East. It seems fairly certain that they came from Crete, or at least that some of them did. It also seems that they had wandered about Asia Minor and that they had something to do with the fall of the Hittite power in that area. Then they turned south, and settled in the southern part of the plain between the 'hill country' and the sea, somewhere about 1220 B.C. They were much more civilized than Israel at this time, and in particular they understood the art of war much better. A hero named Samson first made headway against them, but they were not subdued until the campaigns of Saul and David. We shall return to them later.

It is necessary to notice that in none of the stories of the 'Judges' do all the twelve tribes gather to meet any foe. In every instance but one, action is taken by one of the four groups of tribes named above. The bands that bound Israel together at this time seem to have been traditional rather than effective. The one exception is in the story of Deborah and Barak. Here, to judge by the list given in Deborah's Song[1] two groups gathered to meet the Canaanites—the groups immediately south and north of Esdraelon, where the Canaanite strength lay. Indeed, the more distant tribes of the northern group failed to muster, while none came from beyond Jordan. Most curious of all, the Song makes no mention whatever of the southern group, Judah and Simeon! Various reasons may be given for this, but it seems clear that the national bond was quite loose.

The course of the battle is plain enough. The strength of the Canaanites lay in their 'horses and chariots'—always alien to Hebrew warfare. But, while 'horses and chariots' could carry all before them on level ground, they could not readily manœuvre in the hills. Barak, therefore,

[1] Judges v. 14—18.

drew his men to Mount Tabor, which was a spur of the northern 'hill country' that stood out into Esdraelon; and the Canaanite in the valley and the Hebrew on the mountain, glared at one another, each challenging the other to 'come on.' Barak notices that a storm is blowing up, and he knows that he will win. One can imagine his crying, 'Hallelujah, here comes Jehovah!' For the rain, as it pours, turns every water-course into a flood, and all their floods teem into the Kishon valley, Kishon overflows, and all Esdraelon is a great swamp! And what can horses and chariots do in a swamp? Down pour the nimble Hebrew foot-men among the plunging animals and men, houghing and slaying. And, if Sisera, the Canaanite captain, is to escape at all, it must be on foot.

One very significant fact must be noted in this period, 'there was no king in Israel.' Throughout the stories it is taken for granted that every other people, except sometimes the Philistines, was ruled by a king, but this was not so with Israel. The Israelites had before their eyes several examples of kingship—the empire of the Pharaohs, the tiny principalities of the Canaanites, the tribal kingship of Ammon or Moab—and they didn't like any of them. The reason may be found in the whole story of Abimelech and especially in Jotham's parable, for this lampoons kingship.[1] The eighth chapter of First Samuel is a later account of the evils of Eastern monarchy. It was always despotic, and always meant oppression and often war. Israel had no stomach for such an institution.

Every race hates oppression; but, what is more significant, on the whole Israel preferred peace to war. This is plainly so, even though the events of the period are almost wholly wars! Behind them all there is Israel's peaceful longing to live quietly in her own loved land. And her 'constitution,' so far as she had one, was suited to peace and not to war. She was ruled by 'elders.' In each village these 'sat in the gate' to settle disputes according

[1] Judges ix.

to old custom. They were probably the heads of the families that formed the village. If any dispute arose that was beyond the 'elders'' skill, appeal seems to have been made to some local man of 'worth.'[1] These men had no executive power. They seem to have been mere arbitrators, like the *kadis* of Arabia. They are called 'judges.'

In time of war, indeed, power fell into the hands of single men, as it always must in war, but Barak and Gideon were more like the Dictators of early Republican Rome than kings. While they were not formally appointed, they held sway by popular support for the time of stress, and, when this was over, their sway ended. The normal way of rule was by 'elders.' We may have some of the customs that they administered in the so-called 'Book of the Covenant.'[2] We do not know how long the period of the Judges lasted, but through its length Israel had no king.[3]

## C. *The First Three Kings*

Yet kingship was bound to come. For kingship, even the absolute kingship which is the characteristic political organism of the East, has two great advantages. First, it secures some sort of order within the realm. The 'elders' of the village might be able to ensure order and the keeping of customary law within the village, but what if a man from one village wronged a man from another? Were the 'elders' of the nation, or even of a tribe, to gather to avenge every one of these? And to arrange each time how their decision was to be enforced? It could not be.

We have two instances of the kind of disorder that might

[1] 'Man of worth' is sometimes a better translation than 'man of might,' or 'man of valour.'

[2] Exod. xxi.—xxiii.

[3] For this paragraph, see further in *The Bible Doctrine of Society*, pp. 26ff.

prevail in the two stories that close the Book of Judges.[1] Here the compiler of the book explains the disorders by saying 'there was no king in Israel.' And, when it is remembered that Hebrew and Canaanite villages intermingled, it is easy to see that wrongs done by a man of one village against a man of another, would be frequent.

Now, a king was supreme judge; and he was a judge who could readily enforce his decisions. For with the king there always went the body-guard,[2] and the body-guard was the king's police. When, for instance, David, having heard Nathan's famous story, swore, 'The man that doeth this thing shall surely die,' he could call up Joab, the captain of his guard, and say, 'Take ten men and go to such-and-such a village and put so-and-so to death.' The first advantage of monarchy—especially when the king's sway, unlike that of the Canaanite kinglets, covered the whole land—was some degree of internal order.

There was a second advantage of monarchy, and it was this that finally produced Hebrew kingship. A king was a soldier, and he was a soldier who was ever ready to meet attack. He could make head at once with his guard against any small attack, and against a larger one he could summon all the fighting-men of the folk,—he could gather 'the host.' So, after the king himself, the two most important soldiers were 'the captain of the guard,' and 'the captain of the host.' Occasionally the guard might be set against the host, as when, in the rebellion of Absalom, the 'servants of David,' i.e. his guard, prevailed against the larger but more ill-disciplined 'host' of Israel. But, as a rule, the guard and host would act together, the former making a valuable nucleus for the latter. There is a partial parallel in the Battle of Hastings; there Harold's 'hus-carls' or body-guard stood fighting and dying around their king, when the 'host' of England had already succumbed to William.

[1] Judges xvii—xxi.

[2] We can see Saul in the act of gathering his bodyguard in 1 Sam. xiv. 52.

The danger that produced the Hebrew kingship was the steady and prolonged struggle with the Philistines. Such comparatively transient dangers as the Ammonite attack or even the Midianite forays, might be met by a temporary captain. The Canaanite menace seems to have been finally broken by Barak. But the Philistines actually reduced Israel to servitude.[1] Their power was constant and it was not enough to defeat them once or twice. A campaign of years must be steadily fought, and this demanded the constant authority of a king. Samuel, the last and best of the Judges, saw this, and looked about him for a likely man.

We shall see later that one of the most illuminating passages in the Hebrew records, from the point of view of religion, is the story of the way in which Saul went 'to look for asses, and found a kingdom.'[2] Here we must only note that it was taken for granted that the king must be a 'man of God.' For in this story the 'prophets' of Israel appear for the first time. We need only say here one thing about them—that they were out-and-out devotees of Jehovah. And, when we read that the 'spirit of Jehovah' 'came mightily' upon Saul, and he 'prophesied,' we must deduce that he too was now specially devoted to the service of the God of Israel. He was 'the Lord's anointed,' or, to use the Hebrew word, 'Jehovah's Messiah.' In other words, the cause of Israel and of Israel's God was one. Patriotism and religion are here the same thing.

Perhaps it is not without significance that 'the spirit of Jehovah' came upon Saul at a spot where there was 'a garrison of the Philistines' in the very heart of the territory of Israel.[3] The sight of his people's shame may have stirred him to the warlike service of his people's God.

[1] There are clear traces of this in 1 Samuel—*e.g.* 1 Sam. xiii. 19-23—though the Hebrew writers do not stay over it. In the story of Saul we find the Philistines holding the very heart of the Hebrew 'hill country,' and Saul driven to gather what Hebrew army he could, down in the Arabah at Gilgal—1 Sam. xiii. 6ff.

[2] 1 Sam. ix. and x.

[3] 1 Sam. x. 5.

It will be remembered too that David in turn was devoted to Jehovah, more utterly, indeed, than Saul. These two broke the power of the Philistines. We have not many stories of their campaigns. We know, however, that Saul left the conquest incomplete. The Philistines had drawn their armies, with their 'horses and chariots,' along the coast and on to Esdraelon, where the ascent into the 'hill country' of Israel was most gradual. Here on the slope of Gilboa they defeated Saul. When he saw that the day was lost, he killed himself, for it was the purpose of an Eastern king to win victories, and when he ceased to do so, his day was done. It looked as if the Philistines would prevail after all.

At this point the southern group of tribes became for the first time important in history. This was not unnatural, for the nearest of the Hebrews to the Philistine land was this southern section. Judah produced David. There is no need to trace David's story here, but some of the things that he effected must be noted.

First, he finally rescued Israel from the perils of subjugation by any of the peoples that surrounded it. From this time there might be wars with Philistines, Edomites, Moabites, and so on, but there was never any danger that any of them would conquer Israel outright.[1]

Next, the struggle with the Philistines drew all Israel together as never before. Only a common effort could meet the need, and, first under Saul and then under David, all four groups of tribes fought together. This national unity only lasted till the death of Solomon, but it was none the less important. From this time forward, even through the centuries of the divided kingdom, Israel thought of herself as a single people.

The 'outward and visible sign' of this unity was David's

[1] Later a more dangerous foe was to rise at Damascus—a foe called 'Syrian' in the English Bible, but more properly called Aramæan—yet even this enemy never came near destroying Hebrew independence.

establishment of his capital at Jerusalem. As seen above, this city remained in Canaanite hands till his day. So long as the Jebusite held it, Israel was cut in two. David set himself to capture it, and not in vain. And when he captured it, he made it his capital. For one thing, the small part of modern Jerusalem that formed his 'city' was an almost impregnable fortress. On three sides there were precipices, or almost precipices, and even on the fourth a slope led down from it. A king needed a stronghold and this was a stronghold indeed. Then Jerusalem lay just where the territories of the two most important of the four groups of tribes met. It lay on the frontier of the 'Judah' and 'Ephraim' groups. It was right at the centre of the 'hill country,' and this was *the* strength of Israel. David made it a religious centre by bringing to it the ancient Ark of the Covenant, the palladium of Israel.

Thirdly, David's reign saw the last stage, or one of the last stages, of the amalgamation of the Hebrew and Canaanite races. It has already been seen that their settlements lay together over much of the land, and that Barak had broken the Canaanites' political power. The Philistine oppression and the capture of Jerusalem did the rest. In their attacks upon the 'hill country' the Philistines would not stop to ask whether a village were Hebrew or Canaanite. Probably, again, intermarriage between Hebrew and Canaanite had long been common.[1] Probably many a village had long held a mixed population. The fact that the Canaanite speech only differed dialectically from Hebrew, would help the process. From this time, therefore, Israel was a people of mixed blood. On the whole it was the Hebrew type that prevailed, for the kings were of Hebrew race, and the god of the mingled people was Jehovah, the Hebrew god. None the less, in the mixed race Canaanite influence was very great. This was especially true in religion, as will appear below. The influence of the Canaanite in Israel may be compared with

[1] *Cf.* Judges viii. 31.

that of the Dane in the north of England or of the Gael in Scotland.

A fourth achievement of David, however, was ultimately more important still. He set the type of Hebrew kingship. Many have judged him by the standard of to-day, and by that have condemned him. But by the standards of his own age he was a great and good king. He conquered Israel's enemies, and gave his people peace. Like all other Eastern kings, he was supreme judge ; and the stories both of Nathan's parable and of the woman of Tekoa, assume that if David knew of a wrong done to a poor man or woman, he would right that wrong.[1] For an eastern monarch to take the trouble to do justice to the poor seems almost a miracle to eastern eyes.[2] Indeed, this kind of justice looked to the poor much the same as mercy ! That is, the contrast between justice and mercy was then unknown.

Critics of David gibbet his sin with Bathsheba, but they miss the point. There was nothing unusual in a monarch's taking what woman he liked and getting her inconvenient husband out of the way. What was unusual was that a 'man of God' was found to rebuke the monarch, and that this particular monarch was a fine enough man to accept the rebuke and confess his sin.

Through all the rest of Hebrew history David stands out as the kind of king that Israel longed to see, and, when men looked into the future and described the king of their hopes, they cried out for another king 'of David's line.' The son of Jesse is one of the greatest men of Israel. And, of course, the Hebrew writers stress the fact that he was loyal to Jehovah from first to last.[3]

[1] In consequence, appeals to the king grew so numerous that it was impossible to deal promptly with them all—a common feature of eastern justice. Absalom played upon this to 'steal the hearts of the men of Israel' (2 Sam. xv. 1-6) but he did not dispute his father's justice.

[2] e.g. Psalm lxxii. 12ff. ; Isa. xi. 3.

[3] We ought also to note that we are first able to fix Hebrew dates with some degree of accuracy about his time. He reigned about 1000 B.C. As will be seen below, p. 46, it is possible to fix the dates

Most of the Second Book of Samuel is filled with the history of David's court. It seems to be written by an almost contemporary writer, and it displays three of the ineradicable evils of eastern despotism—the inherent factiousness of the harem with its practice of polygamy, the danger of a son's successful rebellion as a king grows old, and the inevitable dispute about the succession as he nears his end. The last ensues from the absence of any rule that the eldest son shall succeed his father.

The first evil is illustrated by the horrible story of Amnon, the second by the rebellion of Absalom, and the third by the formation of factions around Adonijah and Solomon respectively, as David drew near to his death. In the last story, the adherents of the unsuccessful faction lost their lives, or at least their fortunes, while the supporters of the successful one won the posts of power and wealth under the new ruler. In all this there is nothing peculiar to Israel.

Solomon gained the throne without any extraordinary difficulty, chiefly because his father declared for him before he died. With him the political power of Israel as an independent realm, reached its zenith. He was suzerain of Edom, Moab and Ammon; the Aramæan kingdom, founded about this time, was not strong enough to trouble him much; with Egypt and Phœnicia he was at peace and away in Mesopotamia there was for the time no great ruler.

So for Solomon's reign Israel enjoyed peaceful magnifi-

of Hebrew kings fairly accurately by comparisons with the Assyrian chronology, but the earlier documents give little help for dates before the Monarchy. The recurrence of the phrase 'forty years' shows this. For instance, each of the greater Judges is said to have given 'the land rest forty years'; Moses is said to have lived three times forty years; the period between the Exodus and the Foundation of Solomon's Temple is given as twelve times forty years (1 Kings vi. 1). It is very unlikely that history fell into such regular periods. It may be that by 'forty years' a generation was meant, but at most these figures are the estimates of later writers. It is not until a nation is fairly civilized that it begins to trouble itself with chronology.

cence. Its typical achievement was the Temple. At first, indeed, this was probably not a popular shrine, for two reasons. It was new and it was built by the oppression of Israel, as we shall see directly. Solomon's Temple was at first chiefly a royal sanctuary. Indeed, it appears as but part of the magnificent group of royal buildings that this king built just north of David's old stronghold. In later days, however, it was to become the loved symbol of Hebrew faith. And from first to last it was the one great building of Israel.

Built on Egyptian models, it consisted of a great open-air court-yard, centring in a relatively small shrine. Into this shrine the people never went. It was reserved for the priests. The Temple consisted of three parts—a porch, the 'Holy Place,' and the 'Holy of Holies,' all in line, the porch lying due east and the Holy of Holies due west. It may have been that, when the sun rose in the east on Midsummer day, its rays shone between the two great pillars on either side of the entrance, and, stretching along the Holy Place, fell upon the Ark in the Holy of Holies.

It is only possible to understand many things in both Testaments if the Temple plan is known in its main outlines. And, in particular, it must be remembered that a great part of its ritual took place in the open-air, at the great altar of sacrifice that stood before the porch.

Hebrew art was never a very great matter, but what there was of it culminated in the Temple, and there is no denying that its colonnades and cedar-wood and gold made it a place of splendour. Only a wall divided it from the palace.[1]

There is another side to the building of the Temple. It was built, like other great Eastern buildings, by forced labour.[2] A royal levy-master brought up the Hebrews in

[1] The best illustration of the importance of this fact is the description of the hiding of Joash and the death of Athaliah. Joash was hidden for six years within a few yards of Athaliah's house!

[2] Following 1 Kings v. 13 rather than ix. 20ff.; *cf.* 1 Kings xii. 18.

regular relays to build the king's shrine. This is the leading illustration of the truth that with Solomon the oppression of the people, which is so ready an evil in eastern despotism, fell upon Israel. In later days people forgot this in wonder at this king's splendour. They recalled, too, that his reign was a reign of almost unbroken peace. But he used the opportunity of peace to oppress Israel by the building of his Temple and his palace, and the lavish expenses of his Court. The Hebrew of his own day probably looked at his Temple with mingled feelings of wonder and hatred.

Yet it ought to be added that he was a just judge. The story of the Two Harlots illustrates his skill on this side. So there was no serious outburst of popular resentment as long as he lived.

### D. *Israel, Judah and Aram*

As soon as Solomon died, however, the storm burst. Headed by an able young adventurer called Jeroboam, 'all Israel' gathered to demand from his successor that the rigour of oppression should cease. Rehoboam was fool enough, not only to refuse the demand, but to send along the most hated man in Israel, the levy-master! The result was swift, but its consequences were lasting. 'Ten tribes' forsook the House of David, and set up a distinct kingdom in the north. Only the southern of the old four divisions of Israel, stood loyal to Rehoboam.

From this time the Hebrews, while religiously one, were politically divided. Yet no later king, either in the north or south, seems to have repeated the utmost rigour of Solomon's oppression. For none of them ever built a city like Solomon's Jerusalem,[1] or a shrine like the Temple.

The two kingdoms lived side by side for two hundred years (ca. 930-722 B.C.). It is not easy to remember their

[1] Probably the nearest approximation to this was Samaria, the capital of the House of Omri (1 Kings xvi. 24).

story. In part this is because of the way in which the compilers of the two Books of Kings arrange their material. Having finished with the story of Jeroboam's usurpation and its sequel, they pass[1] to Rehoboam and the other kings of Judah that were Jeroboam's contemporaries till they reach Asa, who outlived him. Then they switch away to the northern kingdom, and tell the story of the other northern kings that were contemporary with Asa. They then revert to Judah, and tell the story of Asa's successor, and so on. Unless a reader is careful, this interlacing of the stories of the two kingdoms is confusing.

Here and there the compilers introduce large sections of the stories of Elijah and Elisha, and this tends to hide the process of the history. For the chief interest of these compilers is with religion. Their one great purpose is to describe the religious movement in Israel. Consequently they give comparatively few historical details, and they hurry over some reigns in a few words, referring the reader who desires to know more to 'the book of the chronicles of the kings of Israel' or 'of Judah,' as the case may be. For instance, it may easily be that historically Omri, the father of Ahab, was more important than his famous son, but the compilers of Kings pass from him in a few verses, as it is Ahab, rather than Omri, who is important religiously.

It is not necessary to say much about the history of Judah in the two hundred years between Rehoboam and Hezekiah. The story of the politics of this little kingdom, of about the size of Yorkshire, was stagnant enough. Her two political ambitions were to maintain suzerainty over little Edom, as this gave access to the eastern seas by the branch of the Red Sea called the Gulf of Akabah, and to hold her own alongside her larger northern neighbour. She had varying success in both endeavours; but on the whole she succeeded in the second, and this was the more important. Wars between the two Hebrew kingdoms were rare and short. During most of the period Judah

[1] 1 Kings xiv. 19–21.

could always rely on Syria, or Aram, to help her against Israel. The northern kingdom is sometimes simply called 'Israel.' As will appear below, there was constant strife between Israel and Aram; and, just as Scotland and France were natural allies against England, through a great part of the Middle Ages, so Judah and Aram were natural allies against Israel.

The two important phenomena in the history of Judah during these two centuries, were religious. First, while Judah had a number both of bad and good kings—kings, in the Biblical phrase, who 'did that which was right in the sight of Jehovah,' or the reverse—it happened that the reigns of the good kings, Asa, Jehoshaphat, Joash, Uzziah, Hezekiah, were long, and the reigns of the bad kings short. The reigns of the five good kings named filled 167 of the 222 years between 917 and 695 B.C. The second important fact was the attempt of a usurper, Athaliah, authoritatively to establish polytheism in Judah. This occurred right in the middle of the period (ca. 840 B.C.). These two phenomena will receive fuller treatment later.

Northern Israel, also called both 'Ephraim' and 'Israel,' was much larger, wealthier, and more populous than Judah. Unlike Judah, however, which remained throughout faithful to the House of David, a succession of dynasties followed each other in Israel. They followed each other in the customary way of eastern despotism, by insurrection and assassination. It is easiest to grasp the history of the two centuries by remembering that two royal houses ruled for almost a century and a half—the House of Omri, for about fifty years (ca. 890 to 843 B.C.), and the House of Jehu for about a century (ca. 843 to 740 B.C.). Both before the first and after the second of these two stable dynasties there was a period of confusion. The chief kings of the House of Omri were Omri and Ahab; and those of the House of Jehu were Jehu himself, Joash[1] and Jeroboam II.[2]

[1] Joash of Israel must be distinguished from Joash of Judah.

[2] In the period between Jeroboam I. and Omri there was one fairly strong king, Baasha.

The political history of Israel in these two centuries centres in two conflicts. The first was the conflict between Israel and Aram. There was now a strong kingdom to the north-east of Israel, whose capital was Damascus, and whose kings included several able men. The struggle lasted almost throughout the period, sometimes one side prevailing and sometimes the other. The chief result was the weakening of both. And both needed to be strong, for the second great struggle of the period was the struggle with Assyria.

### *E. The Assyrian Period*

When Assyria came west, the history of Israel entered on a new phase. It became involved in 'world politics.' In the chapter on Geography we looked at the little land of Palestine by itself, and then we looked at it as a part of a larger world. So far the history of Israel has been confined to Palestine and the little kingdoms around it. What of the world beyond ?

The fact is that for several centuries there had been an abnormal position in world politics. Neither Egypt nor Mesopotamia had been strong enough to set out to conquer. But both the land around the Nile and the great plain between the Tigris and Euphrates are natural seats of empire, and Palestine lay along the road that led from one to the other. What may be called the 'normal position' in the ancient east, shows a great power seated in Egypt striving to pass east and overpower Mesopotamia, or a great power seated in some part of the Mesopotamian plain, seeking to pass west and subdue Egypt, or great empires in both areas, struggling together for the mastery. This is the history of millenniums. For the first few centuries of Hebrew history there was an exception to the rule. On the whole, during these centuries, both Egypt and Mesopotamia left Palestine and its little neighbour states alone. It was in this period that little Israel grew strong.

In the ninth century before Christ, the empire of Assyria began to reach the zenith of its greatness. As its power waxed, its limits spread west. Its armies conquered, one after another, the small kingdoms which lay at this time in the north of what we now call Syria. Its ultimate goal was Egypt. The next little kingdoms that lay in its way were Aram and Israel. Its attack fell first on Aram. In consequence the kingdom of Damascus weakened, and she ceased to threaten northern Israel, which now reached the height of its prosperity under Jeroboam II. But it was clear, for instance, to Isaiah, that, when Assyria had subdued Aram, its next victim would be Israel. This proved to be so. Damascus fell to Assyria in 732 B.C., and northern Israel in 722.[1]

The Biblical records tell us that northern Israel was 'carried captive,' and that strangers from Babylon and elsewhere were brought in to people the vacant land. These new inhabitants became the 'Samaritans.' It was policy, and not cruelty, that led the Assyrians, as well as other ancient empires, to carry captive conquered peoples.

[1] By the aid of the Assyrian inscriptions, fairly exact dates for Hebrew chronology now begin to be possible. An Assyrian king named Asshurbanipal, belonging to the Seventh Century B.C., gathered a great library at Nineveh, much of it written on tablets of fired clay, and among its records there is a history of Babylon and Assyria. In this history there is an exact chronology. The years of this chronology and our own are harmonized in the following way. The Assyrian records name an eclipse of the sun. Astronomy tells us that there would be an eclipse 'visible at' Nineveh in 763 B.C. Scholars, therefore, know which year in the Assyrian chronology corresponds to 763 B.C., and working from this, they can fix other dates. The Assyrian records name Hebrew kings and their doings fairly frequently; consequently the dates of Hebrew history at this time can be fixed. The first mention of a Hebrew king tells of a battle at a place called Karkar, or Qarqar, between Assyria and a confederacy of kings in the 'Westland' (i.e. Syria), for Ahab is named among these kings. Curiously enough, this battle is not named in the Bible. Its date is 854 B.C. and it marks the beginning of the impact of Assyria on the Westland. On the whole, the Assyrian records bear out the chronology of the Books of Kings. By the help of the last, dates can be worked out for all the kings back to David.

The purpose of the transference was to kill nationality. It was calculated that if a conquered population, or rather, the whole of the 'people that counted' in a conquered population—for the 'poor of the land,' the inconsiderable folk, were usually spared—were carried to a distant part of the empire and mingled with the alien people there, they would lose their patriotism and sink into quiescent subjects. Ancient empires found that, wherever there was patriotism, rebellion seized every likely opportunity. The history of the dealings of Assyria and Babylon in turn with the two Hebrew kingdoms, abundantly illustrates this. The purpose of 'captivities' was usually served. In almost every instance the captive people was absorbed in the alien population and lost its separate nationality.

Judah, when its turn for captivity came, survived the ordeal. The Jews have survived it to this day. They are almost the only people that have done so. The Parsis perhaps furnish the nearest parallel. The northern Israelites as a people—apart, that is, from such individuals as Tobit and Anna—disappear from history with their captivity.

Judah survived her northern sister nearly a hundred and fifty years (722–586 B.C.). Near the beginning of this period an event occurred that is very important in the story of Hebrew religion, as will appear below, but probably it only seemed an incident in the eyes of an Assyrian king. Sennacherib, one of the many able Assyrian monarchs, set his heart on the conquest of Egypt, and led armies to assault it more than once. His way, as has been seen, led along the coast of Palestine. The little kingdom of Judah lay in its hills on his flank. Its king was ready to admit Assyrian suzerainty and 'pay tribute' whenever Assyria seemed likely to enforce it. On one occasion, however, Sennacherib had reason to mistrust the loyalty of Hezekiah, the king of Judah, and, not wishing to leave even so small a foe on his flank, sent off a detachment of his army to besiege Jerusalem. The fall of the city was imminent, and with it the fate of Judah, when plague broke out in the main Assyrian army as it neared Egypt. At least, this is what the account of Herodotus, the Greek historian, whose histories now begin to give us some help, suggests. It is easy to see that, amid the masses of an eastern army, with its ignorance and disregard of sanitary rules, Asiatic plague, when once it broke out, would spread 'like wildfire.' Sennacherib, therefore, was obliged to withdraw.

To-day we should say that there was Providence at work in the outbreak of plague, for we can see that the fate of Judah, and with it, humanly speaking, of the Christian religion, hung in the balance. The Hebrew said the same thing in his direct way—'The angel of Jehovah' swept down on the hosts of Assyria, and saved Judah. This means the same thing, for there are no 'accidents' to a believer in God.[1]

A king called Manasseh succeeded Hezekiah. He reigned over fifty years, and is the first bad king of Judah who reigned a long time. His policy was simple for its way was plain. Assyria now reached the climax of its might, and the one policy of a small kingdom was to submit patiently to its suzerainty and 'pay tribute.'

A signal event marked this climax. An Assyrian army fought its way into Egypt at last, marched three hundred miles up the Nile, and captured Thebes (664 B.C.). But this was no enduring conquest, and the decline of Assyria followed speedily upon her greatest triumph, and was remarkably rapid. Some, at least, of the reasons for the decline are clear. The continual campaigns of generations had sapped this great people's strength. Now a swarm of barbarians, usually called Scythians, swept in from beyond the northern borders of civilization, and for a moment carried almost everything before them.[2] Again, a new power

[1] See Chapter IX.

[2] It is necessary to remember that, through several millenniums the civilized world was ringed by a dim, uncivilized region where hordes of barbarians roved. These might at any time break in a

was rising in the mountains beyond Mesopotamia. This was the Medes. Assyria was their natural foe. Once more, as soon as Assyria weakened, Babylon was sure to rebel. For the great empires whose seat has been Mesopotamia, were sometimes centred in the north of the great plain, but more frequently in the south. Babylon was the southern capital, the inevitable rival of Nineveh. She had memories of ancient empire, or rather, of empire after empire. Assyria had for a while subdued her, but now she rose in rebellion. Her natural allies were the Medes.[1] But something quite exceptional now happened. Egypt, which had already shaken off the sway of Assyria, took her side. This help was too late. Nineveh fell in 612 B.C. Some relics of the Assyrian armies held together for a few more years, and then Assyria disappeared from history. The little Book of Nahum shows with what a whoop of triumph Judah hailed her fall.

### *F. The Babylonian Period*

For Judah, however, the fall of Assyria was not in reality victory but respite. An era of world-empires had come to stay, and the tiny state in the Judæan hills could not hope to be independent. It was only a choice of suzerains! And, if she chose the wrong suzerain, or rebelled against a suzerain at the wrong moment, she would inevitably perish.

There was now a king in Judah called Josiah, the last of her important rulers. He reversed the religious policy of

tumultuous wave over the borders of civilization, carrying destruction wherever they went. The fear of such invasions lay always on the mind of civilized man. Other instances occur in the stories of the Tartars, the Goths, the Huns, and the Angles and Saxons. Sometimes the barbarians came, plundered and retired into their ancient darkness. At other times, they came and settled, slowly becoming civilized themselves. The Scythians belonged to the first class, and the forefathers of the English race to the second.

[1] The inter-relation of these three powers, the Scythian, the Median, and the Babylonian, is still obscure in some details; but it is clear that, in the main, they were all enemies of Assyria.

Manasseh, and was inclined to reverse his political policy too. For Judah had always to decide whether she would prefer a Mesopotamian suzerain or an Egyptian suzerain, and woe to her if she chose the wrong one! The choice was now between Egypt and Babylon. The first had regained her power under an able king called Necho. On the other hand, Babylon was, for the present, in alliance with the Medes, and Palestine fell within her 'sphere of influence.'

Josiah hesitated. His successors wobbled from one side to the other as they tried painfully to read the signs of the times. Babylon won a victory at Carchemish, which gave her the command of Syria. Still the kings of Judah wobbled. In consequence Nebuchadnezzar, the great Babylonian, laid siege to Jerusalem and captured it. After a first capture (597 B.C.) he 'carried captive' a great number of Judæans. For us the most interesting of them is Ezekiel. Then in 586 B.C., he came again and made a 'full end' of the independence of Judah, carrying captive a great number more.

Judah became a mere province of Babylon. What were left of 'the poor of the land' were given a sort of governor of their own blood. Among them Jeremiah—left in his own land by Nebuchadnezzar's general because he had upheld the suzerainty of Babylon—alone interests us. Even this feeble folk fell into factions, and many of them fled at last to Egypt.

For nearly fifty years the history of Palestine is a blank. We only know that it was part of the Babylonian empire. It will be noticed, however, that there were now companies of Jews—for the name 'Jew' may from this time be rightly used—both in Babylon and Egypt. This was the beginning of the Jewish 'Dispersion' which has continued in varied ways till to-day.

We must now turn to the Medes. This people, like the Persians, were not Semitic, but Aryan. That is to say, they belonged to the same ultimate stock as many of the peoples of Europe and of India. As already hinted, their seat lay in the mountains between Mesopotamia and the Caspian Sea. In the period that we have now reached their conquests spread rapidly, and in a part of the world that we have not yet named.

Their Empire presently reached south to the eastern shores of the Persian Gulf; in other words, it included the Elamites and the Persians. It also spread north and then west, till it reached the river Halys in the middle of Asia Minor. A glance at the map will show that this means that it lay in a great curve, chiefly mountainous, overhanging the rich and fertile plains of Mesopotamia. It became more and more evident that there would come a clash between Babylonia and this new-born empire, and that, when the clash came, the victory would not fall to Babylon. The clash was deferred for a while, partly because of the league between the two realms, named above, and partly because of the internal struggles in the Median realm itself.

A Persian prince, named Cyrus, of one of the small principalities of Persia, emerged from these struggles. He is one of the greatest men in the history of the world. For a while he left Babylon alone, devoting himself to other conquests. The most important of these, for world history, is his conquest of the western half of Asia Minor, for this brought him to the confines of Europe and set Persia face to face with Greece. As for Babylon, Cyrus needed to do little more than wait until it fell like ripe fruit into his lap. He seems to have entered the city almost without resistance. This happened in 538 B.C. The last empire of Babylon had lasted less than a hundred years.

### G. *The Persian Period*

The Persian empire lasted for two hundred years (555–331 B.C.). It differed in several ways from the empires that preceded it. First, it was much larger. A Persian king fulfilled the long hope of the Mesopotamian rulers and added Egypt to his empire. With this event the greatness of Egypt ended. It has rarely since been ruled by native kings. On this side the empire of Persia reached the Soudan. On the east it touched India and Siberia. On the west it spread into Europe.

The Persian empire, say under Darius the Great (ca. 500 B.C.), was probably the largest the world had yet known. It was probably also the best. We look at the Persian through the eyes of the Greeks, and it is true that, if the Greeks had lost the battles of Marathon and Thermopylæ, not only would the history of mankind have been different, but civilization would have been infinitely poorer.

If Persia, however, be compared with her predecessors, the look of her improves. For she understood the art of government far better than they. The chief factor in their idea of empire was force. They ruled in the main by fear. In modern eyes this means that they subdued rather than governed. But Persia governed. She understood that it is possible to keep a subject people in comparative content, and that this is better than abject fear.

There is an instance in her treatment of the Jews. Cyrus allowed them to return to their own land. A later ruler even gave them a governor of their own race, Nehemiah, and did not interfere with him when he re-built the defences of Jerusalem.

Persian skill in government explains why for so great a part of her two centuries of sway, so many of the subject peoples betook themselves to ways of peace. There was a 'Persian Peace' as well as a 'Roman Peace.'

Like Rome, too, Persia was a great maker of roads. In particular, a great road led from her native capital, Shushan, to her western capital, Sardis. It was one of the wonders of the world. Along it, and along auxiliary routes, a regular system of posts kept the Persian monarch in touch with the various parts of his mighty empire.

It is true that, as with all eastern despotisms, there was in the Persian a tendency to stagnation, and the allegiance of the submissive peoples was passive rather than active.

If the masses of the Persian empire had been actively loyal to their ruler, it is hard to believe that Alexander would have won his victories. Like the huge armies of the Indian rajahs, in such fights as Plassey, the battalions of the last king of Persia had little stomach for fight. They had not the patriotism of death. Yet, when all is said, the Persian empire was better than its predecessors.

Of the history of Israel in this period we know comparatively little. As we shall see, it was very important religiously, and many of its books belong to this time, but they do not include a history. We have only two glimpses of Jewish story in the period, one at its beginning and the second in the middle of it. They are given us in the Books of Ezra and Nehemiah. Neither of them, however, is a typical glimpse. Both of them describe, on the contrary, an exceptional bit of Jewish history. The first lasts for about twenty years, and the second possibly for about forty. The chief figure politically in the first is Zerubabbel, and in the second Nehemiah. Neither of these, however, was an independent prince.

Through the rest of this long period, the state of the Jews was worse than these glimpses show. The greater part of the little race was scattered through the Persian empire, in forlorn and despised groups. Some lived in their own land, or rather in part of it, clinging around Jerusalem, their one city.[1] It was a city shorn of its glory. Probably for most of the period, if not for all, ruins mingled with the dwellings of its people. Nehemiah repaired Jerusalem, but it is doubtful whether even he undid all the havoc of Nebuchadnezzar. It would not have been wonderful if Israel had murmured 'The glory is departed' and expired.

[1] During this period the Jews ceased to speak Hebrew and began to use Aramaic in daily life like their immediate neighbours. This was an ancient Semitic language, nearly akin to Hebrew. It is called 'Syrian' in 2 Kings xviii. 26 (*cf.* Gen. xxxi. 47, R. V. marg.). Ezra iv. 8—vi. 18; vii. 12–26; and Dan. ii. 4—vii. 28 are written in it.

But she never quite lost hope, and sometimes it gleamed clearly. She looked persistently for redemption from the Persian yoke. She believed that she would once again be independent. Indeed, some of her sons expected that a day would come when she, and not Persia, or Babylon or Assyria, or any other power, would rule the world! But this hope, even in its smaller form of national independence, was continually and continually postponed.

Politically the Persian period was for the Jew almost wholly a period of patient submission. It did not seem worth while even to write its history. It is doubtful whether the Jews in Palestine even kept any exact chronological record.[1]

There are, however, two Jewish books that deal with the Jews of the Dispersion in this period; and, at least at first sight, they seem to present a different picture. They are the Books of Daniel and Esther. The scene of the first is laid in the time when the Babylonian empire was giving way to the Persian, and that of the second eighty or a hundred years later. Whether they are history or fiction, many of their chief episodes suit the Persian period well enough. It would be quite possible for such an one as Daniel, or Haman, or Mordecai, to become vizier in Shushan; for it is by no means uncommon that an eastern despot should 'lift up the poor from the dunghill, to set him among princes,' or that he should 'put down the mighty from their seats,' and send them, like Haman, to be hanged. Again it was by no means impossible that a beautiful girl, of any nationality, should become, like Esther, chief queen at Shushan, if only she were beautiful enough. Life at a despotic court had its own excitements.

The real emphasis of the stories lies elsewhere. Behind both there is an implied background of a scattered, despised and seemingly helpless people, who might at any moment,

[1] In Daniel ix. 24–27, the period of 367 years between 538 and 171 B.C. seems to be reckoned as 'three score and two weeks' of years, i.e. as 434 years.

in spite of the normal toleration of Persia, be subject to a capricious and sporadic persecution. They were all the time true to their religion; and their God, who was God above all empires, was taking continual care of them. The fact that God is never mentioned in the Book of Esther does not deny this conviction, but heightens its effectiveness in the background.

In brief, these books, whatever their date, are books of the survival of Israel in exile. Alike in the Babylonian, the Persian and the Greek periods, she—and she only among the captive peoples—was working the miracle of survival, and she was working it through her faith. Flung, as it were, into a den of lions, she escaped! Thrown into a 'burning, fiery furnace,' she was not consumed. The wonder of these centuries is that Israel survived. Politically there is, in the Persian period, no more to say.

### *H. The Grecian Period*

In 334 B.C. Alexander of Macedon crossed into Asia Minor, and in three years the Persian empire was gone! His success was so rapid and the consequent changes so numerous and overwhelming that it looked to people like the Jews, to whom the Persian empire had come to seem almost as inevitable as the hills, that the world was falling to pieces. In a passage in the Book of Daniel, the onrush of Alexander is symbolized as the swift charge of a he-goat,[1] and any one who has seen that animal suddenly put down its head, level its horns, and crash 'bang' at its obstacles, will recognize the aptness of the symbol. And the obstacles went down before the horns. The far-flung empire of Persia, from the boundaries of India to the Sahara deserts, passed in a moment to Alexander. The Greek period had begun.

Perhaps the nearest approach we can make to the understanding of the change that ensued, is by studying the

[1] Dan. viii. 5.

state of India or China to-day. With Alexander the civilization of the West made its first great attack on the East, and to-day it is making its second. The first attack lasted for a thousand years, for it was not until Muhammed that the East threw back the West.

Meanwhile it looks, at first sight, as if Greece were triumphant in everything. The Greek tongue came to be universal, or nearly so. Greeks were everywhere the rulers. Greek cities sprang up through all the old Persian realm. And with them came Greek art, Greek athletics, Greek culture and Greek literature. Gods with Greek names filled the ancient shrines.

Yet beneath this Greek flood the old East lived on. In consequence there was medley indeed. Alongside the more or less 'free' Greek city there was Asiatic despotism, albeit the despots were Greek. Popular religion used Greek names for the gods, but they were Eastern gods. Greek art and culture, already past their zenith, ran in the East into unrestrained riot. The Greek dynasty of the Ptolemies betook itself at last to the ancient Egyptian cult. Ultimately a flood of Eastern religious mysticism swept west and permeated Greek life. While everything turned Greek, nothing turned entirely Greek. For a millennium East and West were fused. Only one thing withstood this fusion—Hebrew religion. And it only succeeded in doing so after a desperate struggle.

After eleven years of splendid and inordinate triumph, Alexander died (323 B.C.). His generals divided his huge empire between them, partly by agreement and partly by war. These generals are called the Diadochi, or Successors. It is difficult to say exactly into how many parts the empire fell, for the number varied. The Book of Daniel counted ten, but probably there were not so many at any one time.

Two, and only two, interest the student of the Bible. Egypt fell to Ptolemy, and he founded a dynasty there, whose kings all bore his name. His dynasty lasted for about three centuries. He made his capital, in a way characteristically Greek, at Alexandria, a city on the sea.

Another general, Seleucus, secured the greater part of Alexander's empire, so far as size goes. He founded a dynasty which also lasted almost three hundred years. His realm stretched from the middle of Asia Minor to the confines of India. He made his capital at a city named Antioch, situated in the north of Syria, a name no longer an anachronism. Antioch stood on the river Orontes, within reach of the Mediterranean. The successors of Seleucus were all named either Seleucus or Antiochus, and his dynasty is called 'Seleucid.' The extent of their realm varied greatly. It was an amorphous and heterogeneous mass, whereas Egypt, the Ptolemaic kingdom, was a compact, wealthy, homogeneous and isolated whole. Both fell at last before the Roman advance. During a great part of its history the Seleucid dynasty was in conflict with a new power in the East, the Parthian, to which it lost a large part of its empire.

If any one will seek out Alexandria and Antioch on a map, it will be evident that Palestine was almost sure to be a 'bone of contention' between the Ptolemies and the Seleucids. In the story of Israel the political rule of the Greeks lasted about two centuries, from the coming of Alexander to Palestine in 331 B.C. until 'the yoke of the heathen was taken away'[1] under Simon the Maccabee in 142 B.C.

During more than two-thirds of this period the Jews were, in the main, though not continuously, under the rule of Egypt; and, though there were occasional insurrections and persecutions, for the most part the Ptolemies treated them well. The dividing date is 198 B.C., when Antiochus the Great took final possession of Jerusalem. Thereafter Judæa was part of the Seleucid dominions. While there were also similar vicissitudes under the Seleu-

[1] 1 Maccabees xiii. 41.

cids, we shall find that one of these, Antiochus Epiphanes who was set upon Hellenising[1] all his realm, tried to abolish the Jews' religion (168 B.C.). Then Jewish patriotism flamed out in a desperate, but ultimately successful rebellion.

For the greater part of the Greek period the materials of history are scanty, though Josephus, a Romanised Jew of the first Christian century, gives considerable help, and for the few years of the Maccabæan struggle we have a very reliable record in the First Book of the Maccabees.

In the story of David a man named Zadok appears, along with Abiathar, as priest of Jerusalem. He was wise enough to choose the winning side when Solomon and Adonijah disputed the succession. Solomon, therefore, made him chief priest when he built the Temple, and Zadok's descendants held this office through the four centuries till the Captivity. At its end the Zadokite priesthood was restored and held office for a second four hundred years. During this period circumstances gave the High Priest the leading position in Judaism. For there was now no king and almost always the local governor was a Persian or a Greek. As has often been said, Israel, at this time, was rather a church than a state. In this church the most important person, the natural representative of the whole people, was the High Priest. When the alien ruler wished to deal with the Jewish people, he turned as naturally to the High Priest as a Turkish Sultan turned to the Patriarch of Constantinople when he wished to deal with his Christian subjects as a whole. When any political power at all accrued to the tiny people that inhabited Judæa, it fell naturally to the High Priest. Again, the obvious token of this people's separate religion was the ritual of the Temple, and the High Priest led the ritual. There is an eloquent description of one of the High Priests of the period

[1] The Greeks called themselves 'Hellenes,' and any people who accepted their language and customs is called 'Hellenist' or Grecian.'

in the Book of Sirach or Ecclesiasticus.[1] The very name 'High'—or more literally, 'Great'—Priest is characteristic of this era.

Some of the High Priests seem to have become their office, but gradually a new situation arose. As the High Priest grew more and more important from a political point of view, the Greek ruler of Palestine, whether he were a Ptolemy or a Seleucid, began to take an interest in the office. These Greek rulers do not seem to have attempted to interfere with the holding of the High Priesthood by the Zadokite family, but when a High Priest died they began to take a leading part in selecting the particular Zadokite who was to succeed. And when a High Priest displeased them, they did not hesitate to depose him and secure the appointment of another. Under these circumstances the High Priesthood gradually became a prize of faction, for it was clear to all that a man who 'played his cards well' at the Egyptian or Syrian court, was likely to be appointed. So at length Israel found its great religious office reduced to a prize of politics.

The situation was complicated by the 'Hellenising' tendency of Greek rule, which has already been described. Its pervasive influence showed itself in Judæa, as everywhere else. In one way the resistance of the Jews was practically unanimous. They all agreed that they must not abandon their religion or submit to its 'Hellenisation.' But the question remained—How far might a Jew betake himself to Greek ways without betraying or jeopardizing his religion? Some claimed that the Jew should resist almost everything that was Greek; others held that there was no need to maintain anything distinctively Jewish except its religion. No doubt many took a middle position.

Among the various descendants of Zadok who disputed and intrigued to gain the High Priesthood there were those who practised the 'Hellenisation' of Israel. For instance,

[1] Ecclus. l. 1–21. This is probably Simon the Just, who was High Priest near the beginning of the Greek period.

some of them, like many other Jews, took Greek names. And it was natural that a Greek over-lord should favour a Hellenising candidate for the chief Jewish office. Antiochus Epiphanes, who succeeded to the Seleucid throne in 175 B.C., appointed first a Zadokite, who called himself 'Jason,' to the High Priesthood, and then another who called himself 'Menelaus.' The first of these, to the scandal of his people, sought to please Antiochus by sending money to Tyre to be spent on sacrifices to Hercules! The conservative party among the Jews grew vehement in opposition to such men.

At length Antiochus determined to destroy the Jewish religion, root and branch, and make an end of Jewish factions. He sent a large army to Jerusalem, set up a Greek image in the Temple (168 B.C.), and ordered that every Jew should sacrifice to his gods. Many succumbed to his systematic persecutions; but opposition found a leader in an old priest named Mattathias, who killed a Jew who was about to sacrifice to a heathen god. Thereupon he and his five sons took to the Judæan hills in open revolt. Mattathias soon died, but his five sons, called 'the Maccabees,' carried on the struggle.

The leadership fell first to the noblest of them, Judas, who won three considerable victories over the Syrian armies, and restored the worship of Jehovah in the Temple. Considering the size of his enemies' forces and the smallness of his own, these victories seemed almost miraculous. But there were several factors in his favour. As he and his small band passed rapidly this way and that in the 'hill country,' nearly every inhabitant could be relied upon to 'give away' the movements of the Syrians. Then every one of his followers was a desperate and determined man, while the Syrian soldiers were mere hirelings. Chief of all, Antiochus was too busy with many troubles in other parts of his huge realm to be able to give his whole attention to the small Jewish rebellion. He had to deal, in particular, with the formidable menace of the Parthians. None the less, the exploits of Judas were wonderful indeed, and the

Jews did right to keep perpetually a 'Feast of the Dedication (really, the re-dedication) of the Temple.'

Judas at length fell in battle. His brothers, Jonathan and Simon, in turn succeeded him as Jewish leaders. The first of these was chiefly a diplomatist. Syria was now a sea of factions; and Jonathan found that by fishing adroitly in the troubled waters at Antioch, he could catch fish of value! He succeeded in getting himself appointed High Priest, though not of the House of Zadok; and the office remained in his family throughout the remainder of the Maccabæan period. His brother Simon gave himself to the development of his small realm of Judæa, and with him this became practically independent. For he captured Acra, the citadel of Jerusalem at this time, where a Syrian garrison had held out through the years of the leadership of Judas and Jonathan. Simon's successors soon lost all real interest n religion and sank to the level of petty Asiatic princelings. They took advantage of the growing weakness of Syria, however, to extend their realm until it covered much the same area as David's, and the later of them used the title 'king of the Jews.' So they were both High Priests and kings.

Their subjects came to hate them. On one occasion, when the royal High Priest was celebrating at the great open-air altar in the Temple, at the Feast of Tabernacles, the worshippers pelted him with the fruits that they had brought with them to fulfil the ritual! The last Maccabee was of as feeble character as the last of many a greater dynasty. The real government began to fall into the hands of an able Edomite[1] named Antipater, the father of Herod the Great. And then the Romans came. One by one, all the western provinces of Alexander's empire had fallen into their hands. In 63 B.C. Pompey, Julius Cæsar's great rival, captured Jerusalem, massacred multitudes of its defenders, and forced his way into the Holy of Holies.

[1] One of the Maccabæan rulers compelled the Edomites to become Jews in religion. The Herods were the result!

## Chapter IV

## THE 'HIGHER CRITICISM'

In most parts of human life there is room for the expert. For instance, in medicine the doctor is an expert, in law the solicitor, in the study of stars the astronomer, in the study of flowers the botanist. Indeed, as the sum of human knowledge grows and grows, we find ourselves more and more driven to the use of experts.

There is a kind of expert who deals with ancient books. He learns their languages, examines their text—for frequently different manuscripts of the same old book have different texts—tries to decide who wrote them, to fix their dates, to estimate their reliability, and to find out whether they are single works of one date or compilations of various dates. This kind of expert, like others, has reduced his methods to a science, with its own phenomena and rules; and, when he wishes to examine any old book, he applies this science to it. This has been done with the Old Testament, as with other ancient literature.

The expert in ancient literature finds it convenient to divide his studies into two parts, though he finds it impossible to keep them quite separate. The technical name for one part is the 'lower criticism' and for the other the 'higher criticism.' The first deals with smaller questions of detail, and the second with larger questions of authorship, composition, date, and so on.

An example of the problems proper to each may be given. There is a well-known song called 'John Peel.' Sometimes its first line is given as 'D'ye ken John Peel with his coat so *gray*?'—and sometimes as 'D'ye ken John Peel with his coat so *gay*?' It would fall to the 'lower criticism' to examine the problem 'Which is original?' There is a play called 'Henry the Eighth' which is usually included among the plays of Shakespeare. But there are good reasons for thinking that Shakespeare only wrote part of it and that other parts belong to another playwright. It falls to the 'higher criticism' to ask 'Were there two authors? If so, which parts belong to Shakespeare and which to another writer? And who was the other writer?'

It will be noticed that the results of such inquiries are often only probable, not certain; though sometimes they are so likely, that many would call them 'certain.' It may also be noticed that the experts may differ about the answers to some of the problems. Both these phenomena occur in the case cited to illustrate the 'higher criticism,' though neither of them in the case cited for the 'lower criticism.' It is certain that 'John Peel' is a Cumberland song, and that there the huntsmen wore 'gray.' It is fairly certain that Shakespeare did not write the whole of 'Henry the Eighth,' though it is not certain exactly where his work begins and ends, or who the other author was.

In this realm, however—as in the realms of other experts—the 'common man' does not reject the help of experts altogether because they sometimes disagree. He accepts the findings of the great majority, if the great majority is agreed, even though he knows that their results are neither absolutely certain nor unanimously accepted.

The experts in ancient literature have long turned their attention to the Old Testament. Of course, it might have turned out that here there was an exception—that the phenomena found in other ancient books did not occur in the Old Testament, and that therefore the experts' methods do not apply to it. It is usually God's way to work through men, not interfering with their ways but yet fulfilling His own purposes. He might have made an exception in the Old Testament. There is no way to decide whether He has done so except to look and see. The experts have done this, and they report that there is no exception here—that the same phenomena occur as in other ancient books—and, so reporting, they proceed to apply their science to this ancient literature, as to others.

The results on which the great majority of them are agreed, have been assumed in this book; and, at least in the conviction of many true Christians, it turns out once more that God has left men to follow their own way, yet has none the less brought His own purposes to fruition. The reader must judge whether this is so for himself.

A few of the phenomena may be named, those being chosen that can be understood without a knowledge of Hebrew. The experts found that in the opening chapters of Genesis there are two accounts of the creation of man, and that the second of these is of a more ancient type than the other.

They found that in a certain set of passages in the first six books of the Bible the God of Israel is called 'Jehovah' from Genesis onwards—yet that in a passage of another type this name is declared to have been revealed first to Moses.[1]

They found that in the story of Joseph's being sold into Egypt two accounts have been dove-tailed together, one speaking of Reuben and the Ishmaelites, the other of Judah and the Midianites.[2]

They found, again, that in the 'Book of the Covenant'[3] there is a code of ancient laws that pre-supposes an agricultural people, but that it is represented as given through Moses to a nomadic race.

They found a curious reference to the 'Ten Commandments' in Exod. xxxiv. 28, which it seemed very difficult to refer back to the Decalogue across the thirteen intervening chapters.

They found that in the Book of Leviticus the Hebrew

[1] Exod. vi. 3.

[2] An English Bible Class struck upon this explanation of the difficulties of this passage without the aid of any experts—see *The People and the Book*, pp. 153f.

[3] Exod. xxi.—xxiii.

priesthood is divided into two orders, priests and Levites, but that the references to the Levites in the historical books do not suit this division.

They found that Moses was credited with the authorship of Deuteronomy, a book that recounts his death.

They found that there are various accounts of the capture of Jerusalem by the Hebrews[1] that seem to contradict each other.

They found that there are two different accounts of the way in which Saul first met David.[2]

They found that, while it is laid down in a passage in Deuteronomy that the worship of Jehovah is to be practised only at one place,[3] in the historical books this worship is frequently practised elsewhere, even by such faithful men as Samuel and Elijah.[4]

They found that in a certain story as told in Samuel, 'Jehovah' is said to stir up David to number the people, but that in the parallel account in Chronicles this is ascribed to 'Satan.'[5]

They found that, in the middle of a story about Darius, a letter occurs that has to do with Artaxerxes, not with Darius at all.[6]

They found that a number of Psalms bear the heading 'according to David,' which do not seem to suit that king.[7]

They found the same prophecy ascribed to Isaiah and to Micah.[8]

They found a large number of prophecies under the name of Isaiah which require the Exile as background, not the kingdom of Judah in the days of Hezekiah.[9]

[1] Josh. xv. 63; Judges i.; 2 Sam. v.
[2] 1 Sam. xvi. 14ff. and xvii. 55ff.
[3] Deut. xii. 13f. The Hebrew cannot mean anything else.
[4] e.g. 1 Sam. i.; vii. 17; 1 Kings xviii. 30.
[5] 2 Sam. xxiv. 1; 1 Chron. xxi. 1.
[6] Ezra iv.
[7] e.g. Pss. xxvi.; xl.; xli.; cx.
[8] Isa. ii. 2–4; Mic. iv. 1ff.
[9] e.g. Isa. xxxv.; xl.—lv.

They found a prophecy ascribed to Amos,[1] who lived about 750 B.C., that seems to refer to the captivity of Judah which did not begin till 597 B.C.

They found a reference to a conflict between Israel and Greece in a prophecy ascribed to a prophet who lived two centuries before the Greek period.[2]

They knew that it is usual in ancient books for old laws and psalms and proverbs to be ascribed to heroes of old time, who lived long before the dates to which the laws and psalms and proverbs seem themselves to belong; and they found that there were such instances in Hebrew literature.

This list only begins to give an account of the phenomena in question. And, finding phenomena that were similar to the phenomena found in other ancient literature, the Higher Critics applied to them the science that deals with just this kind of phenomena. None of their results can be proved like a proposition in Euclid. They may, therefore, all be called 'probable' rather than 'certain.' But a Euclidean certainty is not possible in such studies.

Again, the experts do not agree in all their findings, though the great majority of them are agreed in a great many. These results are pre-supposed in this book. It does not fall within the present purpose to show how they are reached. This is done in books that are devoted to the purpose.[3] Here, as in almost all introductory books on almost every subject, it is assumed that the findings of the experts are reliable.

It ought here to be said that, of those who follow this course, there are a few who reject the findings of the great majority of their fellow-experts, and accept the opinions that are called Fundamentalist or Traditionalist. They believe for instance, that the first five books in our Bible were all written by Moses; that every Psalm that bears

[1] Amos ix. 11–15.
[2] Zech. ix. 13.
[3] The English reader will find a good account of them in Buchanan Gray's *Critical Introduction to the Old Testament*.

David's name was written by him ; and that all the sixty-six chapters that fall in our Book of Isaiah were written by that prophet. As already stated, however, the great majority of the experts are on the other side.

It is worth while asking, 'How does the plain man deal with the findings of experts ? ' Of course, if he wishes to test them thoroughly, the best way, or rather, the only way is for him to become an expert himself. This means, in the instance before us, that he must learn Hebrew and study the science that deals with ancient documents.

If a plain man hasn't the time or the capacity or the inclination to become an expert himself, how does he deal with expert opinion ? In other realms he uses a method that is compounded of testing and trusting. For instance, in the realm of medicine he trusts the expert doctor, but he tests, too, for he notices that, on the whole, more sick people recover who call in doctors than those who do not—that more sick people recover, say, in England than in China. Again, when the expert first told him that the evidence of his eyes was mistaken and that the sun does not move daily across the sky, but that the phenomenon that looks like this is really due to the fact that the earth is round and spins rapidly on its axis, he found it hard to trust them. Gradually, however, he came to think that the experts were right ; and at length men were found who so fully trusted them that they set out over the ocean, believing that if they kept on long enough, they would sail round the world. It does not appear that Drake was an expert astronomer, but, when he had completed his famous voyage, nothing could have persuaded him that the earth was flat. He had both trusted and tested.

In varying fashions this is the usual way of the plain man with expert opinions. It is a mingling of 'trust' and 'test.' He cannot test everywhere ; but, if he finds that the experts are right where he can test them, he accepts their findings where he cannot.

The same dual method may be applied to the findings of

Old Testament experts. The plain man cannot test all their results, but he can test some; and, in particular, he can apply a crucial test. He has found the Old Testament to be a religious book of immense value, the proper prelude, indeed, to the New Testament. Do the findings of the experts undermine this value? Many have feared, and not a few have claimed, that they do. It is hoped that this book, like many others, will serve to reassure the doubtful, and to show that when the 'higher criticism' has done its work, the Old Testament is not a less valuable book of religion than before, but a more valuable—that it does not form a less satisfactory prelude to the New Testament, but a more satisfactory. At least the author has found it so for himself.

In many a cathedral town there are people who worship in the great minster and find it to be a veritable 'house of God,' but who know nothing of the science and art of architecture. It sometimes happens that one of these wishes to know something of the history of the great shrine. He knows another of its worshippers who introduces him to an architectural expert. The three go together slowly through the cathedral; and, as they go, the expert tells the plain man that in the building there is a little bit of Saxon work, hidden perhaps in the crypt. He takes him to see it and tries to explain why the experts assign it to Saxon times. Then he shows an aisle that is largely Norman work, but he points out that there is a window of the fourteenth century in the Norman wall. Next he takes him to a transept that is chiefly of thirteenth-century work, and he can point out to his friend some of the tokens of the workmanship of that era. But he has to say that there is at one corner a bit of tracery which some experts assign to that century and some to the fourteenth. He may show him the spire next, and point out the characteristic features of Decorated Gothic. And finally he may tell him that the great west window belongs to the fifteenth century.

When they have finished their survey, the plain man may

ask, 'Who then built the cathedral? The Saxons who first planned a minster here? Or the Normans who laid the lines that all since have followed? Or the men of the fourteenth century who built the greater part? Or who?' What is the answer to the question?

If the plain man is of a logical turn of mind, he may say, 'Well, but if this crocket were taken away, or this font, or even that side chapel, would the building still be the cathedral?' And his friend might reply, 'This is not a place for exact logic; as for me, I would not take away any single part! It has stood as it is for century after century, and for many generations of worshippers. History is more than logic; let it serve for centuries still. I know it will!' And the plain man, if he loves God, will kneel again and find that the great, old shrine is more than ever a 'house of God' because of the lore of his expert friend.

The Old Testament is far more like a great cathedral than it is like a modern book. The parallel is not complete, but it is perhaps suggestive. The reader, as he follows this book, may be able to watch the builders, period by period, at work, selecting stones, rejecting old pieces of masonry, rebuilding here and there, until the shrine is complete. And over all there is ever the spirit of the architect, who is God.

## CHAPTER V

# JESUS AND THE OLD TESTAMENT

As the subject of this study is the Old Testament, and not the whole Bible, New Testament questions are excluded. The topic discussed in this section, therefore, might have been omitted. But it is not wise, or even candid, to evade the main issue raised by the acceptance of the results of the higher criticism. It is this—What opinion did Jesus Christ hold of the Old Testament? Is it the same as the findings of the experts, or not? If it is not the same, what is to be said?

Jesus said little directly about the structure and authorship of the books of the Old Testament. About the authorship of many of the books He said nothing, either directly or indirectly. But there is one great exception. I do not think it possible to deny, when all His references to Moses are considered, that He shared the common opinion of His time that Moses wrote the first five books of the Bible.[1] Here His opinion clearly contradicts that of the Higher Critics. What is to be said?

It is plain that this raises another question, Was Jesus omniscient? And, as all theological students know, this is part of a still wider problem, that has defied scholarship for many centuries. This wider question is, How could Jesus be both God and man? If He was and is God, He must have been omnipresent; but was the man Jesus of Nazareth in England and China, as well as in Galilee, as God is? Or again, if He was and is God, He must have been omnipotent; how then can it be true that He was

[1] It is also true, for instance, that in Mk. xii. 35-37. He takes it for granted that David wrote Ps. cx.

'wearied with His journey,'[1] for omnipotence cannot be weary? Or again, if He was God, He must have been omniscient; how then could He be said to 'advance in wisdom,[2] or how could He say that He did not know 'the day or the hour' when the 'Son of Man should come'?[3]

There is no agreed answer to these questions. Indeed, it is impossible for men completely to answer them, for there is a mystery in the doctrine of the Incarnation that is beyond human understanding.

There have been those who have believed that the doctrine requires that our Lord was omnipresent and omnipotent and omniscient even when He nestled, a babe of a few days old, in Mary's arms. On the other hand, there have been those who believed that He was wholly like other men, and that His power and knowledge were no greater than those of other men.

Probably in the realm of power the prevailing opinion—and, in particular, the belief that the 'ordinary Christian' has 'worked with' throughout the centuries, though he may never have thought it out in set terms—is that Christ was neither omnipotent nor as weak as other men, but that He had such power as He needed for the purposes of His mission. For example, the ordinary Christian has believed that He could be 'weary,' yet that He worked wonders far beyond the power of other men. This is the belief of the writer of this book. Its usual Biblical basis is the famous passage in the Epistle to the Philippians where Paul declares that, when our Lord became man, He 'emptied Himself.'[4]

A similar creed is possible in the realm of knowledge. Under this, Christians have believed that Jesus could 'increase in wisdom' and could be ignorant of the 'day and the hour' of His own Return. But, while He could be ignorant, could He be mistaken? Not a few have hesitated at this point. They have said that, whenever our Lord

[1] John iv. 6. [2] Luke ii. 52. [3] Mark xiii. 32. [4] Phil. ii. 7.

either expressed or implied an opinion, that opinion must be true; and that, on any questions about which He was ignorant, He refrained from saying anything at all. Does this belief fit the facts of the Gospels? There is not very much evidence, and for the most part it concerns small things. But I think myself that the right conclusion is still the same in the realm of knowledge as in the realm of power. This means that our Lord's self-emptying applied to omniscience; that in many things He was a 'child of His times'; that there were subjects on which He could be mistaken; but that He had such knowledge as He needed for the fulfilment of His mission.

To pass to the instances: Jesus seems to have shared with His fellow-countrymen the belief that the mustard-seed is 'the least of all seeds,' but botanists know that it is not. He seems to have believed, like His contemporaries, that the sun and stars are comparatively small things whose motions centre in the earth.[1] He not only believed in 'demons,' but thought that they disliked 'waterless places.'[2] While He did not know the 'day nor the hour' when 'the Son of Man should come,' He thought it would be soon.[3] Even in one or two references to the Old Testament He is mistaken, if the records are reliable. In referring to the story of David and the Shewbread, He says that it took place 'when Abiathar was high priest,' but the story itself requires that Ahimelech was principal priest at the time.[4] In referring to the martyrdom of Zechariah, He calls him 'the son of Barachiah,' while the Old Testament record calls him 'son of Jehoiada.'[5] If, then, our Lord's knowledge was relative to his mission,—and many who believe that He was God Incarnate hold this—the question follows, 'Was it necessary for the fulfilment of His mission that He should know who wrote the Pentateuch?' It does not seem to me that it was.

There is more to say. One of the remarkable things in

[1] Mark xiii. 24f. [2] Matt. xii. 43. [3] Mark xiii. 30.
[4] Mark ii. 26; 1 Sam. xxi. 1. [5] Matt. xxiii. 35; 2 Chr. xxiv. 20.

the New Testament is the way in which every one—the Jew, the Judaizing Christian, the Gentile Christian, the writers of the various Epistles, the Apostles, Jesus Himself—appeals to the religious authority of the Old Testament. All parties appeal to it, and no one disputes the validity of the appeal.

There is considerable difference, however, in the manner of the appeal. The first Christians, in particular, used, broadly speaking, three methods. One method was to collect 'proof passages' that could be used in supporting the Christian claims about their Lord. There is evidence that there were collections of these 'proof passages' and that they were called 'Testimonies.' Probably two of them were from Isaiah vi. and Psalm cx. In quoting these the disciples were following in the footsteps of Jesus,[1] and something deeper was involved than a mere verbal applicability. But sometimes there was nothing more. For instance—to quote from the first two chapters of Matthew's Gospel, where there seem to be a number of early Christian 'Testimonies'—a phrase from Hosea, 'Out of Egypt have I called My Son,'[2] was applied to Jesus, though it is plain that Hosea himself was speaking of the Exodus.[3] To us this kind of quotation seems arbitrary. Jesus never uses it.

There was another way of quoting the Old Testament in the first century. The greatest exemplar is Philo, the philosophic Jew of Alexandria. Under this many of the historical parts of the Old Testament were interpreted symbolically or allegorically. There is an example in Paul's saying, 'They drank of a spiritual rock that followed them, and the rock was the Christ.'[4] Here the water that flowed from the rock in the wilderness when Moses struck it, is taken as a symbol of the Messiah. So long as it was recognized that the original story did not bear this meaning, there was no harm in this kind of quotation. Sometimes more can be said in its favour, for quite often an ancient

[1] Matt. xiii. 14ff.; Mark xii. 35ff.
[2] Matt. ii. 15. [3] Hos. xi. 1. [4] 1 Cor. x. 4.

teacher's message means more than he himself knew. The writer to the Hebrews, for instance, takes hold of the two Old Testament passages where Melchizedek is mentioned[1] and uses this ancient priest-king as a symbol of Jesus. To use the story of Genesis in this way seems to us artificial[2]; but the writer of the Psalm had at least the concept of a Messiah who is priest as well as king, and this concept found its fulfilment in Jesus.

Our Lord's characteristic way of using the Old Testament was not this. His characteristic way is perhaps best illustrated from a part of the Sermon on the Mount.[3] Here there is a saying that is very difficult if it is taken literally. He says, 'Verily, I say unto you, Till heaven and earth pass away, one jot or one tittle shall in no wise pass away from the law, till all things be accomplished.' If this be taken literally, how could Paul claim that Jesus abrogated the ceremonial law? Or how did Jesus Himself 'make all meats clean'?[4] There is very little in the Sermon on the Mount that is to be taken literally. What Jesus here means is that there are principles underlying the law that are eternal and that these are to inform all the details of the good life.[5] And this is consonant with the whole passage. It opens with the words, 'Think not that I come to destroy the law or the prophets; I came not to destroy, but to complete.'

Jesus goes on to select certain great examples from the Old Testament—taken for the most part from the Ten Commandments—and to show that there is in each of them a great principle, imperfectly worked out; and to illustrate its perfect working. For instance, He shows that the command, 'Thou shalt not kill,' is an imperfect application

[1] Gen. xiv. 18; Ps. cx. 4.

[2] The quotation affects, however, the form and not the substance of the writer's argument.

[3] Matt. v. 17–48.

[4] Mark vii. 19.

[5] Similarly with the saying 'The Scripture cannot be broken'—John x. 35.

of the deeper and wider principle, 'Thou shalt not hate,' and displays its application in life. In other words, our Lord's customary way with the Old Testament is to treat it as an imperfect but necessary preparation for Himself; and that is the way in which it is treated in this book.

## CHAPTER VI

# THE THREE ELEMENTS IN RELIGION

MANY definitions of religion have been attempted, but no one definition fits all the various and multitudinous phenomena. I do not propose to suggest yet another definition, but to ask what elements go to make up religion, as it obtains among ourselves. I think that three elements may be distinguished, which may be called respectively 'spiritual,' 'ethical,' and 'ritual.'

It is very hard to say what is meant by the 'spiritual element,' for probably the word denotes one of the primary experiences of men—one of those things about which we say that, if a man does not himself experience them, it is of no use trying to explain them to him. Who can explain what sight is, or thought, or love? But, whenever a man knows that he is in fellowship with God, he has a 'spiritual experience.' It is a form of consciousness, and, as we are learning more and more surely, states of consciousness are among the things of which we can most confidently say that they 'are.'

To use other words, the 'sense' of God is primary in man. Of course, as we shall find, man may not be able to express this experience in psychological language, or he may misinterpret it, or misunderstand what kind of a being God is, and so on. But, in spite of all these imperfections and failings, if a man has any conscious dealings with God at all, the spiritual element in religion is not altogether absent.

If a man's dealings with his god,[1] and his god's dealings

[1] The word 'god' is only spelt with a capital letter in this book when the people who used it were monotheists.

with him, are not merely formal—if, that is, the fellowship is a living one—it will make a difference to the man's conduct. And, if his religion is very active, it will make all the difference! This difference in conduct is here called the 'ethical element' in religion. Usually it will take its texture and colour from the man's concept of his god. If, for instance, he worships the Hindu goddess Kali 'with all his heart,' his conduct is likely to be cruel, for Kali is cruel. This has a leading instance in the Thugs, who practised murder as a religion. If, again, a man is Muhammedan, and believes in a just, solitary God, who rules by the force of omnipotence, and if he takes his religion seriously, he will believe that the best form of government is the despotism of a just despot, and that even home should be a kind of small, just despotism. If, again, he thinks that the word 'Father' best describes God, and if his belief is not merely otiose, he will be likely to try to 'love his neighbour as himself.' And so on. There is, in every living religion, an ethical outcome.

The third element in religion has just been called 'ritual,' but this word must be taken in a very wide sense. There is a wider word of a technical kind, *cultus*. It denotes everything that has to do with the outside of worship. For instance, if Englishmen to-day buy a piece of ground, put up a church upon it, and so decide that on that spot the worship of God shall take place, that is part of the Christian *cultus*—or, in the wide sense, it is a piece of ritual. Or, if a particular tune is consecrated to the worship of God, it is a piece of ritual.

Ritual has to do with everything used in worship that belongs to the world of the senses. So used, it includes temples, images, priests, altars, vestments, sacrifices. Indeed, *cultus* really includes also such a custom as the keeping of sacred days and seasons, the setting apart of priests or sacred men, and so on.

It would be out of place here to discuss the *rationale* of

the use of ritual.[1] It is enough to say that no religion has ever done without it. It has often been the cause of a religion's degradation, but it is also a chief means of true worship. Its purpose is to express and nourish the 'spiritual' element in religion.

It will be seen that on this account the spiritual element is paramount, that the ethical element is its outcome, and that the ritual element is its tool.

This analysis, of course, is quite modern. No Hebrew of David's day would have been able to understand it. Probably, indeed, the abstract term 'religion' would itself have been beyond his understanding. Similarly, indeed, he would have been quite mystified by a modern account of his government, or his art, or even his agriculture—for what did he know of chemistry?

None the less, though he did not know it, his government illustrated certain political ideas, his art exhibited certain tendencies, his agriculture illustrated certain chemical laws, which modern study can analyse. Similarly, it is possible to analyse his religion.

As the distinction between the three elements in religion did not exist for the ancient Hebrew, he thought it just as important to offer his god the right kind of sacrifice as to tell the truth when he called his god to witness in oath. And he had no conception whatever of the spiritual as a separable thing in religion, just as he would have no thought of 'fellowship' as a separable thing. He knew his god, and he knew his friends—but 'the spiritual,' 'fellowship'?

Yet, in studying his religion, we may try to analyse it for ourselves, and ask the questions: Is there here anything spiritual, or even anything that might some day develop into the spiritual? Is there here anything ethical, however confused with ritual? And the ritual, what was it and what did it mean? It will not be possible to keep the

[1] The writer has discussed much of the subject in a volume called *The Sacramental Society*.

three elements distinct below, for they persistently intertwine, but it will help if they are kept in mind.

In the next chapter it will be found that, in the main, a discussion of the spiritual element—or rather, of that from which it grew—comes first; then a discussion of ritual; and finally one of ethics.

# THE RELIGION OF ISRAEL

## CHAPTER VII

# THE RELIGION OF ISRAEL BEFORE ELIJAH

WE might begin with Adam's religion, proceed to Noah's then to Abraham's, then to Moses', and so on. We shall begin by asking, instead, 'What was the religion of an ordinary Hebrew—by preference, a Hebrew who lived in a village—about the time when Asa was king of Judah and Omri king of Israel, about 880 B.C. ?'

There are two chief reasons for this. In the first place, what is true of other races, is true of Israel—the further historians trace back their history into the remote past, the less the historians agree, and the more often they say, 'We don't know.' But secondly, and this is more important, the distinctive contribution of Israel to religion—the thing that makes Hebrew religion unique—did not become indubitably clear till the day of Amos, or, at earliest, of Elijah, about 870 B.C. Whether it existed earlier in an embryonic form, we need not now ask. It is its developed form that matters for the whole human race. If Hebrew faith had never advanced beyond what it was in the days of Asa, it would only be a subject for scholarly reseach. We need to know what Israel was thinking then in order to get the background for the great prophets. What is meant by this will become clearer later, but it will be remembered that we said that Israel's religious pre-eminence is slight at first but great at last.[1]

What documents have we to go upon ? Though some of the books of our Bible contain ancient material, it is unlikely that any of them, taken as a whole, is as old as Asa.[2] But we have certain documents that profess to tell the story

[1] Ch. I. [2] See Appendix B.

of Israel from the days of Abraham, and even to begin with the story of the first man. And then we have two brief collections of laws.[1] Perhaps, too, the Decalogue belongs to this period.[2]

While it is probable that none of these were written down, as we now have them, till about 850 or 800 B.C., they give us stories and laws that were then already old. We may therefore take it that they tell us what stories were told in the 'gate' of Hebrew villages 'in the cool of the evening,' and what laws passed as customary among the elders of the villages in the days before Elijah. In addition, we have the records of Israel in Canaan from Joshua to Elijah.[3]

Are the early Hebrew stories of Abraham, Moses, Samuel, and so on, history, or legend, or myth, or what? I believe that Moses, and all the great leaders of Israel that followed him, were real men, but not that everything that we read about them, is history. The same is probably true of Abraham, Isaac and Jacob. On the other hand, it seems to me that the stories of Adam and Noah and the other stories of the times before Abraham are myth.

It may be asked, in consequence, what value these stories can have for religion, and how we are to distinguish the historical from the legendary and the mythological? The answer is that, for the purpose of the present discussion, it does not matter. For we are trying to discover, not *what events happened* in the long period before Elijah, but *what the Hebrews thought* just before his time. And, in order to understand the *thought* of early peoples, the very best materials are their legends and myths.

[1] Exod. xxi.–xxiii.; xxxiv. 10–27.

[2] See also in Chapter xi.

[3] The chief parts of the books from Genesis to First Kings that may be quoted for this chapter may be gathered from the table in Appendix B. They include the J and E documents for the Hexateuch and the non-Deuteronomic parts of Judges, Samuel and 1 Kings i.–xvi.—for these see further in Appendix B. A great many of the most famous stories of the Old Testament come in these books—stories that have often rightly been used by preachers to illustrate the weaknesses, trials and heroisms of religious men.

The day is past when mythology and legend could be swept on one side as unimportant. Anthropology has made that idea 'out of date.' If the history of *events* is being traced, it is usually very difficult to decide how much in early stories is reliable, but if the history of *thought* is in question, whether it be what early men thought about religion or anything else, a myth or a legend is like a photograph. It pictures accurately the *mind* of the people among whom it was popular. There may never have been a King Arthur or a William Tell, but the stories about them portray the thoughts of mediaeval knights and of the early Swiss.

For our present purpose, therefore, we may examine the stories of early Israel quite freely, without deciding at all how much of them is history and how much is myth and legend. Here that question is irrelevant. It need hardly be said that, as a rule, the later the period of which a story tells, the larger will be the historical element. For instance, there is much more history in Judges than in Genesis, and hardly anything but history in Samuel.

The stories of early Israel are very familiar. It is obvious that for those who told and loved them religion was the nerve of life. This is just as true of the early Hebrew, and indeed of the Hebrew always, as it is of the modern Hindu. For the stories are stories of the god of the Hebrew race.

It will be best to gather the rest of this chapter under a few great questions.

First, *what was the early Hebrew concept of religion*, that is, of the relation between Jehovah and his people Israel? It may be summed up in the word 'covenant.' Abraham was in covenant with Jehovah, so were Isaac and Jacob, and so was the people Israel that was descended from them. Covenant with Jehovah, however, did not obtain because Abraham and his descendants were in some physical way descended from their god—a common early idea—but because Jehovah chose to make covenant with them. What were the terms of the covenant? They were quite simple—Abraham undertook to do just as Jehovah told him to do; and Jehovah, on his part, undertook to care for Abraham. And both kept their word.

At the beginning of the story we find Abraham in Ur, a city in the lower Mesopotamian plain. Jehovah tells him to go to the distant land of Canaan—and Abraham goes. It is quite wrong to think that this was to behave as nomads always do. The typical nomad has a round of wells and pastures, to which he leads his flocks and herds in given seasons, as his fathers have done 'from time immemorial.' These wells and pastures are in definite areas, and these areas are just as much the 'fatherland' of the ordinary nomadic tribe as England is the fatherland of Englishmen. The nomad does not normally journey to unknown and distant places. When Abraham 'trekked' to Canaan, he was doing a very unusual and venturesome thing. But he obeyed his god, and his god took care of him.

It is easy to gibbet this idea of 'covenant' as commercial —but that is because we are a commercial people! Other comparisons are much more to the point. If one thinks for a moment, one sees that, underlying every true home, there is a kind of covenant—the father undertaking to care for his children, and they owing obedience to him. Is this a kind of commercial bargain? Between every true king and his people, or between every good general and his troops, there is a kind of covenant; on the one side there is the promise of obedience, on the other the pledge of care. Is this commercial? These analogies come far nearer than bargain to the ancient Hebrew idea of 'covenant.' On the one side there is the concept of obedience, on the other of providence—in the literal sense of that word.

According to the ideas of the early Hebrew, none of the three Patriarchs, having entered into covenant with Jehovah, refused to do what Jehovah told him to do. And Jehovah, on his side, cared for each Patriarch in turn in every vicissitude. Whether Abraham is crossing the

Desert, or Isaac is contending with the alien for wells, or Jacob is seemingly 'under the thumb' of Laban or in stress by famine, Jehovah provides for him. Perhaps the outstanding instance is in the story of Moriah. Abraham is bidden to sacrifice the son on whom all the promises rest; he sets out to do so; Jehovah thereupon delivers Isaac. In a crucial instance the covenant holds.

It will be seen that, in however naïve, in however crude a way, there is here the idea of fellowship between god and man; there is here soil in which that which we have called 'spiritual' may grow.

Next, we find the story that the Hebrews 'went down into Egypt' and were a slave race there. Any one who thinks that early stories ought to be logically consistent, may ask what Jehovah was doing to allow this; but early thought does not trouble itself about logical consistency.

The Hebrew records leap in a verse or two from Jacob to Moses. It is not easy to over-estimate the greatness of Moses, for he is one of the very few men in history who have made a nation. He made it out of a slave-race. He made it by telling of a living god. And he was able to make it because that god showed the slave-race that he was alive indeed. For, as soon as Moses comes on the scene, the phenomena of covenant recur. Moses meets with the god of his forefathers in the wilderness, and Jehovah sends him on an almost impossible task, and he undertakes it.

There is no need to follow the story further in detail. But we must note the occurrence of a new phenomenon. The 'people' are often disobedient to the will of Jehovah. This is the primitive Hebrew account of sin. The story of the Exodus is the story of the way in which a single leader, who was obedient to Jehovah, prevailed with a people who wanted to be disobedient.

The chief episode of the story of Moses, however, tells how he, and Israel with him, entered, or re-entered, into covenant with Jehovah at Sinai. They are to be his people and he is to be their god. This does not mean that the early Hebrew was a monotheist. He believed that there were other gods beside Jehovah. For instance, there was a god of the Moabites called Chemosh.[1] But with these other gods Israel had, or ought to have had, nothing to do. Israel was not in covenant with any one of them. Israel, therefore, did not owe them obedience, nor did it belong to any of them to care for Israel.

This idea that a given nation and a given god, as it were, belonged to each other, is sometimes called monolatry or henotheism. How far the idea prevailed among the ancient peoples—in particular, how far it prevailed to the exclusion of the worship of other gods—is doubtful; but the early Hebrew thought that he ought to worship Jehovah and not other gods. We shall see that probably many early Hebrews failed to practise this idea; but the idea, none the less, obtains in the early stories. Has any nation always practised its faith to the full?

Again, the early Hebrew seems to have believed in other divine beings who had something to do with Israel—such beings as the 'evil spirit' that plagued Saul—but these he conceived to be under Jehovah's sway. He spoke also of 'the angel of Jehovah' and 'the spirit of Jehovah'; and, while sometimes these phrases seem to be practically synonyms for Jehovah himself, at other times they seem to refer to distinct beings; yet, even so, they are under his control—they are not gods of Israel.

In the primitive stories of Joshua and the Judges the concept of Israel's obedience is in the background, and the prominent notion is that Jehovah took care of his people in every kind of peril. Yet the other idea in 'covenant' was not extinct.

For instance, it recurs in the story of Achan and the story of Saul. In both stories a notion occurs that seems to us repulsive. Jehovah bade Joshua exterminate the people of Jericho and Saul to exterminate the Amalekites. The word is translated 'utterly destroy'; but 'death-

[1] Judges xi. 24.

devote' would suit better, for it is a sacrificial word.[1] But we find both Achan and Saul refusing to do all that Jehovah told them to do. Both keep back part of the spoil to do as they chose with it. In both, therefore, there is disobedience. And in both Jehovah shows His displeasure.

The twin ideas that underlie the notion of covenant—obedience and providence—run right through all the stories of early Israel from Abraham to David. This is their mark. There is no need to show how they form the *motif* also of the two stories of Adam and Noah, which fill so great a space in the stories of the days before Abraham.

These twin ideas are vital in religion. If there were a nation that began with them, and practised them, and tried, and tried, and tried to find out what obedience to the will of God means, that nation might at last be able to learn that God is the Father of every man. Or if it were not a nation that did this, but only certain people within a nation, for those people the great law would hold that 'To him that hath shall be given,' and at last they would learn, when they prayed, to say 'Our Father.'

But to return to our Hebrew villager in the early monarchy. If he thought that it was his business in life to do the will of Jehovah, he needed to know what it was. *What did he think his god's will was?* And how did he find out what it was?

In answer to the first of these two questions, it will be useful to recall two stories about David. One tells that, when he had decided to make his capital at Jerusalem, he wanted to carry thither the ancient Ark of Jehovah—the very *palladium* of Israel. This was a wise thing to do, for as yet Jerusalem was an alien city to Hebrew eyes; but if the Ark were there, it would begin to be a holy place. But there is no doubt that David, quite apart from this piece of worldly wisdom, was devoted to Jehovah, the god of Israel. His whole life illustrates this.

[1] Something more will be said about the non-ethical content of the idea later.

The story[1] makes it quite clear that David thought that, where the Ark was, there was Jehovah. On a first attempt to move it up the hills to Jerusalem, a man named Uzzah touched it and fell dead. For David this is a clear sign that Jehovah does not wish to go to Jerusalem. So he leaves the Ark in a neighbouring house for three months. Next he hears that no evil, but only good, has befallen that house; and, to put the truth plainly, he supposes that Jehovah is now 'in a good temper,' and he repeats his attempt. And we find him celebrating a sacred dance all the way up the hill—a dance that seems to have had little restraint in it; probably the kind of dance that bands of 'prophets' used—for he supposes that Jehovah likes this ritual, and that it will keep him in good temper. This is one story.

The other is the story of Nathan's parable. David has committed adultery with Uriah's wife, and secured Uriah's death in battle. 'And Jehovah sent Nathan unto David.'[2] And Nathan said 'Wherefore hast thou despised the word of Jehovah, to do that which is evil in his sight?' We know the rest of the story.

If now the two stories be put side by side, we see that in the eyes of the early Hebrew either to touch the Ark or to commit adultery was to 'sin against Jehovah.' And he seems to have made no distinction between the two kinds of 'sin'! In other words, the distinction between the ritual and ethical elements in religion was not yet made. In technical terms, they had not yet been 'differentiated.' To us, the difference between them may seem as 'plain as a pikestaff'; but this is because we are the heirs of the great prophets, who made the distinction clear once for all. Before their days, the distinction hardly existed—perhaps it did not exist at all.

This fact has been illustrated by putting two stories side by side, but the evidence for it is widespread. For example, while the ancient collection of laws in the thirty-

[1] 2 Sam. vi. [2] 2 Sam. xii. 1.

fourth chapter of Exodus seems to be wholly ritual, in the collection known as the 'Book of the Covenant,'[1] ethical and ritual rules lie intermingled. It is plain that for those who drew up this code there was no conscious intermingling of two radically different things. For them every law alike declared the will of Jehovah.

The same is true, though not in quite the same way, of the Decalogue. Those who call it 'a simple ethical code' speak incorrectly. The first four commandments have to do with ritual, the other six with ethics. It is true that the two seem here to be distinct—but it is not the ethical that comes first!

This great example leads to two other remarks. First, sometimes people speak as though there were nothing ethical at all in the customs of early peoples. This is a mistake. There is something ethical in such customs—and particularly in those of Israel—but it had not yet been taken out of the general mass of custom and recognized as a thing of a distinct kind. And second, it is a mistake to under-rate the value of ritual. We ourselves take the first four Commandments and say, 'Yes, these are ritual rules; but then they embody and serve spiritual values, and in religion the spiritual is primary.' This is true; and it is true, in cruder ways, of many a piece of ritual that we find useless or even repulsive. David's dancing before the Ark did mean that he was Jehovah's faithful servant and that he vowed to do his will in Israel. And this was to say that politics is subservient to religion! Behind the crude there lay a great principle, after which men were groping.

Again, it seems to us merely barbarous that Jephthah should sacrifice his daughter to his god. We should agree that Jephthah, having made a vow, ought to keep his word, but we should add, 'Of course, God would not insist on his keeping the *letter* of the vow, for He would know that when Jephthah vowed, he had not intended such a sacrifice

[1] Exod. xxi.–xxiii.

as this. He would only expect the vow to be kept in *spirit.*' But the early Hebrew had not reached this distinction between 'letter' and 'spirit,' and for him the issue is, 'Shall I put my daughter or my god first?' And he held that he must keep his word to Jehovah. There is here a dim groping after another great principle—'He that loveth son or daughter more than Me, is not worthy of Me.' In many a crude custom, which at first sight seems wholly mistaken, closer examination reveals a certain 'feeling after' a high principle.

It is perhaps clear now that in early days men did not distinguish between the spiritual, ethical and ritual elements in religion; still less did they seek rightly to relate them to each other. This appears again when we go on to our next question, *How did the Hebrew of the period between David and Elijah get to know the will of his god?*

Like other primitive peoples, he thought that Jehovah had talked with the great men of old time, in much the same way as two men talk together. For instance, Jehovah with two angels came to visit Abraham one evening and, Abraham having waited on them while they had a meal, Jehovah told Abraham what he thought of doing to Sodom.[1]

But, while this happened in far-away days, the Hebrew villager of Asa's day knew quite well that it did not happen now. How, then, was he to learn the will of Jehovah? The answer was—using our phrases—'Through particular kinds of men, who were, in various ways, in touch with Jehovah.' Of these three types may be named—the law-giver, the prophet, the priest.

They are put in this order merely for convenience in treatment. There is a risk in naming them separately, for in this early period they were not clearly differentiated. For instance, both Moses and Samuel were law-givers, priests and prophets. To try to draw hard-and-fast lines between these three kinds of 'holy men' is almost like

[1] Gen. xviii.

trying to draw a hard-and-fast line between a bird's beak and wing and tail in the yolk of a new-laid egg! Clear distinctions come later.

Among many early peoples law is religious. In other words, every law is thought of as an expression of the god's will. This is often so too with informal customs, for custom is just traditional law. In the thought of Israel, Moses was the first law-giver. Even if we were not told this, we should deduce it; for, as soon as the slave-people Israel reached the desert, manifold questions for which there had been little or no precedent while they were in Egypt, would arise, and an authoritative decision would be needed.

We have an instructive picture of the origin of Hebrew law and custom in the eighteenth chapter of Exodus. Here, when any two men have a dispute, they come to Moses 'to inquire of God,' and so Moses 'judges the people.' In other words, the giving of law is a religious function.

In later days we find Samuel 'going in circuit' year by year to four holy places to judge Israel.[1] Eli, another man of God, is also said to 'judge.' In the Book of Judges quite a number of other people are said to 'judge Israel.' There has been much debate about the meaning of the phrase in this book, because the chief 'judges' here are soldiers rather than law-givers. But it looks as if any man, whom people recognized for any reason to be a 'man of God'—whether because he was a prophet like Samuel, or a priest like Eli, or a saviour of his people like Gideon, or merely a man whom Jehovah had evidently prospered, like Abdon[2]—might 'judge.'

The meaning of the word is nearly what we mean by 'arbitrate.' When two Hebrews quarrelled, or when two Hebrew villages quarrelled, they could, if they chose—and often they did choose—go to some man in the neighbourhood whom every one knew to be a 'man of God,' and ask him to decide. And, while he had no police or other 'secular

[1] 1 Sam. vii. 15–17. [2] Judges xii. 13ff.

arm' to enforce his decision, it was thought of as Jehovah's decision.

But this indefinite and sporadic kind of law-giving ultimately broke down. There was a tendency for 'every man to do that which was right in his own eyes,' because 'there was no king in Israel.' In other words, an early people thought of a king as a man who not only gave decisions but was able to enforce them. As already seen, he had police in the shape of a body-guard. With the coming of monarchy, justice passed to the king.

But this did not mean that it ceased to be a religious function, for the king was Jehovah's 'Anointed,' and it was expressly recounted of Solomon that he was a successful king because Jehovah gave him special capacity as a judge.[1] Solomon's decision in the instance of the Two Harlots recalls the stories of acute Arab *kadis*; but it is given as an example of how Jehovah gave him 'wisdom' to 'judge this people.'

The evidence is sporadic, but there is enough to show that with Moses there began a system of law-giving in Israel, which went on and on and on, and that as one decision after another was given through the generations, each was regarded as a decision of Jehovah. We may ask whether anything was done to gather the series of decisions together, what was done when one decision conflicted with another, and how the customs of many scattered villages could all portray the will of Jehovah. Little can be said certainly in answer to such questions, but something is suggested below.[2]

It is now perhaps clear that, whether or not we can point to any particular laws of Israel and say 'These go back to Moses,' he played a greater part in the history of Hebrew law than King Alfred, for instance, in the history of English law. Moses was the first law-giver of Israel. And, as in other early races, the codes of traditional law were ascribed

[1] 1 Kings iii. 4–28. [2] Ch. xiv.

to the first law-giver. He is the spring of Hebrew law rather than its reservoir.

We pass to the second kind of 'holy man' in early Israel—the prophet. Here it is best to begin by reading the ninth and tenth chapters of the First Book of Samuel. They tell the story of Saul's search for some lost donkeys. Two kinds of 'holy men' appear, though there is a comment that suggests that they were much alike. The first is called a 'seer,' who turns out to be Samuel; the others are called 'prophets.' Saul and his bondman go to the seer to find out where the donkeys are. If the story occurred in any other early record, we should say that the seer was thought to have 'second sight.' As to the second kind of holy men, the prophets, they appear in a group, apparently dancing a sacred dance to music near a holy place, almost in a kind of frenzy. When Saul meets them 'the spirit of god' comes mightily upon him and he 'prophesies.' Perhaps the nearest thing in to-day's life is the 'dancing dervishes'—unless it be true that these have degraded the dance into a means of *baksheesh.*

These phenomena are not peculiar to Israel. Similar groups of holy men appear among many races. Two things, in particular, may be said about them. They are out-and-out devotees of the god whom they serve; and prophets are not prophets by heredity. The 'spirit of god' may 'come upon' any one. In our speech, the prophet's was an individual call. In the word of an onlooker when Saul began to join the excited band, 'But who is their father?'—that is, prophecy is no matter of heredity. Utter devotion to a given god, and an individual call—these are marks of a prophet. We shall find that, as Israel learnt more and more what the will of the true God is, these two phenomena become very important. But, considered by themselves, they are not peculiar to Israel.

The prophets, however, had other functions beside the excitement that comes so often, though in various ways, to men of all periods who believe that a god has 'visited' them. The prophet was a man who told other men what Jehovah's will was. We are not told how the prophet himself learnt the will of his god. Probably we should say that he learnt it by meditation and prayer. But at any time a prophet might burst upon a king with the words 'Thus saith Jehovah.' The message might be a rebuke for some ritual disobedience, as when Samuel denounced Saul for his failure to 'death-devote' Agag and the Amalekite cattle; or it might be such an ethical challenge as Nathan flung in David's face after his sin with Bathsheba; or it might be the giving of an answer to a king's question, such as, 'Shall I go up to battle against Ramoth Gilead or not?'; or it might be a reply to a private man's question, as, 'Where are my father's lost asses?' Just as we found that ritual and ethics were not differentiated in law, so now we find that they are not distinguished in prophecy. Neither are politics differentiated from either. The idea is that Jehovah has to do with all human life, and the prophet is a man who can tell a man or a king his will in cases where law and custom are not much help.

I have already quoted a passage that lies just outside our present period, but it illustrates the place of the prophet in early Hebrew life almost better than any other. It is the story how Ahab and Jehoshaphat 'sit in the gate of Samaria' asking a great band of prophets to tell them whether to declare war on Syria or not.[1] There are some difficulties in the story, but we can see the two kings on their thrones in the open-air; we can see a vast crowd of Hebrews surging about as the cry runs, 'Is it war or peace?'; we can hear the prophets declaring for war in the name of Jehovah; we can see one of them careering about with horns on his head to act a parable of victory; we can see, as a psychologist would say, that if once the conviction lays hold of the crowd of hearers that this is the will of Jehovah, there will arise a confident 'will to victory' that may do much to bring it; we can see, too, the solitary

[1] 1 Kings xxii.

prophet who waxes sarcastic with Ahab himself. At this point we can see three other things—how readily the prophet's call might degenerate into mere time-serving; how difficult it must have been sometimes to decide between the 'oracles' of different prophets; and how courageous a man a true prophet, even of these early times, might be. We see, too, that, when he is driven to explain how the other prophets come to tell lies, he does not say, 'They are not prophets'—for the outward phenomena of early prophecy were there—but that Jehovah himself has deceived them through 'a lying spirit,' because Jehovah is set on the destruction of Ahab.

When we remember what prophecy ultimately came to be in Israel, we can see that there is here a good example of the principle that Israel is chiefly unique, not at the beginnings of her story, but at the end—not in what she at first was, but in what she ultimately came to be. None the less, we can also see, in the retrospect of history, that Samuel saved Israel when he gave her the Monarchy; that Nathan was the precursor of the great ethical prophets of later days when he rebuked David; and that Micaiah told Ahab the truth when he denounced Jehovah's curse upon him. Already prophecy was a great power in Israel.

When we turn to the third kind of holy man, the 'priest,' we naturally think of Jerusalem and the Temple and the sons of Aaron. But were there no priests in Israel before there was a Temple at Jerusalem? And what was it that made a man a priest? The evidence is sporadic and difficult to systematize, but it appears that a priest was primarily a man who carried out the ritual at a holy place.

How many holy places were there? We must remember that Israel at this time was settled in many scattered villages and that each village largely lived its own life. Had every village, then, its own shrine? This is likely, though it cannot be proved. If we may judge from such passages as the ninth chapter of First Samuel, the shrine, called 'the high place,' stood on rising ground outside the village. In the same story we find a festival being celebrated at it, as though a feast went with a sacrifice.

Besides these many village shrines, there were a few shrines of greater importance. The chief of these were Beer-sheba, Hebron, Gilgal, Bethel, Shechem, Shiloh, and Dan. This gives a list from south to north. When David carried the Ark to Jerusalem, that city would begin to be a chief holy place too. It will be noticed that most of these places were famous in the national lore of Israel. At Hebron Abraham lived and was buried; at Gilgal Joshua crossed the Jordan, and so on. Even the far northern sanctuary at Dan claimed some connexion with Moses.[1] We find, therefore, as in so many other countries, a multitude of local shrines and a few great shrines.

In the two earliest codes of laws we find that Israel is bidden to gather at three seasons of the year to worship.[2] It is unlikely that all the people gathered at one place, but it is not at all unlikely that each of the four groups of tribes mentioned in the third chapter, was accustomed to gather at one of the chief shrines in its own area at such times.

Who were the priests at the shrines, local and central? There are instances where men seemingly of any tribe might be priests—Micah's son, for instance, or David's sons.[3] At Shiloh, however, it is assumed that Eli's priesthood would naturally pass to his sons; and at Dan there was an ancient priesthood that claimed to trace its line back to Moses.[4] Again, Samuel, an Ephraimite, offers sacrifice, but it seems to be counted sacrilege for Saul to do so.[5] Then again, 'Levites' are named here and there, but it does not appear what this word meant, for it is only in later times that we find it clearly associated with the son of Jacob called Levi. In other words, here too there was much fluidity in this early period and little uniformity. This is parallel to other instances of the kind. As to the

[1] Judges xviii. 30.
[2] Exod. xxiii. 14ff.; xxxiv. 23.
[3] Judges xvii. 5; 2 Sam. viii. 18.
[4] Judges xviii. 30.
[5] 1 Sam. xiii. 8ff.

priesthood at Jerusalem in particular, something has already been said.[1]

To return to an earlier question—How did a priest get to know the will of Jehovah? Apparently by casting some kind of sacred lot by means of an 'ephod'—whatever an 'ephod' was.[2] In this period the priest is of little importance. It is possible, however, that it was through his activity that the first collections of Hebrew laws began to be made.[3]

*What was worship like at a typical 'high place'?* We naturally think at once of the Temple, but we have no description of its *cultus* at this time and we don't know how far the *cultus* there was typical. To get the best idea of how the early Hebrew worshipped, we must gather what we can from two sources—the references to worship that occur incidentally in the Hebrew records, and the discoveries of archæology about the worship of the Canaanites.

At this point it is important to remember that the race that inhabited Palestine at the time of Asa was a mixed race. This has already been shown in an earlier chapter, and the fact is of capital importance for the story of Hebrew religion. In later days the prophets and Deuteronomists looked back to this mingling of races as the source of the corruptions of Hebrew religion. For instance, Ezekiel says, addressing the people of Jerusalem, 'Thy origin and thy nativity is of the land of the Canaanite; the Amorite was thy father, and thy mother was a Hittite.'[4]

It is not difficult to see how this happened. When the Hebrews broke into Canaan, they seized a large number of villages, and with them, of course, their various 'high places.' Turning out the local Baal, they began to worship Jehovah on the old spot. And, as they amalgamated with

[1] Pp. 58-60.

[2] e.g. 1 Sam. xxiii. 9ff.; xxx. 7ff.; and the LXX. (see Chap. xiv.) translation in 1 Sam. xiv. 18f. 41. Some passages that name the 'ephod' seem to describe a priest's garment and some a solid object.

[3] See Chap. xiv.

[4] Ezek. xvi. 3; *cf.* Judges i; Exod. xxxiv. 11ff.; Deut. xii.

the Canaanites, the old Canaanite ideas might begin to gather round the old shrine, and this would be all the easier because in many ways the two cults were alike. Even the name 'Baal' could be used of Jehovah, for its meaning is simply 'Lord.'

I remember visiting a Roman Catholic church in India where there was a famous image of the Virgin. It was a high day, and I saw many Hindus taking their offerings in the long procession that passed the image. For a whisper was current among them that this image was really the image of a goddess of their own, which had been there long before any Roman Catholics came, and which had been flung aside but had mysteriously come back.

Something of this kind happened in Israel. We cannot trace its course in detail, for we have not the materials, and doubtless it would come insidiously, but we know what its ultimate outcome was, as we shall see when we reach the story of the great prophets. Ultimately the two gods tended to be indistinguishable. This identification of two gods with each other, with the consequent blending of their two cults in one, is technically called 'syncretism.' The word is just Greek for 'mixture.'

According to the writer or editor of the Book of Kings, 'Jeroboam, the son of Nebat,' 'made Israel to sin' by setting up two bull-images at Bethel and Dan—that is, at two of the chief old shrines in his new northern kingdom, the one at one end of it and the other at the other end. It is important to notice that these bulls were images of Jehovah, not of some 'strange god.' There can be no doubt that similar images would be found at other shrines, at least in the north. Was this act of Jeroboam's the beginning of image-worship in Israel? The experts cannot agree about the answer, for the evidence is conflicting, and it may be that sometimes the editor has carried back the ideas of his own age, by anachronism, into a time when they were unknown or at least not prevalent.

It is agreed that in primitive religions worship by means

of images is not the earliest kind of *cultus*, and this seems to be true of Israel. For instance, Abraham met Jehovah at the 'oaks of Mamre,' Isaac at the well of Beer-sheba, and Jacob at a great natural stone at Bethel. This is consonant with early Semitic practice. In this practice there was no image; but the great tree, the notable spring, the great stone were thought of as marking favourite haunts of the god.

But, while worship by means of images was not the earliest form of cult, it arose practically everywhere in the world. It is possible that there were always some voices raised against it in Israel, but it is certain that ultimately it became quite common. An instance of the conflict of evidence may be given. There is a record that two prophets protested against Jeroboam's bulls at the very time that he made them[1], yet neither Elijah nor Elisha says one word against them. It is enough to know that there would be a constant tendency to make images of Jehovah, especially where Canaanite influence was strong, and that at last it became very common indeed.

As to the Temple, the accounts we have tell that there were at first images of cherubim in it, but no image of Jehovah himself; some, however, hold that Moses' brazen serpent was an image of Jehovah. This may be so; but any one who has seen the way in which images of secondary gods have gradually found their way into Indian temples—even into those temples of Shiva in which the great god himself is represented, not by an image, but by a rounded stone—will perhaps hesitate to admit that this is proved. However, Israel began this long period without images of Jehovah, and ended with them.

Both in Hebrew and Canaanite shrines there were altars and in many ways the sacrifices offered on them were alike. The sacrifices were of different kinds—oxen, sheep, goats, corn, oil—but the chief of the usual sacrifices were of animals. A double phrase describes them at this period

[1] Kings xiii. and xiv.; *cf.* Exod. xxxiv. 17.

in the Old Testament. They are called by two words that are not too happily translated 'burnt-offerings and peace-offerings.'

The first of these was wholly burnt on the altar. In early days the god was thought of as enjoying the smell of the burning animal.[1] In later days we do not know in what way the sacrifice was counted to reach the god by being burnt; perhaps here it sufficed the Hebrew to say, 'This has always been so.' But it is clear that, when an ordinary Hebrew brought one of his few precious animals and gave it to his god, he was offering something that cost him a good deal. This is the good element in the practice.

In the so-called 'peace-offering,' on the other hand, part was burnt on the altar and given to the god, but the worshippers ate the rest in a sacred feast at the 'high place.' Sometimes, apparently, the priest ate with them, and sometimes he had a distinct share.[2] Here the good idea amid the crude ritual was that there is fellowship between god and his worshippers, for the common meal is the ancient symbol of fellowship.

We do not know how often sacrifices were offered, but we are told that 'three times a year' every male was to appear before Jehovah.[3] These three special seasons were all harvest festivals. One was celebrated when the barley was ripe, at about our Easter; the second when the wheat was ripe, at about our Whitsuntide; and the third when the grapes and figs and olives had been gathered in, at about our Michaelmas.

It is clear that these festivals suit an agricultural people rather than a nomadic one, and it may be that they were one of the better things that Israel learnt from the Canaanites. On the other hand, the Hebrews seem to have brought the Sabbath and the Passover from the Desert.[4] The

[1] Gen. viii. 21; 1 Sam. xxvi. 19 (R.V. marg.)
[2] 1 Sam. ii. 12ff.; ix. 22ff.
[3] Exod. xxiii. 14-17.
[4] Exod. xvi. 25; xii. 21ff.

second of these became practically amalgamated with the first of the three agricultural festivals. This celebrated, therefore, both the Exodus and the barley harvest. Ultimately the three festivals came to be called the Feast of Unleavened Bread (with the Passover), the Feast of Weeks (seven weeks after Passover), and the Feast of Tabernacles.

Was human sacrifice practised by the Hebrews? There is no doubt that the Canaanites practised it, especially in the instance of new-born children. The story of Jephthah shows that it might occur in Israel, but the story of Abraham on Moriah seems to add that Jehovah did not *require* it. Such practices may be either required, or permitted, or forbidden. Israel seems already to have reached the second stage. Similarly, while all first-born creatures, whether of men or animals, belonged to the god, like the first-fruits of the harvest, yet our earliest records say that in Israel a lamb was to be offered instead of a first-born child.[1] By the time of Micah at latest, the better kind of Hebrew at least, had learnt that, whatever other nations might do, Jehovah loathed human sacrifice.[2] It must be remembered that the practice, however horrible it seems to us, is one of those customs that have good elements in them. When a man sacrificed his child he was giving up his most precious possession; he was 'denying himself' to the utmost for the sake of his god.

There is need to name two other sacred objects in Canaanitish worship, the 'pillar' and the 'Asherah.'[3] The archæologists have found quite a number of 'pillars' among the remains of Canaanite shrines. They were upright stones, usually three or four feet high. Their use is not clear. The Hebrews seem also to have used them, Jacob's stone at Bethel being a famous example.

[1] Exod. xiii. 13.

[2] Mic. vi. 7.

[3] The latter is very unhappily translated 'grove' in the Authorised Version.

Did the Hebrew also use the Asherah? This was a sacred pole, and it stood for a Canaanitish goddess. It seems very likely that a Baal and an Asherah—that is, the local god and his wife—were constant elements in Canaanite religion. It is clear that there is here one kind of polytheism[1]; clear, too, that there is here the definite assertion of sex in god. The Canaanite religion was what is called a 'fertility cult'; that is, it identified the processes of growth in nature—the growth of plants and harvest—with the sexual process in animals and men. This is an ideal that clearly suits an agricultural people rather than a nomadic one. It is unlikely, therefore, that the Hebrews brought it with them into Canaan. It readily lends itself to the idea that there is religion in lust. We do not know how ancient this notion is. We do know that it is millenniums old, and that it is by no means extinct in heathenism to-day.

What response did the Israelites make to it when they mingled with the Canaanites? There is evidence that the Hebrew quite frequently—some think perpetually—copied his neighbours here. But there is also evidence that there was in Israel constant protest, both against polytheism and against sacred lust.

A number of instances may be given. For example, just as Israel was on the point of entering Canaan, the Moabites led them astray in the 'sin of Baal-Peor'; here the priests rose up in very vigorous protest.[2]

In the story of Gideon, which illustrates in more ways than one the inter-mixture of Hebrew and Canaanite, we find his father worshipping the pair of Canaanite gods, a Baal and an Asherah; and it is Gideon's first task to destroy them at Jehovah's behest.[3]

[1] Solomon, to please his foreign wives, practised a second kind of polytheism—he built temples to foreign gods at Jerusalem (1 Kings xi. 27), and these remained for three centuries (2 Kings xxiii. 13).

[2] Nums. xxv.—here early and late accounts are dove-tailed.

[3] Judges vi. 28.

In the story of Eli, again, we read that his sons fell into sexual sin 'at the door of the tent of meeting,' and that Samuel cried out against their 'iniquity' in the call of Jehovah.[1]

Again, when Rehoboam became king, the southern Hebrews fell into this horrible custom, with its accompaniment of 'sacred women' and worse; but Asa set his face against it.[2]

For the northern kingdom the most signal instance, though probably by no means the first, occurred in the days of Ahab, as will appear below. All the evidence that we have, therefore, goes to show that the practice was common, but that there were always some to protest that this was not the way of the worship of Jehovah.

We may add here that there is general agreement that the religion of the nomad held a higher ethical level, to use our word, than that of the agriculturalist. In the Old Testament documents, the leading evidence for this is the story of Abraham and Lot. Lot betakes himself to 'the cities of the Arabah'—the very word 'cities' denoting in those days agriculturalists—and we read that 'their sin' was 'very grievous.'[3] In this passage, indeed, we come as near the purely ethical as anywhere in the records of this period.[4]

The typical sin of Sodom was grossly sexual. Whenever a Hebrew looked from his hills on the Dead Sea, the dreadful story of Jehovah's judgement on the ancient cities of sin would spring to his mind. He never wholly succumbed to a belief in sacred lust. It is difficult for us to understand how much this ultimately meant. Almost everywhere else—some would say, everywhere—popular

[1] 1 Sam. ii. 22-26; iii. 11-21. It is quite characteristic that Hophni and Phineas are also charged with a ritual offence (1 Sam. ii. 12-17). The last paragraph in 1 Sam. ii. probably belongs to a later source.

[2] 1 Kings xiv. 21-24; xv. 12ff.

[3] Gen. xviii. 20.

[4] Note the words 'righteous,' 'wicked' and 'right.'

religion ascribed the sexual to god, and so turned fatally from the path of progress.[1]

Finally, we ask the crucial question—*What was the Hebrew concept of the nature of god in this early period?* The answer has already been implied. The early Hebrew held ideas about god that were not logically consistent. He held some ideas that were true, so far as they went, and that would furnish a good starting-point for progress in religion; but he also held other ideas that, if they became dominant, would be fatal to progress.

In this period the Hebrew did not finally choose which of the two paths he would follow. He stood through this long period at the parting of the ways. He did not know that, if he took one path, he would be as the rest of the races of the world; and that if he took the other, he would give the world its final religion. But so it was.

Some illustrations of this early acceptance of logically incompatible ideas may be given. And in passing, it may be remarked that to this day there has never been a people that did not cherish some logically incompatible ideas!

First, then, Jehovah was a 'living god.'[2] This means that he was active all the time. The whole story illustrates this, for it is just as much the story of Jehovah as the story of Israel.

Further, he was so effectively a living god that he could do as he liked. Throughout the records there is never the suggestion that Jehovah wanted to do something and could not. This is not the later and semi-philosophic concept of omnipotence, for Israel was not yet even semi-philosophic. But it was an idea out of which the concept of omnipotence

[1] A further remark may be added. In a large part of Asia three things go together in immoral cults, the woman, the serpent and the tree. The story of Eden has these three. It probably passed through many changes before it reached its present form, but at any rate Israel associated the frequent triad with the beginning of sin.

[2] It is possible that this idea is the root meaning of the name 'Jehovah.'

could grow. Yet the idea is inconsistent with the other Hebrew idea that there were other gods. For instance, in the story of Jephthah we have a piece of early diplomacy whose basis is that Moab's god Chemosh has given Moab its land, just as Israel's god, Jehovah, has given Israel its land.[1] It was hardly possible, however, that two gods, living side by side for centuries as their peoples did, would never wish to do incompatible things! Similarly, the Hebrew records assume that, if Jehovah wished, he could fetch Abraham from Mesopotamia, call Israel out of Egypt, break the power of the Philistines, and so on. Yet in all these lands the Hebrew believed that there were other gods. Did they just let Jehovah have his own way? The question hardly emerges. That is to say, in practice Israel treated its own god as able to do anything he wished, just as if there were no other gods at all.

It was not merely that Jehovah could do as he liked with men. He could also do as he liked with nature. Indeed, some of the chief stories about him were just of this sort. He delivered Israel from Egypt by sending 'plagues'; he destroyed Pharaoh's army by flood; he divided the Jordan before Joshua; he struck Barak's enemies from the storm-cloud. It is true that with the founding of the kingdom these stories almost cease, but it was on them that the Hebrews fed their minds as they thought of their god. In particular, the story of the Exodus and of flaming Sinai never faded from their minds. For them, Jehovah was their god because he had 'brought them up out of the land of Egypt.' He was a god of wonders, who could do as he liked with clouds and hail, locusts and quails, river and sea.

It is often said that in this period Jehovah is a 'local' god—and this in three ways. First, he is thought of as frequenting certain favourite places, as Sinai, Bethel, Shechem. Then he is thought of as accompanying the Ark. Thirdly, he is thought of as god of the land that he has given his people 'to possess.' Yet not one of these

[1] Judges xi. 14ff.

ideas is consistently held. Jehovah is not confined to the sacred spots; for he calls Abraham in Ur, comes 'riding on the wings of the wind' to help Joshua or Barak, and so on. Nor is he to be found only where the Ark is, as the same examples show. Nor is he confined to the land of Canaan, for he rescues Israel from Egypt; his chief seat is Sinai, which lies outside Palestine; and so on. In other words, there lie here side by side the ideas of a localized god, and the idea of a god who can be anywhere that he wants to be. If the last idea ultimately prevails, it will give place to the later concept of omnipresence.

The passages already quoted suggest that Jehovah was a 'national' god, and that he had nothing to do with any nation except Israel. Yet the Hebrew, taking over the stories of Eden and the Flood from Babylon and giving them his own stamp, represents Jehovah as maker of the first man, and god of the world of men! The two ideas are quite incompatible. Which was ultimately to prevail? In this period there is no answer.

It is customary to say that in these early days Jehovah was a 'war-god'; and certainly the picture of Joshua's campaigns, the wars of the Judges, and David's victories, imply that he could fight indeed. Yet behind all this there is something else. It is very remarkable that the three Patriarchs, the ideal heroes of Hebrew story, are men of peace. In this respect these stories of early heroes are probably unique in the world. And the purpose of all Jehovah's wars was to give his people peace and prosperity in Canaan. Under Solomon he achieved this, and it is noted as the chief glory of Solomon's time. In other words, we have here an early instance of the concept that war is just a means of peace, and that it is better to be at peace than at war.

Is the concept of Jehovah ethical at all? In two ways it may be held that he is not. He is not ethical if he is capricious; he is not, to our minds, ethical if he makes ritual as important as ethics. There are one or two stories that make Jehovah capricious,—for instance, the story, already quoted, of David's bringing of the Ark to Jerusalem.[1] And, to take a wider issue, why did Jehovah choose Israel at all, and not Edom, or the Philistines? No answer is given in the documents, and this choice looks to us like mere caprice.

As to the distinction between the ethical and the ritual, it has already been pointed out that these were not differentiated at this period. Jehovah, for instance, demands the performance of the ritual of the 'devoting' of spoil to him in the story of Achan, just in the same way as he demands that David shall not take another man's wife. Yet there is more of what we call 'ethical' than is sometimes allowed. The story of Abraham and Lot has already been instanced. It is difficult to read the story of the Flood without concluding that the wickedness of the drowned world was 'ethical.' The story of Jehovah's anger with David because of Bathsheba is another instance. Again, both Nathan's parable and the story of the woman of Tekoa[2] take it for granted that David was a king who cared for the poor. If a rich man stole a poor man's lamb, or if a widow were going to lose her only son, it is assumed that David would step in to help the helpless. And this was because the king was supreme judge, and to do justice was a religious act.[3]

This leads to another instance. The collection of early Hebrew laws called 'the Book of the Covenant'[4] has often been compared with other early Semitic codes, for instance with the Babylonian Code of Hammurabi,[5] and some have said that there is no difference between them. But the Hebrew code is distinctive in this—that in every instance except perhaps one, it takes the side of the poor and helpless against the rich and powerful. The Code of Hammurabi by no means does this. To take a single

[1] G 90, *cf.* 2 Sam. vi.
[2] 2 Sam. xiv.
[3] See pp. 93 f.
[4] Exod. xxi.–xxiii.
[5] This code probably dates from *ca.* 2300 B.C.

example, the Book of the Covenant has no instance of capital punishment for theft. Now theft is normally the crime of the 'have-nots' against the 'haves.' But it is the 'haves' that makes most laws, and they are usually severe indeed upon theft. But neither the earliest Hebrew code, nor any of the later, decrees death for this crime. Is there any other code of the days before Christ that has this distinction?

It is true that the Book of the Covenant, like the whole literature of the period, does not distinguish between ritual and ethics, but this does not mean that there were no ethical elements in the religion of Jehovah at this time. The ethical and ritual elements lay together unseparated. As yet the question remained unsolved—or rather, un-asked—Which element is fundamental in the concept of religion?

It will be seen, therefore, that while at this early time there were seeds of possible progress in Israel, it was not yet certain that they would germinate.

## Chapter VIII

# ELIJAH AND JEHOIADA

The compiler of our Books of Kings traces the story of the Hebrew monarchy down to the Fall of Jerusalem at the hands of the Babylonians in 586 B.C. The writer, therefore, must have written some time after this date. In his account of the kings of Israel and Judah from the days when Jeroboam rebelled against Rehoboam onwards, he knows of four kinds of kings. For him they fell into classes according to their religious policy, not according to their secular achievements.

For him the best kings were those who abolished the old 'high places' or local shrines, concentrated the worship of Jehovah at Jerusalem, and kept it pure from the use of any kind of image. Of these kings he knows two, Hezekiah and Josiah: their story belongs to the following chapter.

The next best kings were those who came short of the writer's ideal only because they tolerated the 'high places.' He says of them that they 'did that which was right in the sight of Jehovah.' There were many of these in Judah, and, as we have seen, it was their reigns that chanced to be long reigns. There are some hints that even under their rule the tendencies to syncretism—to the image-worship of Jehovah, to the admission of a goddess alongside him and the consequent immoral cult—described in the last chapter, kept cropping up in the southern kingdom.[1] But it seems that a king who 'did that which was right in the

[1] e.g. 1 Kings xxii. 46.

sight of the Lord,' according to our writer's standard, must have withstood these tendencies at least in the Temple itself, for only a wall separated it from the palace.

In the third class there fall the kings who 'made Israel to sin' in the way that Jeroboam did; that is, they encouraged and followed the worship of Jehovah under the form of a bull, with all the dangers that went with it. Under these kings, that is, syncretism flourished. They include some kings of shorter reigns in Judah, and *the whole* of the kings in the north.

When we come to the story of the House of Omri, the writer describes a worse apostasy still. Here we reach his fourth kind of king. The great villains of the piece are Ahab and Jezebel in the north, and their daughter Athaliah in the south. We may quote the writer's own words about Ahab—'And Ahab the son of Omri did that which was evil in the sight of the Lord above all that were before him. And it came to pass, as if it had been a light thing for him to walk in the sins of Jeroboam, the son of Nebat, that he took to wife Jezebel, the daughter of Ethbaal, the king of the Zidonians and went and served Baal and worshipped him. And he reared up an altar for Baal in the house of Baal, which he had built in Samaria. And Ahab made the Asherah; and Ahab did more to provoke Jehovah, the god of Israel, than all the kings of Israel that were before him.[1] It is necessary to ask what exactly it was that made this a new and final form of apostasy.

Ahab did not propose to abolish the worship of Jehovah, for the names of his own sons contain the name of the ancient god of Israel.[2] He proposed—apparently guided by his Zidonian wife Jezebel—to introduce the worship of a pair of Phœnician gods, and put their worship *alongside*

[1] 1 Kings xvi. 30–33.
[2] The first syllable of 'Jehoram' and the last syllable of 'Ahaziah' are forms of the name that we pronounce 'Jehovah.'

*that* of Jehovah. These gods had their separate temples,[1] their distinct 'holy men,'[2] and so their distinct worship. In other words, Ahab deliberately tried to make all his people polytheists. This meant that they were to do what all other nations have done. If Ahab had succeeded, Israel would not have given mankind the true religion, for the true religion is monotheistic. It was a critical moment for the world.

Ahab's attempt might easily have succeeded, for it would find allies among his people. It has been seen that the Canaanites called their god Baal, and that this word, as it simply means 'lord,' could be used for Jehovah. But with Ahab's story it appears definitely as the name of a rival god. This god was much like the old god of the Canaanites, and would appeal to those who had, under the influence of syncretism, long worshipped Jehovah much as their fathers had worshipped the Canaanite Baals. Again, side by side with the Zidonian Baal there was a goddess Ashtart or Ashtoreth. This word is not the same as 'Asherah'; and while the Asherah was a sacred pole, Ashtart was worshipped under the form of a female image, usually of a gross kind. But the two might easily both be used, and it is clear that in the Phœnician cult the gods were sexual. Those, therefore, who liked to use the Asherah would readily pass to the worship of Ashtart.

All the evils of syncretism were here, with the addition that a second principal god was set up alongside Jehovah. If Ahab had succeeded there was an end of what we have called monolatry. It was possible that this should either degrade into polytheism, or ennoble into monotheism. Ahab's success would have decided the issue and decided it disastrously. To speak 'after the manner of men,' the fate of religion hung in the balance.

'And Elijah the Tishbite . . .'[3] At this point our

[1] See quotation above. [2] e.g. 1 Kings xviii. 19.
[3] 1 Kings xvii. 1.

author begins to interpolate large extracts from a different kind of book into the records that he was gathering from 'the books of the chronicles of the kings of Israel.' Even an English reader is aware that there is a change of style. The right adjective for this document is 'prophetic.' Since the days of Samuel and Nathan there had been a dearth of great prophets. The chief name is Ahijah's, but few Englishmen know who he was. The exact student can name one or two more, such as Gad and Shemaiah. But every one knows Elijah. And this eminence is not an error. We must ask where Elijah's true greatness lay. If we had known nothing of him, for instance, except that he was said to have raised a widow's son to life and to have gone to heaven in a chariot of fire, these things would not make him important in the story of religion. His great achievement lies elsewhere.

While the number of prophets of any importance in the period before Elijah is small, it is assumed in the records that the prophetic order had continued all the time, for Elijah and Elisha themselves appear in close connexion with the group of men called 'the sons of the prophets.'[1] It is assumed, too, that the prophets, being devotees of Jehovah, opposed Ahab's polytheistic policy, for Obadiah hides them from the king in caves. Yet at the same time Elijah, in particular, is a solitary figure. He appears as a great and lonely individual. In other words, both the corporate and individual sides of human nature appear in the story of the prophets. This is to repeat what was said above, that the prophets appear in groups, yet that each prophet was 'called' individually.[2] But in the story of the prophets it was the individual that counted. This is pre-eminently so in the instance of Elijah. His story is the story of a duel between a prophet and a king, or rather, between a prophet and a queen. Elijah and Jezebel front each other. And the issue is, Shall Israel become definitely and finally polytheistic or not?

[1] *Cf.* 1 Kings xxii. [2] P. 95.

There are three important stories, the story of Elijah on Carmel, of Elijah at Horeb, and of Elijah and Naboth's vineyard. There is no need to recount the first.[1] The point to note about it is that from Elijah's point of view, his attempt on Carmel failed. This is the only place in the Bible where Mount Carmel figures prominently. In choosing its site for his challenge to Baal, Elijah was probably carrying the war boldly into the enemy's country, for Carmel lies at the point where the road takes along the coast to Jezebel's homeland. The scene itself is one of the bravest in history. A single man faces a king, a nation, and a religion. And there is no doubt what his challenge was. 'How long hop ye on two branches?'—this is perhaps the right translation of his words—'If Jehovah be god, follow him; but if Baal, then follow him!' In other words, for Elijah it is one god or the other; it cannot be both gods at once. And for a moment it looks as if he had won. All Israel shouted 'Jehovah, he is god; Jehovah, he is god.'

Ahab acquiesced, for the long delayed rain was sweeping up from the west. His chariot must race up Esdraelon to Jezreel before Esdraelon becomes, as in Barak's day, impassable for chariots. As it hurries along, the haggard, famine-bitten people are creeping out of the villages to greet Jehovah and the storm. They see Elijah running with girt loins before the chariot, and they cry 'Jehovah, he is god; Jehovah, he is god.'

But Elijah had yet to reckon with his chief foe. Amid all the enthusiasm for Jehovah, Jezebel stood like a rock for Baal, and Elijah knew which would win if it came to a tussle between Jezebel and the people. And he ran away! Carmel was failure.

He ran to 'Horeb the mount of God.'[2] The reason is clear. This was Jehovah's ancient seat, the very spot where the covenant between Jehovah and Israel had begun.

[1] I Kings xviii.    [2] I Kings xix.

It was fitting that here it should end. In the far-away days of Moses a whole people had here plighted troth with Jehovah; now the one man who was still faithful to that covenant, the only one, came to report a universal apostasy. To Elijah the story of Israel seemed to be finished. Israel had forsaken its god, and what else mattered? The religion of Jehovah seemed to be dead.

But at Horeb Elijah learnt that Jehovah was not beaten, and that the truth was that at Carmel he himself had taken the wrong way. In the days between Moses and Elijah Jehovah had been thought of chiefly as a god of wonders, a god who, time and again, as need arose, asserted himself in extraordinary acts. Perhaps the most prominent of his ways of manifestation was by a mysterious smoking flame.[1] On Carmel Elijah appealed to Jehovah under just this concept. He was to do a great marvel, to descend in flame, and win. But he did not win! What then?

While Elijah brooded in despair on Horeb, the scene in which in Moses' day Jehovah had made himself known to Israel, with its fire, and earthquake and tempest, was repeated. But now 'Jehovah was not in the wind,' or 'the fire,' or 'the earthquake.' 'And after the fire' there was 'a sound of gentle stillness.' This, and not 'a still, small voice,' is the meaning of the Hebrew.[2] In other words, Elijah learnt that, when Jehovah seemed to be doing nothing, and even to be absent, he was none the less there and none the less working his will. To use yet other modern terms, he learnt that Jehovah was god of the ordinary as well as of the extraordinary, god of history as well as god of wonders—even more god of history, indeed, than god of wonders—and that through what men call 'the ordinary events of human life,' he was working his will and getting his way.

The sequel of the revelation on Horeb exhibits this.

[1] e.g. Gen. xv. 17; Exod. iii. 2; xiii. 21; xix. 18; 1 Kings viii. 10.

[2] 1 Kings xix. 12.

Elijah is bidden to 'anoint' Elisha to be prophet after himself, Jehu to be king of Israel, and Hazael to be king of Aram. At the same time he is told that there are 'seven thousand' left in Israel who had not 'bowed the knee to Baal.' Of these the prophets are to be the leaders, and there is a young fellow ploughing in a Hebrew village who will rise to leadership when Elijah is gone. Again, Jezebel and the strong house of Ahab have not beaten Jehovah. He is already getting a man ready to rebel against that house and destroy it, and with it Phœnician polytheism, Jehu, the son of Nimshi. Even for the enemy realm of Aram Jehovah has his plans. A usurper is to succeed there, too,—a man called Hazael, and he will be Jehovah's whip to chasten Israel.

We should say that on Horeb Eljiah developed a new policy; the Hebrew said that he had received a revelation. For a Christian theist, the two phrases mean the same thing, for he thinks of Elijah as seeking and receiving a policy from God. The historic parallels are such stories as those of Muhammed in his mountain cave in his earlier and better days, or the Buddha wandering in the forest to brood upon religion. Only Elijah is in the succession of the one race that did not ultimately lose its way in the search for God, and Muhammed and the Buddha are not.

It is worth while looking at the story of Horeb still more closely. When it is said that the idea of Jehovah as god of history begins here to predominate over the idea that he is god of wonders, it is not meant either that the first named idea had no anticipations or that the second idea became extinct. Ideas do not just arrive on given dates, like an Act of Parliament. Great ideas have always anticipations; they are usually at first the ideas of a few and take long to permeate the mass of common thought; and they rarely altogether eclipse old ideas, especially if, as usually happens, the old ideas have some truth in them.

The notion that Jehovah was god of ordinary life,

whether in the story of individuals or of the nation, was not altogether new. Nor did the idea that Jehovah was god of wonders immediately pass. It is prominent, indeed, in the stories of Elijah and Elisha themselves, and it is by no means altogether untrue. What is meant is that on Horeb a great and true idea became dominant in a single man's mind, and that later it became dominant in other men's minds. It is one of the dominant ideas in Christian minds to-day.

Three other points are important. First, on Horeb the idea of a 'godly remnant,' of a faithful minority, and of a faithful minority who in the end counted for far more than the ungodly and vast majority, emerged in the 'seven thousand' that Jehovah 'left him' in Israel in Elijah's day. This concept was recurrent and important in later days. Jehovah was rejected by the many, but he would win by the few.

Again, in the reference to Hazael a new thing appears, or rather a very old thing re-appears. We have seen that for a long time Jehovah had been thought of predominantly as a national god, though the idea that he had to do with other nations besides Israel lay undeveloped in the stories of Adam and Noah.[1] In practice, as distinct from ancestral tale, he had been god of one nation and of one nation only. But now he begins to take part in the history of other nations. He decides who is to rule in Aram. This idea will meet us again later.

Thirdly, we ought to note how the prophets proceed to carry out this idea of Jehovah as lord of history. Elijah himself fulfils only one of Jehovah's three behests. He calls Elisha from his plough. But Elisha is heir of the idea. He waits his time, or, as a man of religion would say, he waits Jehovah's time. At last he sees that the hour has struck for Jehovah's final reckoning with the House of Omri, and he sends one of 'the sons of the prophets' to

[1] P. 108.

anoint Jehu. And Jehu, whom we should call a ferocious soldier, extirpates the Phœnician cult.[1]

Similarly, Elisha himself goes at a given moment to Damascus and meets Hazael. The story of their meeting is a psychological study. By the use of 'suggestion' the prophet puts the idea of rebellion into Hazael's mind, or crystallizes an idea that was already 'sub-consciously' there, and the thing is done![2] Hazael, too, is a ferocious soldier to our thinking. But, on examination, it will be found that the idea that God works through history, always involves the concept that God works His will through bad men as well as good, and chiefly through men who, like Jehu, are a mixture of bad and good.

If we return now to our discrimination of three elements in religion, spiritual, ethical and ritual, to which does Elijah's revelation relate? It might be presented as a matter of ritual, for the question was one of the number of objects of worship. Yet, since the cult of Baal involved immoral worship, it is clear that ethics enter too, though there is no sign that the prophets yet made the distinction between ritual and ethics. But what of the spiritual? The word would have seemed strange to Elijah. Yet on Horeb there was that immediate contact between God and man that we call 'spiritual.' The prophetic frenzy that we met with in the story of Saul has here grown to something nobler, to something that is 'spiritual.'

To return to the ethical. There is another signal instance of the truth that this was now an element in prophetic religion. It is the story of Naboth's vineyard.[3] Here Jezebel and Ahab conspire to rob Naboth of his family plot of land, and to secure his death. Elijah repeats the protest of Nathan in the parallel case of David's sin, but he repeats it with a stern message of doom. Once again, the remarkable thing is not that an eastern monarch should seize any piece of land that he liked, but that a prophet should be

[1] 2 Kings ix. and x. [2] 2 Kings viii. 7–15.
[3] 1 Kings xxi.

found to arraign him in the name of God. It is remarkable too that in the prophetic account of the struggle, Ahab's sin against Naboth should be bracketed, as it were, with his apostasy, as twin cause of the doom of his house. Ethical ideas were not yet differentiated in Israel, but they were there.

The same Phœnician peril threatened the kingdom of Judah. For Athaliah, a daughter of Ahab and Jezebel, married a king of Judah, and became the evil genius of the south as her mother of the north.[1] For fifteen years, first under her husband, then under her son, and finally under herself, Judah sinned against Jehovah with the polytheism of Ahab. But deliverance came in the south, not from the prophets, but from the priests. When Athaliah usurped the throne, she attempted to stamp out the House of David, in the way of eastern usurpers. But during her six years of reign, a single boy of the house, Joash, was living in the Temple that adjoined her palace! The priest Jehoiada had him in his secret care, until the time came when he could win over the royal bodyguard to his side. When once the guard failed her, Athaliah was doomed. The 'city' was on her side, but it could not stand against the guard. She was murdered as she tried to flee. And we find that the 'people of the land,' the country folk, were on the side of Jehovah and Jehoiada. It certainly looks as if polytheism were not yet popular in the south,—outside the 'city' Jerusalem, that is. Cities often take up with new ways while country folk are slow to change.

After Athaliah's death, the 'people of the land' tear down the temple of Baal, which was clearly a distinct shrine, and slay its leading priest. And the new king, Joash, proceeds to restore the Temple.

Under the prophets in the north and the priests in the south, Israel refused to be definitely and finally polytheistic. The danger had long been present, and it recurred in Hebrew history, but it never again came so near final

[1] 2 Kings xi.

victory. Just as Nelson won a decisive victory at Trafalgar at a crisis in the middle of England's long struggle with Napoleon, so Elijah and Jehoiada won a decisive victory for Jehovah at a crisis in Israel's long struggle against polytheism. It began to appear that there was to be one people, or rather a 'remnant' of one people, that refused to take the fatal way of the worship of many gods.

## CHAPTER IX

# THE MIRACLES OF THE OLD TESTAMENT

THIS is a good place to say something about the miracles of the Old Testament. First, it is necessary to ask what we mean by 'miracle.' The word itself means 'wonder.' Broadly speaking, there have been three accounts of what 'miracle' is.

The first is the account accepted by all the peoples of the world before the era of science. They thought that a god, or the gods, were active in the universe, and that now and then men could see what they were doing. For instance, millions of Hindus have believed that, when an eclipse occurs, a great monster tries to swallow the sun, but that ultimately the sun-god splits the monster in two and resumes his sway. Or again, men have thought that, when a man is struck dead by lightning, it is some god that strikes him. Or they have thought that, when plague befalls a city, it is because some god is angry with it.

People who think like this, are not troubled with the difficulty that a god seems to be 'breaking the unbreakable laws of nature,' or 'interfering with the course of nature,' for they do not think of 'nature' as a fixed system in which there are unbreakable laws. They do not face the difficulty because they are not aware of it. To them it seems just as possible that a god should kill a man with lightning as that a man should kill him with an axe. God is busy in the world, or the gods are busy in the world, just as men are busy in the world, only gods can do things that men cannot. And now and then men can see them doing something.

This was the idea current in ancient Israel. When a

great plague of locusts swept down upon Egypt, Jehovah was doing something for his people. When the Jordan shrank until Joshua and the host of Israel could pass through it, Jehovah was doing something. When a vast number of Sennacherib's troops died, Jehovah was doing something. So far, Israel shared the ideas of other ancient peoples. We will ask whether there is any truth in the concept later.

A certain tendency goes with this concept of miracle—a tendency for the stories of miracles to grow with the years. Where there is a real wonder, other stories of wonders easily gather round it, as a snow-flake gathers round a speck of dust. Again, the account of the actual wonder, as it passes from mouth to mouth, tends to grow more and more wonderful.

There is an instance of the first tendency in Prestcott's *History of Mexico.*[1] It seems to be fairly certain that, not long before the coming of Cortes, there were strange 'natural phenomena,' as we should call them, that alarmed the Mexicans. But presently there was also a story of how a dead princess came alive!

The stories of the 'stigmata' of St. Francis furnish an example of the second tendency. There seems to be little doubt that Francis' long and intense brooding upon the five wounds of our Lord, did influence his own body. Psychologists tell us that this is not impossible. But, as the story was repeated in the Franciscan Order, the wonder grew greater, as at once appears if the latest accounts are compared with the earliest.

These phenomena occurred also in Israel. There is no question of intentional fraud, only of credulity; and, before the era of exact science, most men were credulous. An example of two may be given. The story of the last Plague in Egypt seems to tell of a great pestilence—a pestilence from which the Israelites were free, for they lived in Goshen, which was separated from the Nile, the

[1] Book II, Ch. IV.

main seat of the Egyptian population, by a stretch of desert. Tradition, however, declared that it was 'the first-born' and no other who died in every home. It seems plain that another great plague broke out in Sennacherib's army. Such a plague would spread with frightful rapidity in the great host of an eastern king, for there was little or no knowledge of medicine or sanitation; but the Biblical record states that all who perished died in one night. Again, scholars have long held that there is probably some historical basis for the tradition of the Flood, and recent archæological discoveries may turn out to give proof of this. But the Bible account states that the Flood covered the world and topped the mountains of Ararat, some sixteen thousand feet above the sea. It seems plain that in this realm Israel was like other nations, not unlike them.

The second account of miracles depends upon a given account of God's relation to His creation. There was a time, notably in the eighteenth century, when 'nature' was thought of as though it were like a great machine which God made once upon a time and then left, for the most part, to run by itself. Under this concept God was counted to have subjected the universe to 'immutable laws of nature,' which are as regular as clock-work. Is it possible for a clock, when it is time for it to strike four, to strike ten? Some said, 'No,' and denied all stories of miracle. Others said, 'Yes,' for every now and then God interferes with the machine that He made, interrupts the action of the 'laws of nature,' and does something that 'contradicts them.' This account of nature, with its consequent account of miracle, needs mention, for it still obtains in many minds. But it builds upon an account of 'nature' that is no longer accepted. It is under this concept that men talk of the 'natural' and the 'super-natural' as contradictories. Under it a 'miracle' is an inruption of the 'super-natural' into the 'natural.'

It will be noted that, under the idea just named, God

stands outside His world and only rarely intrudes into it. But, if any one believes in what is called 'immanence'—and for a theist who believes in any form of evolution, this is an easy belief—he denies that God is merely outside his world. He asserts that God is also 'inside' it. He says that God is at work in it all the time. He says that the sun could never rise without God, nor a rose bloom, nor a man think.

Men of science used sometimes to scoff at this idea, but now they are not so sure. For one thing, they know that under the concept of a 'fixed system' nothing new could ever happen; and they see new things happening all the time. Also, they know that, when they have done their best to describe the processes of nature and to account for them, there is still something or someone behind them all, unreachable by science, and not a few of them are willing to call this 'something' or 'someone' God.

Under this concept Christian theists claim that God is always and everywhere at work—that He takes His share in everything that happens except sin. But if this be so, what becomes of the distinction between the 'super-natural' and the 'natural'? We may either say that both are always there, or we may say that the distinction between them lapses. Is not the 'natural' also the 'super-natural' if God is in it?

What then is a miracle? Everything is a miracle, for God is in it. He is in the sunrise as well as in the eclipse; in the regular tide of the Red Sea as well as in its failure once upon a time; in the life of Sennacherib's multitudes as well as in their death. If, however, the term 'miracle' is to be kept, under this account, for a few events, the only account that we can give of them is that they are events in which men see with especial clearness that God is at work. This definition means, not that God only occasionally 'does something,' but that men only occasionally notice that He is doing it. A miracle is then only a peculiarly clear instance of the works of a God who is working all the time.

It is worth while to pursue this idea a little further. There is a story that when Luther was a young fellow, he was much impressed because a companion was struck dead in a thunder-storm while he escaped. Some later writers have said, 'Pooh! All that was just an accident.' But can a theist believe in 'accident'? If he does, he must mean that there are events in the universe whose full effects God does not foresee or control. This is no theism. A theist must believe that, though he himself cannot say why God allowed Luther's companion to be struck dead, yet God had something to do with it. On the other hand, if he is a Protestant, he thinks he can see God's purpose in the escape of Luther, for this man was to be of great importance for religion.[1]

For a believer in 'immanence,' therefore, a miracle can only be a peculiarly clear instance of the way in which God secures His purposes in the world. There are people who see God at work chiefly in disasters. Jesus did not deny that there were examples of this[2]; but His characteristic attitude was to see God at work in the beneficence of the sun and the rain.[3] For Him these daily events were acts of God. They are not less miraculous in the only true sense, because they are frequent.

Earth's crammed with heaven, and every common bush
Aflame with God! But only they who see
Take off their shoes.

It is plain that this third account of miracles is fatal to the second. Is it fatal to the first—that is, to the account that prevailed in Israel? Not at all. The third account says that the first account is true as far as it goes, but

[1] A friend supplies an illustration from the life of Archbishop Whateley. Someone told him that he had been in a ship-wreck and by a wonderful Providence he alone had escaped. Whateley replied that he knew of a more wonderful case—where Providence had taken a ship, with its cargo and crew and passengers, all safely across the ocean.

[2] Luke xiii. 1–5.

[3] Matt, v. 45.

that it does not go far enough. It is incomplete, not untrue. It is incomplete because it fails to allow sufficiently for the truth that God is always and everywhere active. It is not untrue, for God was active in the events that it calls miracles.

Miracles do not occur everywhere throughout the Bible. There are three great groups of them, and a few sporadic ones. The three groups cluster respectively round the names of Moses and Joshua, Elijah and Elisha, and Jesus and the Apostles. There are instances of the sporadic in the story of Isaiah.[1]

So far as the Old Testament is concerned, it is true, as already explained, that from the time of Elijah onwards, miracle plays a diminishing part in the story of the religion of Israel. God is still a god of wonder—and who would deny this ? But He is principally a god of history. For early Israel Jehovah was chiefly the god of the wonders of Sinai ; for Isaiah He was the god who used Assyria for His own purposes ; for Jeremiah the god who used Babylon for His own purposes ; and so on. Elijah is the hero of a number of miracles, but he is greatest on Horeb, where he discovered that Jehovah is master of what is called the 'ordinary course of events,' and not merely or chiefly of the 'extraordinary.' He is master of both ; but from Elijah's time the two concepts began to be rightly related in Israel.

It does not fall within the scope of this book to examine the Old Testament miracles one by one ; but, taken as a whole, they seem to suit the third definition of miracle given above. At the same time, the process, also described above, by which traditional accounts of miracles add to their number and wonder, seems clearly to have been at work. This process seems to have gone further in the group of miracles associated with Elijah and Elisha than in the group that gathers round Moses and Joshua. A comment may be inserted about each group.

[1] For Jonah and Daniel, see Chap. xiii.

In the 'Elijah and Elisha group,' a number of the wonders suggest that the prophets had greater medical knowledge than was usual at the time. It is quite in accordance with early ideas that such knowledge should be associated with religious men. This is an instance of an incomplete truth. For does not God play His part, for a Christian theist, in every cure that medicine ever works? This explanation, however, does not cover the greater miracles of this group; whatever their origin, in their present form they are not historical.

The characteristic mark, on the other hand, in the 'Moses and Joshua group' is the number of miracles that have to do, not with the world of men, but with the world of nature. Parallel phenomena can be found to most of them in the phenomena of the Nile Delta. For instance, under certain circumstances the Nile runs red; or again, there is some evidence that an upheaval of the sandy bottom might make it possible to cross the north-western tongue of the Red Sea where it is usually impassable.

The theist will say that God is at work in all these things. But, while he finds it impossible to say exactly what purpose God is serving in many such phenomena, in the instance of the two great groups of Hebrew miracles it is possible to discern His purpose. The phenomena of Egypt coincided with the Exodus—or rather, occasioned the Exodus. And, so far as history can see, if there had been no Exodus, there would have been no Israel and, to speak 'after the manner of men,' no Christ. Here, therefore, a believer in immanence can not only see God at work, but he can see what God is doing.

Similarly, in the days of Elijah and Elisha, as we have already noted, the religion of Israel all but perished, and its survival depended upon the survival of the 'godly remnant' that the prophets led. We have not the details of all the story, but it is plain that the 'sons of the prophets,' who gathered round Elijah and Elisha, and in whom the hope of Israel lay, clung together in forlorn trust. They survived because Jehovah meant them to survive. And they were not wrong in seeing His workmanship in many strangely helpful things that befell them.

We, too, in the retrospect of history, can see not only that God was at work, as He always is but what His purpose was. At two crises He so worked that the way was open to the coming of His Son. It was no accident that 'Moses and Elijah' were with Jesus on the Mount of Transfiguration. In their days, as in His, unusual events happened—unusual, not unnatural—and in those events it is still possible to see the purposes of the God who plays His ineradicable part in every single thing that happens except sin. A miracle is just one of His rarer and clearer works.[1]

[1] It does not belong to this study to discuss the miracles of Jesus; but, to avoid misunderstanding, I may add here that I believe that He worked miracles. It may be difficult for any one who thinks that Jesus was no more than a good man, to believe in His miracles; but it does not seem to be difficult for one who believes, as I do, that He was Divine, to accept them. For God to 'become man' does not seem to me to be 'an interruption of the laws of nature,' but the consummation of God's work of creation. It is 'natural,' that is, as well as 'super-natural,' if the last misleading word is to be retained.

Again, in Jesus' miracles the purposes of God are exceedingly plain. They form 'part and parcel' of His Son's life and work—an inevitable part, as I think. This is not the place to develop this statement, but one point may be named—Jesus' unerring selection of miracles. It is just as wonderful to examine the miracles that He refrained from working as to examine those that He worked. The story of His Temptation falls here.

## Chapter X

# THE FIRST GROUP OF WRITTEN PROPHETS

We have seen that Jeroboam I. set up two bulls, one at Bethel and one at Dan, and that these two shrines were centres of syncretism. Of the two, Bethel was far the more important, for Dan lay away in a remote and isolated corner of the distant north. About the year 760 B.C., when the bull at Bethel had stood for almost two centuries, there was a priest in charge of the 'royal shrine' called Amaziah.

One day a man named Amos,[1] who belonged to a place called Tekoa, which lay some twenty miles south, in the heart of the barren mountains of Judah, took his stand near the bull and began to denounce its worship and to preach Jehovah's doom on Bethel and the whole north; and, not only on the whole north, but on all the small nations whose land lay around the Arabah, and upon Aram as well. There was an altercation between the priest and Amos. Amaziah bade the new prophet begone to his own land. The prophet replied by declaring an awful doom on Amaziah himself. With this scene the greatest period in the story of the religion of Israel began.

It is necessary to recall the historical background. The reigning king in the north was Jeroboam II., the most splendid of the House of Jehu.[2] Both in the north and south it was a time of wealth, prosperity and luxury. The House of Jehu, according to the compiler of the Books of Kings, followed consistently the policy of 'Jeroboam, the son of Nebat, who made Israel to sin.' So did the few

[1] Amos vii. 10–17. [2] See p. 46.

feeble rulers that followed in the north until the Fall of Samaria in 722 B.C. This means that the compiler accuses these kings of syncretism rather than polytheism; but, as has already been seen, the one might readily pass into the other, and there are signs in the Book of Amos that outright polytheism was sometimes practised.[1]

The old line of 'the sons of the prophets' does not appear in the picture; indeed, they never again appear as true exponents of the will of Jehovah. There are signs that they had succumbed to the easy temptation to prophesy 'to eat bread'[2]; that is, they suited their prophecies to the desires of their patrons so as to gain a living.[3] With Amos a new series of prophets began, with whom the individual call of Jehovah is peculiarly clear. Their watchword was the old one, 'Thus saith Jehovah,' but with them it rang with a new revelation and it rings still.

The line of these prophets lasted, with one great interval, for about two hundred years. There is a development in their teaching, yet fundamentally they all said the same things. This will appear as their story is rapidly sketched. Apart from one of them, Isaiah, they are not mentioned in the Book of Kings. But they have left us written accounts of their testimony. In other words, we have now reached the 'written prophets.' An idea of the message of each of them may be gathered from a comparatively few passages in their books. A short list of 'selected readings' from the oracles of each prophet, as well as from some other books, is suggested in footnotes.

We gather from the Book of Amos[4] that there was a common belief that a 'day of Jehovah'[5] was near—a 'day,' that is, when Jehovah would show his might as he had not done for many a day. Amos agrees with this

[1] Amos v. 26.
[2] Amos vii. 13.
[3] The story of Micaiah (p. 97) and the story of Gehazi (2 Kings v. 26) illustrate this.
[4] Selected readings: Amos vii. 10–17; i. and ii.
[5] Amos v. 18.

expectation, but he declares that Jehovah will show himself in the judgement of Israel, not in its triumph. In his own words, he preached that 'the day of Jehovah is darkness, and not light.'[1] For him the peculiar seat of Jehovah is Jerusalem.[2] He pictures it as a lion's lair, and he says that the lion is bestirring himself; and that, as every living thing shuddered when it heard a lion's roar ring over a countryside, so Israel and all its neighbours will shudder as Jehovah takes the path of doom.

Amos does not say what world event will fulfil this prophecy, but there is little doubt that he refers to the nearing menace of Assyrian power. Amos cries out against two chief evils. First, he denounces the ritual at such shrines of Jehovah as Bethel, Gilgal and Beer-sheba.[3] In other words, he denounces syncretism. For the first time a prophet sees and gibbets its evils. Second, he demands, or rather he testifies that Jehovah demands, righteousness. In doing this, he distinguishes ritual from ethics, and declares that by itself the first is worthless, and that the second is the essential element in the religion of Jehovah. The ethical issue is clearly taken at last.

If there is one sin against righteousness that Amos pillories more than another, it is cruelty. In the series of oracles against peoples that fills his first two chapters, the capital charge against nation after nation is cruelty. So long as he is talking of the neighbour peoples, he condemns the cruelty of nation against nation. But when he comes to Israel, for whom he reserves his worst woe, he tells of the wrongs of the poor. In his day, as in many another, luxury and poverty culminated together. Many of the yeomen that made up the bulk of the population, were being driven, first to the money-lender and then

[1] Amos v. 18.

[2] Amos i. 2. Some, however, think that the few references to Judah in this book are later insertions. This applies particularly to the last paragraph, ix. 11–15, with its message of hope after captivity.

[3] e.g. Amos v. 4f.

to slavery. The slave-markets were so glutted with slaves that a man might be sold at the same price as 'a pair of shoes.'[1] Amos cries out again and again against these enormities. For him it is sin not only to oppress the poor, but to neglect them. He has a fierce oracle against the 'idle rich,' the people who enjoy their own luxuries and care nothing for the plight of their neighbours.[2] Amos is sometimes pictured as a hard-hearted man, but he is stern to the rich because he has pity on the poor. As for the present prosperity of Israel, it is like a 'basket of summer fruit,'[3] lovely and luscious to look at now, but already ripe for the rottenness of quick decay.

A second prophet, Hosea,[4] belongs to the same period. Probably he prophesied a little later than Amos, in the last few years of the northern kingdom, when king succeeded king in spasmodic disorder.[5] Assyria had then drawn very near; and we can see the people of the little Hebrew state now hoping that its coming will bring security and now trembling lest it should bring calamity. For Hosea there is no doubt. He foretells the destruction of the state and captivity in distant lands.

In reading his book two things need to be remembered. First, that, as with Amos and other prophets, his oracles, as at present arranged, are not in chronological order; and second, that, since his style is very allusive,[6] and since the meaning of the Hebrew text is not always clear, it is sometimes difficult to follow him in detail. But his general message is quite plain. It is just Amos' message over again, with differences in emphasis and manner.

For instance, even more plainly than Amos, Hosea dismisses the whole business of images of Jehovah and bulls of Samaria as sheer idolatry and apostasy.[7] As for the 'calf' at Bethel, 'the workman made it, and it is no

[1] Amos viii. 6. [2] Amos vi. [3] Amos viii. 2.
[4] Selected passages: Hos. i.–iii.; xiv. [5] Hos. viii. 4; x. 7.
[6] That is, he makes allusions that his hearers would readily understand, but which are obscure to us. [7] e.g. Hos. viii. 4–6.

god . . . it shall be broken in pieces.' So much for the ancient image of Jehovah Himself!

But the best way to compare Hosea with Amos is to put side by side the two consecutive passages that begin their two books. The two first chapters of Amos tell of the doom of people after people, culminating in the doom of Israel; Hosea's first three chapters tell of his own ruined home and the likeness of Israel to it. Hosea's wife was a harlot. For him she was a parable of Israel. Jehovah had wooed Israel for his bride long ago, and now she was a harlot. This parable recurs in later prophets, but it is never so poignant as with the man whose own wife was faithless.

If we try for a moment to look into such a home, with its loyal husband, its sinful wife and its hapless children, we can understand why in Hosea cries of woe alternate with cries of love and forlorn hope with despair. Would not just such illogical moods alternate in the heart of such a man? And for Hosea his own agonies are but a small copy of the agonies of Jehovah over sinful Israel. Yet Hosea's hope never utterly dies, and neither does Jehovah's. There shall return to Jehovah and Israel the happiness of their far-away wooing, when Jehovah companied with Israel in the wilderness and there were as yet none of the vile entanglements of Canaan to bewilder and degrade his bride. For Hosea, Jehovah is tender as well as righteous.

Meanwhile, after more than two centuries, there was a great prophet in Judah. His name was Isaiah, the son of Amoz.[1] We have his own story of his call, and he tells us its date.[2] 'In the year that King Uzziah died, I saw Jehovah.' In the eyes of the compiler of the Books of Kings, Uzziah was a good king. Isaiah, on the other hand,

[1] Selected readings: For Isaiah's general message—chs. vi.; i.; ii. 5–22; xxxii. For his oracles before the Fall of Samaria, 722 B.C.—chs. v.; vii. For his oracles at the crisis of Sennacherib's invasion—chs. x. 5–34; xvii. 12–14. Chs. ii. 2–4; xi. 1–9 should be read, though perhaps they belong to some later prophet.

[2] Isa. vi.

tells us that he himself 'dwelt in the midst of a people of unclean lips,' who had eyes but would not see, had ears but would not listen, had hearts but would not understand,— who were so evil, indeed, that blow after blow must fall upon them until only a small remnant, like a tiny shoot springing out of the stump of a tree on which the axe has plied, and plied, and plied—only a small remnant shall survive. The difference between the two accounts is that between the judgement of a historian who has merely searched the records of past kings and the insight of a contemporary. To the compiler Judah was respectable enough in the days of Uzziah; to Isaiah it was an unclean thing.

Obviously, in Judah as well as Israel, there was sometimes a difference between a king's policy and a people's practice. In Judah, as well as Israel, in spite of a number of good kings, syncretism and polytheism were degrading the worship of Jehovah. Judah may not yet have been as sick with this disease as Israel. The Temple at Jerusalem, in particular, may have retained a purer form of cult; but the evil was there, deep-seated and pervasive.

This appeared clearly four or five years after Isaiah's call. Ahaz then came to the throne, and he was one of the kings of Judah who 'did that which was evil in the sight of Jehovah.' We are told that he 'made his son pass through the fire,' which may mean that human sacrifice recurred in Israel. The compiler traces this to the influence of the Canaanitish leaven. Isaiah shows us the people betaking themselves to wizards and traffickers with 'familiar spirits.'[1] Some of these tendencies came from the east,[2] and indeed it is obvious that, when the Assyrian empire spread west, many such influences would come with it. The compiler illustrates this tendency in another way when he tells us that Ahaz made a new altar for the Temple in the Assyrian style.[3] In brief, evils that had been always

[1] Isa. viii. 19. [2] Isa. ii. 6. [3] 2 Kings xvi. 10ff.

present now flaunted. The king's practice now marched with the desires of the mass of the people. The disease that killed the north, was rampant in the south.

With the accession of Hezekiah, who followed Ahaz, there was a change in royal policy. Hezekiah strove to maintain the independence of his little kingdom, chiefly by playing off Egypt against Assyria. And his religious policy was in line with this policy of independence. He was one of the two kings for whom the compiler has unstinted praise. He tells us that he not only 'did that which was right in the eyes of Jehovah' like earlier kings of Judah, but that he waged a strenuous fight against the whole use of images. It is not unlikely that there had always been some relics of a tradition against this in the south, and now at last there came a king who saw the extent of the evil and grappled with it. We are told that he 'put away the high places.'[1] This means that Hezekiah saw that his people were so prone to image-worship that the only way to extirpate it was to abolish every shrine of Jehovah except the one that always lay under his eye, the Temple at Jerusalem. Such a policy of the concentration of worship was, of course, much easier in so small a realm as Judah than it would have been in the north. In the very Temple there was an old, old image of a serpent which tradition ascribed to Moses himself. But the people were making a subsidiary god of this serpent; so Hezekiah broke it in pieces.[2] Hezekiah struggled to rid Judah of syncretism and all its ills. Are we to suppose that he succeeded?

It is tempting to simplify history by supposing that the reign of Ahaz was altogether evil and Hezekiah's altogether good, and to ascribe all Isaiah's oracles of doom to the first

[1] 2 Kings xviii. 4.

[2] 2 Kings xviii. 4. There is an opinion that this serpent was an image of Jehovah Himself, which had for centuries been the principal object of devotion in the Temple. It will be seen that I am one of those who do not incline to this opinion.

of the two reigns, and all his oracles of hope to the second; but the situation was more complex than this. In both reigns two parties were in constant conflict—the 'godly remnant,' for this term is now very much in place, and the mass of the people. Under Ahaz the second class had the benefit of royal support and under Hezekiah the first. Both parties were there throughout the whole period. We may compare the way in which there were both Romanist and Protestant parties in England during the reigns of Edward VI., Mary and Elizabeth; but now one, and now the other, was favoured by the monarch. No doubt, in Judah, as in England, there were many who were content merely to look on and watch other people struggle.

The Book of Isaiah is a very long one, and there is no book in the Bible about whose contents experts have differed more. A large part of its oracles are now ascribed by the great majority of scholars to other writers than the son of Amoz. There are three considerable collections of oracles which are his.[1] The elements that are common to the prophetic message of this great period are all manifest in his oracles. Indeed, if an English reader wishes to learn what this common message was, he cannot do better than read the first five chapters of the Book of Isaiah. The number of unexplained allusions to contemporary events and concepts is here small, and the exposition is comprehensive and clear.

But, in addition, we may ask—What is there distinctive in the preaching of Isaiah? In particular, how did his preaching advance upon that of Amos and Hosea? The answer depends on the two facts that, with the coming of a world-empire, a crucial practical problem

[1] Isa. i. 1–xi. 9; xiii.–xxiii. (except the oracles about Babylon); xxviii–xxxii. There is much difference of opinion, however, about the date of three famous predictions of world peace, ii. 1–4; xi. 1–9; xix. 16–25. Some writers think that this concept does not suit Isaiah's time. Another view is taken below. Other passages are ascribed to Isaiah; but his message can be learnt thoroughly from these three sets of passages; or, indeed, from the first and last of them.

faced every believer in Jehovah, and that Isaiah had a passionate love for Jerusalem and the House of David. It was in relation to the first fact that Isaiah made his permanent contribution to religion. The second conditioned the particular expression that he gave to his ideas. The two intertwine so continuously in the story that they cannot be kept separate, but it is worth while to note them now.

When some great upheaval happens in human history, men only slowly adjust themselves to it. This was so in the days when the mighty Assyrian empire arose and shook 'all nations.' Let us pass to the particular issue that it raised in religion. The question at once was asked, 'What is an Edomite, or a Moabite, or an Aramean, or a Hebrew to say now about his national god?' For, as Assyria herself claimed,[1] national gods were as helpless as nations before her. Down they went in common ruin with their peoples! What about Jehovah? Only two ways were open. One was to admit the Assyrian claim and to allow that Jehovah was at best a feeble and helpless god; the other was to claim that Jehovah was master of Assyria, and indeed of the whole world of men, all the time!

It has been seen that in the earliest stories of Israel, the last idea was not altogether absent[2]; but also, that for centuries before Isaiah's day, Jehovah had in practice been a local and national god. It has been seen, too, that in Elijah's vision on Horeb the idea appeared that Jehovah was master of Aram as well as of Israel. With Amos this idea had widened to include all the little neighbour nations,[3] and Hosea had asserted that the coming of the Assyrian was Jehovah's way of punishing his apostate people. In other words prophetic thought had been feeling its way in a certain direction. The ideas that Jehovah is god over all the nations of the world; that he dictates their fate; that, in particular, overweening Assyria is but his tool, and a tool that he will fling away

[1] Isa. x. 8–11; xxxvi. 19ff. [2] Pp. 107f. [3] Amos i. and ii.

when he has finished with it—these ideas appear full-grown with Isaiah. In other words, he strode boldly down the path that ended in monotheism. Indeed, he himself was in practice a monotheist, whether he had worked out all the theoretical statement of the great concept or not.

There are illustrations of this idea in his many oracles about foreign nations. These oracles are not merely, as with Amos, about the small neighbour peoples, but about ancient Egypt,[1] wealthy Tyre,[2] the distant and mysterious Soudan,[3] and, chief of all, the seemingly omnipotent Assyria.[4] Perhaps the best single illustration of the idea is the passage that begins at Isaiah x. 4. Here Isaiah, anticipating the name that was later given to Attila, the 'scourge of God,' declares that Assyria is but 'the rod of' Jehovah's 'anger,' with which he scourges Israel for her sins; and that, when once this rod of his has served this purpose, Jehovah will break it in pieces! Assyria thinks that it has power of its own, but it is just a thing in his hands! It thinks that it is going to capture Jerusalem, does it? It never will, for Jerusalem is the city of Jehovah. A rod might just as well take it into its head that it wields the hand that grasps it! Poor little Sennacherib! What can he do against Jehovah—Jehovah, of whom the prophet learnt long ago that 'the fulness of the whole earth is his glory.'[5] The omnipotence of the one God seems to us as obvious as the existence of America. None the less, it was once a discovery, and Isaiah is greater than Columbus.

Sennacherib failed to capture Jerusalem. At the time this was the vindication of Isaiah and his doctrine. It would startle and delight all Judah and no doubt it stimulated a temporary return to the worship of Jehovah and of no other. For once, too, a prophet would be popular. Indeed, a belief seems to have become current that, in any event, Jehovah would save his Temple. We shall find

[1] Isa. xix. [2] Isa. xxiii. [3] Isa. xviii.
[4] e.g. Isa. xvii. 12–14. [5] Isa. vi. 3.

that this idea proved a stumbling-block to Israel in the days of Jeremiah.

But the true vindication of Isaiah's certainty was not the escape of the city from Sennacherib, dramatic and signal as that was. In many another instance a great conqueror has failed to capture some town or other, and it has meant nothing for the world. The true basis of Isaiah's assurance that Jehovah was master of Assyria was Jehovah's character. Why is it that the god of one little people can still be thought of as God of the whole earth? Because that people's god was righteous. In other words, Isaiah added ethics to monotheism in his concept of his nation's god. This idea, of course, he shared with Amos and Hosea. It cannot be said that he here added to their ideas, but he does expound the nature of righteousness at greater length than they. It can now be seen that it has four chief elements—justice, mercy, truth,[1] and peace. I have laid out all that this four-fold concept implies elsewhere.[2]

It will be obvious that all four ideas are social as well as ethical. Indeed, ethics always has a social content. For Isaiah's own exposition of the first three ideas, reference may once more be made to his first five chapters. It will then be clear that, from the point of view of a poor man of those days, the ideas go together. For instance, justice and mercy were not, for him, contradictory, as so often with us, but complementary.

The prophetic doctrine of righteousness now approached completion. It is difficult to exaggerate its importance for the world. To-day, for instance, the current concept of right character and conduct in the white world is just this four-fold concept of righteousness. We all believe that a man ought to be just, merciful, true and peaceable. Anticipations of this teaching and approximations to it may

[1] This concept means something farther reaching than the mere speaking of the truth; it is a reliability that permeates character.

[2] *The Bible Doctrine of Society*, ch. iii.

be found elsewhere. But historically the white world has learnt it because it is in the Bible, and its roots in the Old Testament concept of God.

A word needs to be said separately about the concept of world-wide peace. As has been seen,[1] many scholars think that this idea belongs, not to the environment of Isaiah's ideas, but to a later period. There is much to say, however, on the other side. In the early ideal of Israel, as portrayed in its ancestral stories, there lay dormant an ideal of peace.[2] This seemed to be eclipsed in the days of the Judges and kings, for Jehovah then appears as a war-god. But we saw above[3] that even here the true notion is that the Hebrew god made war that he might give his people prosperity and, as an element in prosperity, peace.

It is allowed that the idea that a god should give his people prosperity was current among ancient races. In the time of Amos, for instance, there was a current phrase, 'the day of Jehovah,' under which Israel expected that its god would triumph, and his people with him. But they might think of him, and of themselves, as flourishing in war, or as flourishing in peace. We do not know how they would have responded to this alternative, but we know that another people, Assyria, responded by asserting that for them and their god prosperity meant war and war and war. This appears in not a few of their kings' records. Had Isaiah any other idea about his God? Like Hosea, and in a way that surpassed Hosea, he did believe that at long last Jehovah would give His people prosperity. This is allowed. But was it a peaceful prosperity? Did Isaiah, at this point, contradict the Assyrian ideal?

This brings us to the second of the facts that ruled his thinking, and brings us to it at a decisive point. He loved Jerusalem and the House of David. In the history of Judah there were many good kings, at least in comparison with the kings of the north. At their beginning there

[1] P. 137, footnote. [2] *cf.* p. 108. [3] P. 108.

stood David, and with him, Solomon. It has been seen that in their story the idea can be traced that the best kind of kingdom is a kingdom at peace.[1] Isaiah foretells more than once that Jehovah will give Israel prosperity under the rule of a scion of the House of David. One of the most famous of these promises runs, 'Unto us a child is born, unto us a son is given, and his name shall be called Wonderful Counsellor,[2] the Mighty God, the Everlasting Father, the Prince of Peace.'[3] Under this description of the 'prince of the four names' Isaiah tells us what he thought a true king ought to be. He would be wise, 'Wonderful Counsellor'; he would be powerful, 'Mighty God'[4]; he would be like a father to his people; his heart would be set on peace, 'Prince of Peace.' In the last name Isaiah seems directly to contradict the Assyrian ideal of a king. Similarly, in a later passage,[5] this prophet foretells that the two great realms of his world, Egypt and Assyria, whose antagonism was the ruling factor in the history of the period, would find peace at last because they would worship the god of little Israel.

Another prophecy,[6] which may not be Isaiah's, for it is found also in the book of his contemporary Micah,[7] extends this idea in the famous picture of all nations 'flowing unto' Jerusalem to worship Israel's god, and to 'learn war no more.' And a third great passage,[8] which appears in our Book of Isaiah as the sequel of the greatest of Isaiah's pictures of Jehovah's mastery of war, proclaims that this war is but the prelude to a universal peace under a scion of David's line. Jehovah will achieve the impossible, —'The lion shall lie down with the lamb.'

[1] Pp. 39, 42.
[2] These two words are to be taken together.
[3] Isa. ix. 6.
[4] That is, he would have the power of God behind his rule.
[5] Isa. xix. 23.
[6] Isa. ii. 2–4.
[7] Mic. iv. 1ff.
[8] Isa. xi. 1–9.

did not fulfil the prophecy, either in the perfection of his rule, or the extent of his triumph. Neither did Josiah; and the other later kings were all 'evil'! Again, there was no other king in Israel till the Maccabees and the Herods! But all the while the Jew treasured this prophecy, for he knew that it must come to pass, if God is God. Not indeed in its immediate detail, for men's wickedness delays God, but in its *principle*. If there is a God, and if He is omnipotent and loving, He must in the end set up a kingdom of heaven on earth. Isaiah declared that He would do so in an 'heir of David's line.' In our speech, he was declaring that there is continuity in the ways of God; that 'salvation is of the Jews'; that it was through Israel and through a Hebrew Messiah that God would rescue the world from its woes. And he was right.

A 'Messianic prophecy' is not a passage which, being wrenched from its context, can be made to fit events that happened centuries after the prophet's time. It is a passage that asserts the great truth that God's sure purpose of redemption will be perfected under a perfect king, the heir and perfecter of the Old Testament doctrine of God's way of rule, and this came to pass in Jesus Christ.

It will not be possible in a book like this to examine other Messianic prophecies in detail. For their exposition reference must be made to the commentaries. But perhaps the historical method of interpretation will be clear enough from this example.

There is one more name in the first group of written prophets. To Amos, Hosea and Isaiah, we must add Micah.[1] Like Isaiah he belonged to Judah; but, unlike Isaiah, he belonged to a village, and not to a capital city. He has a special animus against cities and all their ways. For him they were capitals of sin. In his Messianic prophecy, therefore,[2] he looks for the future king, not from David's city, Jerusalem, but from David's village Bethlehem.

[1] Selected passages: chs. iii.; vi. i.-vii. 6.
[2] Mic. v. 2; some, however, ascribe this passage to a later writer.

His book falls readily into three parts.[1] Each is a fair example of a certain literary arrangement of material, which is common—of course, with considerable variation—in many of the Old Testament prophecies, as they stand in the several books. First, there is a description of a national apostasy; next Jehovah's judgement falls; then we read of the survival and prosperity of the faithful 'godly remnant.' We do not know whether we owe this arrangement to the prophets themselves, or to those who arranged their oracles, or sometimes to one and sometimes to the other; but there is no doubt that it tends to repeat itself.

If a single oracle of Micah is to be selected for quotation, it would be the first paragraph of his sixth chapter. These eight verses epitomize the message of the four great prophets of the Assyrian epoch. Jehovah does not require ritual.[2] Even the harrowing ritual of the sacrifice of the first-born means nothing to Him. His will for a man is 'to do justly, to love mercy, and to walk humbly with (his) god.' These are great demands, but they are also the 'good tidings,' the gospel, of the prophets.

Their message may now be easily summarized. Jehovah is God of all nations. He is righteous, and demands righteousness of all nations, but especially of His chosen people, just because they are His chosen people. Without righteousness, He will accept none of the ritual of worship. He will judge and punish the multitudes of the unrighteous, even though they be His own people. To the righteous He will give prosperity, however few the righteous remnant may be. These truths are current coin now, but it was the prophets who mined the gold.

[1] Chs. i. and ii.; iii.-v.; vi. and vii.

[2] This is probably so even with the reference to Balaam, for it is in close connexion with his story that we find the Hebrew first going astray in the way of immoral worship.—Num. xxv.; *cf.* xxxi. 16.

## CHAPTER XI

# THE SCHOOL OF DEUTERONOMY

ON Hezekiah's death there followed the darkest half century of the southern kingdom. For at least forty-five years Manasseh reigned. The Compiler finds it hard to discover words to describe his wickedness.[1] The sin of the Son of Nebat is a small thing here. Manasseh was as bad as Ahab. To the sins that Israel learnt from the Canaanites he added sins that Ahaz had borrowed from the east, and multiplied and multiplied them. Worst of all, he desecrated the Temple itself, as even Athaliah had not done, and turned it into a polytheistic shrine, where the enormity of the old Canaanite Asherah elbowed the enormity of the new Babylonish cult of 'the host of heaven.' Wizards, soothsayers and charmers swarmed; and, in addition to all this, Manasseh was forward to 'shed innocent blood.' In his reign the religion of Israel sank to its lowest ebb.

The faith of Jehovah survived, though we do not know how. The Compiler suggests that there were prophets in Manasseh's time, but he does not give any name, and none of our prophetic books belongs to this half-century. Still, the question arises—How did the oracles of Amos and Isaiah survive? How did any books that told of the religion of Jehovah survive? There must have been those who loved and copied and preserved them. The 'godly remnant' did not perish. When the long night was over, we find that there were still faithful priests of Jehovah, ready to cleanse and restore the Temple. Just as the evil

[1] 2 Kings xxi. 1-18.

kind of religion survived in Hezekiah's day or Josiah's day, so the good kind survived in Manasseh's. And this dismal half-century schooled the remnant for the greater ordeal of exile.

After this dark period, the last good king, Josiah, came to the throne. He was only eight years old, and we do not know much about his first seventeen years of rule. But we find that in his eighteenth year the Temple was being restored and repaired under the direction of a priest of Jehovah, Hilkiah. At this point Josiah takes very decisive religious action on the side of Jehovah.

Here again religion and politics were one. During Manasseh's reign the power of Assyria had reached its zenith, and there seemed nothing to do but submit; but, as the seventh century neared its close, it began to appear that Assyria might not rule for ever. As we saw above,[1] the Scythian, the Median, the Babylonian and the Egyptian all played a part in the story. Josiah, like others, began to surmise that Assyria's day was done, and with the surmise the hope of the restored independence of Judah sprang too. And this would mean, in ancient and eastern eyes, the restoration of her national cult. It is not suggested that Josiah was a mere time-server, for he was a sincere worshipper of Jehovah and he would see Jehovah's hand in the doom of Assyria. For him, as for all men until comparatively recent times, religion and politics did not seem to be two things, but one.

The compiler of the Books of Kings gives us a long account of the reformation of Josiah, but there are not many elements in it. We are told that the king purified the Temple from the abomination of heathen worship; that he cleansed it both from the defilements that went back historically to Canaanite influence, and from the more recent abominations of the east; that he abolished the unclean worship that once more flourished in the Temple itself; that he 'defiled Tophet,' the seat of human sacrifice;

[1] Pp. 48 f.

that he destroyed every 'high place'—that is, every shrine except the Temple—and in particular the 'high place' at Bethel,[1] which the Son of Nebat had set up; and that he led his people in the celebration of a great Passover unto Jehovah. It will be seen that this was to repeat more thoroughly the measures that the compiler had already assigned to Hezekiah a hundred years before.

We are told that Josiah did all this in obedience to the teaching of a 'book of the law of Jehovah' which Hilkiah, the priest, had found in the Temple. What book was this? It is the opinion of the great majority of scholars that it was a large part of our Book of Deuteronomy.[2] There are several reasons for this. For one thing the literary style of Deuteronomy is quite distinctive, as even an English reader will feel if he will read, say, the sixth and twenty-eighth chapters straight through. It is much like the style of the compiler himself, not least in the very passage that describes the reforms of Josiah. Our earlier documents are not written in this style. But the chief reason is that Josiah's reforms tally in several ways with the teaching of this book,—and with its teachings, where it has no anticipations in earlier law-codes.

In particular, in one passage at least Deuteronomy[3] lays it down that Jehovah is only to be worshipped at a single place; and, until Hezekiah's time, there is no trace of this idea in any historical book. It is plain that, in Josiah's eyes, the 'place which Jehovah, thy god, shall choose' is Jerusalem; yet the Judges and Samuel, for instance, and Solomon and Elijah, had all worshipped him elsewhere without any suggestion of sin or even of irregularity. Indeed, until David had taken the Ark to Jerusalem, it was not a 'holy place' for Israel at all. Had all Hebrew worship in pre-Davidic times been sinful? And ought there then to have been no worship at all? 'The law

[1] His realm seems to have stretched as far north as this.
[2] Chs. xii.-xxvi. and xxviii. at least.
[3] Deut. xii. 2-14.

of the single sanctuary' seems clearly to link the 'Book of the law of Jehovah' that Hilkiah found in the Temple, with the Book of Deuteronomy.[1]

In discussing the Book of Deuteronomy it is best to think of a school of preachers and writers rather than of a single author. We do not know when this school originated. Possibly the reign of Hezekiah is as near as we can get. If so, they were at work during the long night of Manasseh's reign, reducing the old laws of Jehovah's worship to writing and not hesitating to add to them, or rather, to apply their principles to new historical situations. For it seems clear that these men were in charge of an old but growing tradition. This will be illustrated presently.

There is good evidence that their work did not cease with Josiah's reign, but continued into the Exile. It is probably to the Deuteronomic school that we owe the Books of Kings in their present form; and not only the Books of Kings, but the Books of Joshua, Judges and Samuel as well. All these contain old material edited by Deuteronomists.

The last event mentioned in the Books of Kings seems to us an unimportant conclusion. It is the fact that the King of Babylon 'lifted up the head of Jehoiachin out of prison' in the thirty-seventh year of his captivity. We can understand its being mentioned if it happened at the time when the editor was at work. The Book of

[1] Selected passages: chs. iv.-vi.; xii.; xxiv.; xxviii. The arrangement of Deuteronomy is not difficult to make out. First (chs. i.-iv.) there is an introduction which tells us that the book is a statement of what Moses said when, just before his death, he rehearsed the Covenant of Horeb to the Children of Israel in the Plains of Moab. Next there follows a prelude of exhortation (chs. vi.-xi.). After this there comes the main body of laws (chs. xii.-xxvi.) ending with a great peroration about the obligations of the whole Covenant. The remainder of the book gathers additional matter, of varying dates, but includes another and even mightier peroration (ch. xxviii.), in which the writer elaborates the one theme that obedience will bring blessing and disobedience will bring disaster after disaster. Near the end there are two songs of Jehovah,—one (ch. xxxii.) in the Deuteronomic strain, and the other recalling an earlier style (ch. xxxiii.).

Deuteronomy is written as if it were a long speech delivered by Moses to Israel in the 'plains of Moab' just before he died. This illustrates the way in which ancient peoples ascribed to their first law-giver codes of law that had taken centuries to grow. Here the Book is treated as the product of a school of writers who were at work from the time of Hezekiah or earlier to the period of the Captivity. It is quite likely that the prelude to the Book[1] belongs to the Exile, for prefaces are often the last parts of books to be written.

The master idea of the book is the old one of Covenant. It has been seen that this was a very old idea.[2] The *word* is common in Deuteronomy; it is not common in the prophets, yet the prophets too had the *idea*. They held, as all schools of Hebrew thought held, that there was a peculiar relation between God and Israel,—that Israel was His people and that He was Israel's God. This meant, as we have seen,[3] that Israel's one duty was to do His will, and that He, on His part, would care for Israel. This idea occurs over and over again in the Book of Deuteronomy; perhaps its greatest illustration in the whole of the Old Testament is the great sermon on the theme that rolls in eloquence through the twenty-eighth chapter. Israel was a Covenant people. Everything in Deuteronomy follows from this.

The Covenant, for the Deuteronomists, as for the writers of earlier documents, goes back to the Patriarchs, to the sojourn in Egypt, and to Moses. There is a good example in chapter twenty-six. Every year the Hebrew is to take his first-fruits to the priest and confess—'A wandering Aramean was my father, and he went down into Egypt and sojourned there, few in number; and he became there a nation, great, mighty and populous; and the Egyptians evil entreated us, and laid upon us hard bondage; and we cried unto Jehovah, the god of our fathers, and Jehovah

[1] Chs. i.-iv. [2] Pp. 85ff. [3] Pp. 85ff.

heard our voice, and saw our affliction and our toil and our oppression; and Jehovah brought us forth out of Egypt with a mighty hand, and with an outstretched arm, and with great terribleness, and with signs and with wonders; and He hath brought us into this place, and hath given us this land, a land flowing with milk and honey.'[1] The passage is a good illustration, not only of the concept of Covenant, but of the distinctive Deuteronomic style. Jehovah is Israel's Covenant God.

Other ideas ensue. Israel has been unfaithful to the Covenant; therefore Jehovah has brought troubles upon her; let Israel return unto obedience and all will be well; let her persist in disobedience, and all will be ill. This is the master idea of the Deuteronomists, as of the prophets.

But there is more to say. A protest was made above against the interpretation of the idea of Covenant in commercial terms. In Deuteronomy we have the true word. It is 'love!' Israel is told that Jehovah 'chose' her because He 'loved her fathers.'[2] It was because of this 'love' that He has done for Israel deeds that have never else been heard of from 'one end of heaven to the other.'[3] On the other hand, Israel is called to 'love' Him—'Thou shalt love Jehovah, thy God, with all thine heart, and with all thy soul and with all thy might.'[4] The term 'love' itself is not found even in the prophets as it is found in Deuteronomy. It is from Deuteronomy that our Lord Himself chose this key-word of His own teaching. Is there anything commercial in love? Yet 'love' is only one of two words. The other is 'fear.' Israel is as repeatedly called to 'fear' Jehovah as to 'love' Him. And 'verily He is a god to be feared.' The description of the theophany of Horeb in the prelude to Deuteronomy[5] tells us how Jehovah spoke 'out of the midst of the fire.'

[1] Deut. xxvi. 5.
[2] e.g. Deut. iv. 37.
[3] Deut. iv. 32; the whole fourth chapter is in place here.
[4] Deut. vi. 5.
[5] Deut. iv. 11ff.

For this school, as for Isaiah, Jehovah is a God of unseen majesty, before whom men must tremble. And He is a God who 'will by no means spare the guilty.' To evil-doers He is terrible, to well-doers He is merciful. It is for Israel to fear and to love Him. These are the two sides of a Covenant with such a God.

We found above that the idea of monolatry had of old time gone with that of Covenant. Was this so now? The answer is that monolatry, in Deuteronomy as in the prophets, had grown into monotheism. We have seen that when once a world-empire came within the orbit of Hebrew experience, monolatry could not survive; that it must either sink into polytheism or rise to monotheism, and that the prophets took the second alternative.[1] The Deuteronomists did the same. 'Jehovah, He is God; there is none else beside Him.'[2]; 'Hear, O Israel, Jehovah, thy God, is one Jehovah.'[3] As for other gods, they are 'the work of men's hands, wood and stone, which neither see, nor hear, nor eat, nor smell.'[4]

It will be noticed that many of the quotations here are from the fourth chapter. It may be that this belongs to the later part of the Deuteronomists' work. With whatever ideas the school began, by the time that they had finished their great book, they were monotheists pure and simple. For them, however inconsistent it may logically seem, Jehovah was both a national god and the only God.

If Jehovah was the one God, could He be the local god? It has been seen that in earlier times, He had been thought of as frequenting such places as Horeb, Gilgal, Bethel and finally, Jerusalem. Could He be any longer so conceived; and, if He could not, what was to be said of His sanctuaries

[1] Pp. 138f. [2] Deut. iv. 35.

[3] Deut. vi. 4. Perhaps this great text took its special form because, so long as Jehovah was worshipped in different places, it would be easy to think that, as each place had, in Canaanite eyes, its own Baal, so each place had its own Jehovah. This shows one more way in which polytheism might readily develop.

[4] Deut. iv. 28.

on earth? The Deuteronomists thought of the one God as having his seat in heaven; or rather, they began to feel after the concept that He cannot be localized at all. For instance, the Hebrew is bidden to pray, 'Look down from thy holy habitation, from heaven, and bless Thy people Israel'[1]; again, in Solomon's prayer at the dedication of the Temple, which has all the marks of the distinctive Deuteronomic style, these words are put into the king's mouth, 'But will God in very deed dwell on the earth? Behold heaven and the heaven of heavens cannot contain Thee; how much less this house that I have builded?'[2] In other words, under monotheism God cannot be localized.

What then is to be said of His sanctuaries on earth? In the same prayer there is the answer; and it moves towards the answer that we ourselves give when we separate a place and a church for the worship of God. But here a famous phrase should be quoted from Deuteronomy itself. A place of Jehovah's worship is called 'the place which Jehovah thy God shall choose to cause His name to dwell there.'[3] In other words, God is in heaven, but He has chosen to localize His worship on earth.

This is not the Christian idea that God is everywhere, and therefore He may be met with wherever His people gather for His worship; but it is an approximation to it. In form it is illogical, but historically it is easy to understand. God is too great for the 'heaven of heavens' to contain; but only in Jerusalem can He be worshipped as He ought.

[1] Deut. xxvi. 15.

[2] 1 Kings viii. 27. In this prayer there is a recognition of the problem suggested above—How can the one God be national?—and a beginning of its solution. See vv. 41-43.

[3] e.g. Deut. xiv. 23. There is dispute whether the Hebrew phrase here means 'the one place' (i.e. Jerusalem) or 'every place.' If the second translation is right, there is here an instance of the older *strata* of ideas in Deuteronomy (see below, pp. 157f.), for the legality of more than one sanctuary is allowed. In Deut. xii. 5-21, the Hebrew phrase is not quite the same, and there is no doubt that there the reference is to a single legitimate sanctuary.

What did Jehovah require of Israel? The answer fills fifteen chapters[1] and cannot here be described in detail; but some outstanding characteristics may be noted. It will be found that, under them all, Deuteronomy takes up and develops ideas that were already found in earlier legislation, and particularly in the Book of the Covenant.[2] First, Deuteronomy is one of the most intolerant books in the world. Whenever it comes in sight of 'other gods' it breaks out indignantly against them. And it knows no mercy for those who would fain serve them. Even a wife who suggests to an Israelite that he should add a second god to Jehovah is to be pitilessly slain.[3] And the whole 'bag of tricks' of Canaanitish worship—images, *asherim*, altars, even the pillars that were thought innocent earlier[4] —are to be ruthlessly smashed to pieces.[5] The prohibition of the image is traced back to Horeb; there, Israel is told, her fathers 'saw no form' whatever when Jehovah spake unto them 'out of the midst of the fire.'[6] Even the sacred 'fire' which, it will be noted, could not readily be represented by an image, is now clearly thought of, not as Jehovah, but only as His environment.[7] The Deuteronomist would not have known what the word 'spiritual,' in our sense, meant; but he is clearly on the edge of asserting what we mean when we say 'God is spirit.'

It is plain that there is here the conclusion of the process that began when earlier teachers cried out against the *asherah* and 'molten gods.' For the Deuteronomist the whole evil of syncretism and the leaven of the Canaanites is as plain as daylight. He is not only a monotheist but he worships the unseen and unseeable God.

Yet though the Deuteronomists are so intolerant of other gods and their ritual, they believe that there is a right ritual in the worship of Jehovah, and that it is an essential

[1] Chs. xii.-xxvi. [2] See pp. 109f. [3] Deut. xiii. 5.
[4] See p. 103. [5] e.g. Deut. vii. 1-11; xii. 2ff.
[6] Deut. iv. 12. [7] Deut. iv. 12.

element in the true religion. They have nothing of the prophets' scorn for ritual. They do not declare that it is useless; rather, they would reform it; or, better still, they would restore it to what they thought, rightly or wrongly, was its ancient form.

If we ask what this ritual was, we find once more a development of earlier ideas. There is an altar of Jehovah, and priests,[1] 'burnt offerings and peace-offerings,' three great annual festivals, and so on. But we have now considerably more detail about them, though this need not detain us here.

There is no *rationale* of the ritual, or next to none. We are not told, for instance, why the God who dwells in 'the heaven of heavens' should desire that He should be offered a slaughtered sheep at given times. It is enough for the Deuteronomist that from of old Jehovah has decreed that it shall be so. Of course, the idea that Jehovah enjoyed the fragrance of the sacrificial smoke is gone for ever; it could not survive when monotheism came. But there is some emphasis on the value of the sacrifices from the point of view of the worshipper. Sacrifice is now chiefly thanksgiving. In it a man and his family 'rejoiced before Jehovah.'[2] It is clear that a sacrifice was a feast at a shrine, a periodical merry-making. In it the Hebrew recognized that every good thing is a gift of God. There is worth in the notion that thanksgiving is good and that there is a merriment that pleases God.

There are 'commandments' in Deuteronomy that refer to conduct, as well as to ritual. They are interspersed, however, among the rules of ritual, without any line of distinction, just as in the earlier law-codes.[3] As with those law-codes, these Deuteronomic rules of social behaviour have behind them, almost without exception, the environment of the Hebrew villages, and not of

[1] In Deuteronomy these are the same as 'the Levites'—*cf.* p. 98.
[2] e.g. Deut. xii. 12-18.
[3] *Cf.* pp. 91, 109f.

Jerusalem or the capitals of the north. In some instances they repeat the statutes of the Book of the Covenant, and it is clear that the Deuteronomists knew of this earlier code. But in a good many instances they do more than repeat the older laws. They apply further the ethical idea that underlies them. And they add many new commands. Both in the enlargement of old rules and in the addition of new ones a religious humanitarianism is manifest that surpasses that of the Book of the Covenant.[1] Deuteronomy has a great pity for the poor. 'The stranger, the fatherless and the widow' is a recurrent phrase, and always the law bids the Hebrew help them.[2] Here, as in the Book of the Covenant, Hebrew law, in the name of Jehovah, always takes the side of the poor. In this the Deuteronomist marched with the prophets.

Illustrations are strewn all over the relevant chapters.[3] A single example may be given of the development of an old law, and one also of the many new laws. There was an old law that if a free-born Hebrew were so hard-pressed by poverty that he was driven to sell himself as a bondman, he should be set free at the end of seven years.[4] The Deuteronomist adds that, when he is set free, 'Thou shalt not let him go empty; thou shalt furnish him liberally out of thy flock, and out of thy threshing-floor, and out of thy wine-press: as Jehovah thy God hath blessed thee, thou shalt give unto him.'[5] In other words, the bondman is not to return to an unplenished farmstead, but his old master is to 'set him up' with stock of this sort and that, so that he may make a hopeful beginning.

[1] Pp. 109f.

[2] Sometimes the 'Levite' is added; it will appear below that he too was dependent on other men's alms. The 'stranger,' or rather, the 'sojourner,' was an alien who came to dwell in a Hebrew village, and who, of course, had no land. He was therefore driven to hire himself out to the yeomen who had land, and he was their easy prey. It is assumed that, when he dwelt in a Hebrew village, he began to worship the Hebrew God.

[3] Chs. xii.-xxvi. [4] Exod. xxi. 2-6. [5] Deut. xv. 13f.

As an example of new edicts, we may take the law that forbade the cutting-down of an enemy's fruit-trees.[1] The implied picture represents the Hebrews as besieging an enemy's village or city. They find it hard to carry the defences. The fruit-trees, of course, are growing outside. The obvious thing to do was to cut them down, for this would not only help to make 'bulwarks' against the city, but would 'take it out' of the enemy in years to come, for freshly planted trees grow slowly. But Israel is bidden only to use for 'bulwarks' the trees that do not yield fruit, and to leave fruit-trees standing, for a tree is not an enemy! In other words, we have here one of the first mitigations of the utter ruthlessness of ancient war. The Hebrew had taken a first step on the road that leads to Geneva Conventions, and Red Cross *corps*, and, at long last, to the League of Nations. There are other illustrations of the mitigation of war; but it is only possible to do justice to this side of the Deuteronomic code by reading it through, and by seeing the picture of the village and its circumstances behind each edict. Perhaps all the social laws of Deuteronomy might be ranged under the last six of the Ten Commandments, which occur in a slightly distinctive form in this book.[2] And perhaps all the ritual edicts could be ranged under the first four Commandments. At any rate, in Deuteronomy, as in the Decalogue and all other Hebrew codes, the ethical and the ritual lie side by side, both alike being the will of Jehovah.

We have seen that in three realms,—in the repudiation of other gods, the rules of right ritual, and the laws of right conduct—Deuteronomy links with and carries further old ideas, and particularly the ideas of the Book of the Covenant. Probably this gives the key to the book. It may be compared to a tree. As we look at a tree, we see some things—the trunk, for instance—that are old; some things that are not so old—for instance, a particular branch; and some things that are quite new—a leaf, for instance, or a

[1] Deut. xx. 19.f. [2] Deut x. 6ff.

flower; yet we know that the tree is an organic whole, the product of a process of growth. So, in Deuteronomy there are some things that are very old, some that are not so old, and some that are quite new; yet the book is an organic whole. It shows what the Hebraism of the more ordinary Hebrew, who belonged to the 'godly remnant,' had come to be at the time of the exile, rather than the religion of those outstanding men, the great prophets. Its writers think that the tree had been the same since Moses; the truth, however, was that Moses had sown the seed from which the tree had grown.

Deuteronomy is important in yet another way. It is the first great example of a great transition—the transition from the idea that God's will may be learnt chiefly from living 'men of God' to the idea that the will of God is enshrined in an authoritative book. We saw that in earlier Israel the leading concept was that Jehovah spoke to men through various kinds of 'holy men'—the judge, the priest, the prophet, the king.[1] The Deuteronomists do not contradict this notion, but in their time it had been found insufficient. The function of the judge passed, as we saw,[2] to the king; but, after Solomon, we do not find that there is any record of Jehovah's speaking through kings. The Deuteronomic compiler does indeed say that a number of kings 'did that which was right in the sight of Jehovah,' but he seems to be thinking of a king as carrying out an already known law rather than enunciating a new law. In the Book of Deuteronomy itself there is a paragraph about the kingship,[3] but its burden is that a king is not to oppress his subjects. In one passage in Samuel, of Deuteronomic style,[4] the evils of kingship are graphically set out; while in another[5] there is promise of a line of Davidic kings who shall be blessed or disciplined according as they do the will of Jehovah or not. The

[1] Pp. 92ff. [2] Pp. 35, 94. [3] Deut. xvii. 14ff. [4] 1 Sam. viii. 10ff. [5] 2 Sam. vii. 8ff.

notion here too is that it is a king's business to carry out the will of God, not to declare it.

Again, there is a passage that instructs the Israelites, when some dispute arises that is 'too hard' for them to settle, to seek a decision from 'the priests, the Levites.'[1] Here too the idea seems to be that the priests are more likely to know the law than the ordinary Hebrew. For the most part they appear merely as the ministers of ritual.[2]

Again, the Book of Deuteronomy recognizes that there has been a great line of prophets in Israel. Indeed, it counts Moses himself to be the first of the prophets[3]; but the same passage recognizes that there are false prophets as well as true ones. Its directions for discrimination between the two, apart from the denunciation of death upon any prophet who 'speaks in the name of other gods,' are not very serviceable. It admits, in effect, that one could not be sure whether a prophet had a true word from Jehovah or not until his prophecy had come true or false. This would not help a man who wanted immediate direction, as Ahab and Jehoshaphat did, for example, when they asked, 'Shall we go up against Ramoth Gilead or not ?'[4] None the less, the Deuteronomists had a living and vigorous belief in prophets, as the compiler's inclusion of the stories of Elijah and Elisha, Isaiah and Huldah, in his history, show.

Yet the chief idea of the Deuteronomists lay elsewhere. Hilkiah came to Josiah with an authoritative book in his hand, for he said, 'I have found the book of the law in the house of Jehovah.'[5] And the king, as advised by Huldah,

[1] Deut. xvii. 8-13.

[2] When any local 'high place' was closed, by Hezekiah or Josiah, a problem would arise about the Levite or Levites that had ministered there. These flocked to Jerusalem, and there are directions in Deuteronomy that they were to minister there (Deut. xviii. 6-8)—directions that Josiah did not fully carry out (2 Kings xxiii. 8ff.). It was probably because of this situation that the Levites are so often represented in Deuteronomy as needy.

[3] Deut. xviii. 15-22.

[4] See pp. 96ff.

[5] 2 Kings xxii 8.

accepts this book as what we call a 'canon of scripture,' a finally authoritative account of the will of Jehovah. This idea was to become more and more prominent in Hebrew religion until, after many centuries, it ruled out all others. For good or ill, it is the dominant concept of the orthodox Jew to-day. Deuteronomy is a 'canon'; it treats the will of God as already revealed. All that needs to be done is to read and obey. This idea did not yet triumph; but with this book it takes clear shape in the Hebrew mind.

There are deficiencies in this concept, as in almost everything that is Deuteronomic. This book has ideas that the prophets could not accept, as will appear in the next chapter. None the less it is one of the great books of the Old Testament. Along with the prophets, it teaches a lofty monotheism; it ultimately rid Israel of all idolatry; it applies, in effect, the prophets' master-principle of righteousness to many of the details of daily life; indeed it is not unlikely that here it deliberately borrowed from them; and it originated or repeated that universal alphabet of conduct, the Decalogue[1]; its great command 'Thou shalt love Jehovah, thy God, with all thy heart, and with all thy mind, and with all thy strength' is the master-key of all religion. Jesus Himself said so. It may be doubted whether any other ancient people produced a religious book as great as this one.

[1] Deut. v.

## Chapter XII

# THE SECOND GROUP OF WRITTEN PROPHETS

'Then Jehovah put forth his hand and touched my mouth; and Jehovah said unto me, Behold, I have put my words in thy mouth, and I have this day put thee over the nations and over the kingdoms, to pluck up and to break down, and to destroy and to overthrow; to build and to plant.'[1] These words are of world-wide scope. They were spoken in the thirteenth year of Josiah to a young Hebrew called Jeremiah. His is an outstanding name in the second great period of written prophecy. In it there are six prophets—Jeremiah, Zephaniah, Nahum, Habakkuk, Ezekiel, and the so-called Deutero-Isaiah.[2] Of these, while the first is the greatest, the last two are great as well. The period lasted for nearly a century.[3] It will be remembered that Josiah's reforms began in the eighteenth year of his reign. Jeremiah, therefore, began to prophesy five years before Deuteronomy was promulgated. His ministry lasted for more than forty years.[4] While the main part of the Book of Deuteronomy belongs to Josiah's reign, the work of the school continued right into the exile. Broadly speaking, therefore, the second group of written prophets was contemporary with that of the

[1] Jer. i. 9f.
[2] Isa. xl.-lv.
[3] *ca.* 635-540 B.C.
[4] Selected passages—for Jeremiah's message in general: chs. i.; vii.; xxii. 20—xxiii. 8; xxvi.; xxxi. 23-40; for the reign of Josiah: ch. v.; for the reign of Jehoiakim: chs. xxxv.-xxxvi.; for the reign of Zedekiah: chs. xxviii.; xxxii.; xxxiv. after the fall of the city in 586 B.C.: ch. xliv.

Deuteronomists, and the two movements, prophetic and legal, must be thought of as going on side by side.

We have seen that we know nothing of the 'godly remnant' during Manasseh's long reign. There may have been prophets, in this half-century, but we know nothing of them. There were also priests, for not only do we find one of them, Hilkiah, leading the Deuteronomic reform, but two of the prophets, Jeremiah and Ezekiel, were of priestly stock. Nevertheless, during this period it seemed as if Jehovah were inactive. Wickedness triumphed, and He did nothing! But, as mighty Assyria's day waned, the hopes of the 'faithful few' revived. This shows itself in the two simple 'visions' with which Jeremiah's ministry began. 'The word of Jehovah came unto me, saying, What seest thou, Jeremiah? And I said, I see a rod of an almond tree.'[1] When a long winter was passing away, the almond was the first tree to put forth shoots. The tree's very name suggested wakefulness.[2] After half a century of winter Jehovah was awake again! 'And the word of Jehovah came unto me the second time, saying, What seest thou? And I said, I see a seething cauldron.'[3] We have all seen a large pot of water, set upon a fire; for a long time the water looks just the same; then, especially if someone takes a bellows to the fire, the water begins to bubble, and suddenly it is boiling! So Jeremiah saw the world. For long it had seemed, from the prophetic point of view, like still water, but now, with the weakening of Assyria, the rise of the Medes, and the stirring of Babylonian revolt, world events are clearly moving again. Now the world is like a boiling pot! Jehovah is busy once more."[4]

[1] Jer. i. 11.

[2] There is here one of the many 'plays upon words' or 'puns' that occur in the Old Testament. See the marginal notes in the R.V.

[3] Jer. i. 13.

[4] The very word translated 'seething' means that someone is taking a bellows to a fire.

In the life-time of Jeremiah there were three momentous historical events. With each of them one of the so-called 'minor prophets' broke into oracle.

The first was the invasion of the Scythians, about 630 B.C. The Book of Zephaniah[1] foretold the doom that they brought. 'Be silent at the presence of the Lord Jehovah: for the Day of Jehovah is at hand! for Jehovah hath prepared a sacrifice: he hath invited[2] his guests.' No nation is to escape in the 'general doom,' but the prophet keeps his worst woes for Judah and Jerusalem. And the reason is clear—'Her princes in the midst of her are roaring lions; her judges are evening wolves: they leave nothing till the morrow. Her prophets are light and treacherous: her priests have profaned the sanctuary, they have done violence to the law. Jehovah in the midst of her is righteous!'[3] It is a terrible indictment. It was in the midst of a people so iniquitous that Jeremiah grew up.

The second climacteric event was the Fall of Nineveh in 612 B.C. For the men of those days it was as great an event as the fall of Napoleon to our grandfathers, or the Great War to ourselves. The little book of Nahum[4] tells us how it struck a contemporary. His third chapter, for instance, is an exultant pæan over the doom of Assyria. He greets the fall of Nineveh with a shout, almost a shriek, of joy. He tells of the rush of war-chariots into the doomed city. To Nahum the sack of Nineveh by Medes and Babylonians was just a deed of Jehovah's. His prophecy could be epitomized in a sentence—'Hurrah, Jehovah has Assyria down at last!' It is monotheism in action.

To the world historian the third epoch-making event was the Battle of Charchemish in 605 B.C., but to the Judæans, and to the readers of the Old Testament, it is rather the Fall of Jerusalem in 586 B.C. The two events

[1] Selected passage: ch. i.
[2] Hebrew, 'sanctified.'
[3] Zeph. iii. 3-5. It is not unlikely, however, that the Scythian attack passed Judah by.
[4] Selected passage: ch. iii.

can be taken together, however, for the second was but a sequel to the first. After the Fall of Assyria it was doubtful for a while whether the suzerainity of the empire would pass to the Babylonian, the Mede or the Egyptian. The Babylonian came to terms with the Mede and crushed Egypt at Carchemish.

In the bewildering decade that followed, Habakkuk stood 'upon (his) watchtower' and wondered.[1] Yet amid the chaos he was certain that the Chaldæans (or Babylonians) as they swept the world were just an instrument of Jehovah's punishment. 'For see, I (Jehovah) raise up the Chaldæans, that bitter and nasty nation, which march through the breadth of the earth, to possess dwelling-places that are not theirs. . . . They are all of them for violence; their faces are set eagerly as the east wind: and they gather captives as the sand. Yea, he scoffeth at kings, and princes are a derision unto him: he derideth every stronghold; for he heapeth up (a bank of) dust and taketh it.'[2] And the prophet is clear about a second truth. Not only is the Chaldæan havoc of invasion Jehovah's punishment for sin, but 'the righteous shall live by his confidence' in Jehovah.[3]

These three prophecies give us the background of Jeremiah's book. The Scythian invasion befell while he was a young man, the Sack of Nineveh in the midst of his ministry, and the Fall of Jerusalem as it neared its end. As one reads these three short books, one sees that certain convictions were now prophetic commonplaces. Prophets took it for granted now that Jehovah was the one God, that He ruled all nations, and that He punished the wicked, for He Himself was righteous. In other words, the first group of written prophets had made ethical monotheism axiomatic for all prophets.

[1] Selected passage: ch. ii. Some scholars, it should be noted, ascribe the whole prophecy to the time of Alexander's invasion (see the commentaries).

[2] Hab. i. 6-10.

[3] Hab. ii. 4. This is Paul's text when he wrote to the Romans. —Roms. i. 17.

No Old Testament book repays study more than the book of Jeremiah,[1] but it needs study. For one thing, its prophecies, like those of other prophets, are not arranged in chronological order. Yet the book, unlike many other collections of prophecies, often gives us the historical picture that explains a particular prophecy. In a way it is an autobiography. It tells many a story of Jeremiah and, in telling them, it illuminates the story of his times.

We can see the little people of Judah, clinging about their one city and their line of Davidic kings, bewildered by the varying course of world events, now sanguine with hope, now hysterical with despair; conforming to Josiah's reforms and worshipping Jehovah alone at one time, falling away to manifold idolatries as soon as there is another kind of king; trusting in the power of Jehovah to save the Temple as He had done in Isaiah's day, yet sinning, and sinning, and sinning against Him; aware that Jeremiah was a true prophet of Jehovah, yet unable and unwilling to believe in his stern gospel of exile; king, and princes, and priests, and false prophets, and citizens and 'people of the land' acting and re-acting on each other, forming factions, falling into other factions, uniting, sundering, disputing—until every man of influence is carried away captive to Babylon, and the forlorn fragment that remains tears itself to pieces in useless strife, and flees frighted into Egypt, carrying Jeremiah with it in its inconsistent despair. We can see all this as we read how, on this occasion and that, Jeremiah prophesied and preached.

Yet his autobiography does not exhaust itself in stories of his outward doings,—it is a spiritual autobiography. It tells how a solitary man communed and interceded and expostulated and wrestled with God. Jeremiah quails before Jehovah, yet He is intimate with Him too. This characteristic appears in the very first chapter, and it is the key to the whole book. Like Augustine's *Confessions* or George Fox's *Journal*, this book tells of the dealings of a

[1] For selected passages see p. 162.

single man with God. Like them, too, it made history.

It is not difficult to state Jeremiah's political message. His prophecies cover five reigns, but two of the five kings only ruled for very short times. Practically speaking, his prophecies fall in the reigns of Josiah the reformer; Jehoiakim, who sinned resolutely 'with a high hand'; and Zedekiah, who sinned as 'wobblers' sin.

Scholars do not agree about the story of the prophet's attitude to Josiah's reforms. Some think that at first he had hopes that the reformation would succeed; others hold that from the first he saw its futility. All agree, however, that he came to see this; and that, at least through the reigns of Jehoiakim and Zedekiah, when most of his prophecies fall, he had a single political message.

He maintained that the one wise policy for Judah was to submit to Babylon; but he knew that Judah was unwilling to do this, and that upon every seemingly good opportunity she would rebel. And he declared, in season and out of season, that rebellion would end in the fall of the city, and the deportation of the people. But he added that Israel would survive in exile, or rather that the 'godly remnant' would; and that, after seventy years,[1] the exile would end and the people return to their land.

To his hearers all this seemed madness. They remembered how Jehovah had rescued the city and Temple from the might of Assyria in the days of Isaiah, and they could not believe that He would fail them before Babylon. Again, it seemed to them, as to all men then, that captivity would be fatal to the nation, and so it would make an end of Jehovah and His people together. To preach captivity, therefore, was treachery; and probably they asked, 'If there is to be a return, why a captivity?' Yet Jeremiah persisted in his policy, and history vindicated his insight. We see him at one moment 'standing in the gate' of the Temple to protest to the people who flocked in through it

[1] Jer. xxv. 11f. This is probably a 'round number'; at any rate, the captivity turned out to be shorter than this.

that even 'the temple of Jehovah' should fall[1]; and at another buying the ancient patrimony of his house when, at the height of the Babylonian terror, it seemed to all others that in a year or two no Hebrew would own land at all.[2]

The story of the Burnt Roll[3] is a good example of the historical situation. Jeremiah, as at some other times, is a captive 'in the court of the guard,' for he has too much influence with the vacillating people to be left at large. So he calls a faithful friend named Baruch to his aid. Baruch writes out Jeremiah's prophecy of doom on a scroll, and, at Jeremiah's bidding, boldly reads it to the Temple crowd. One of the 'princes,' or ruling class, hears it, and hurries Baruch and his dangerous roll out of the Temple and into the palace, which lay next to it. Here a company of the 'princes' are gathered in some sort of council chamber. Baruch is bidden to read Jeremiah's sermon to them, and, as they hear, they fall into consternation. It will never do for the people to hear such messages! Yet some of the council feel uneasily that it may all be true! But they feel too that they must carry the roll to King Jehoiakim. Yet they know his temper, and they do not want him to turn on Jeremiah and kill him. So they bid Baruch hurry away to the prophet and take him into hiding. Apparently they could somehow get him out of prison if they would. Meanwhile, they go off into the king's apartments in the royal buildings of Solomon. They find Jehoiakim in 'the winter palace' warming himself at a brazier. They stand round with varied feelings while the roll is read for the third time. Jehoiakim calls for a knife, rips the parchment into strips, and throws them on the fire. Some of the 'princes' try to dissuade him, for they feel that they are watching sacrilege, yet he persists. And then he makes hue and cry to find Jeremiah and Baruch—but 'the Lord hid them.' So the prophet escapes with his life. And, being the only man who dares to stand up to the resolute king, he bids Baruch to re-write his commination

[1] Jer. vii. 13f. [2] Jer. xxxii. 6-15. [3] Jer. xxxvi.

and to add thereto. For all these words are words of Jehovah, and who is Jehoiakim to confront God?

But Jeremiah's chief contribution to religion is neither in his courage, nor in his political sagacity, nor even in his insistence that Jehovah is a righteous God who rules the world and demands righteousness in His chosen people. In all these things earlier prophets had anticipated him. To understand his distinctive contribution to religion we must remember two things—his own religious experience and a proverb current in Israel at his time. The proverb ran, 'The fathers have eaten sour grapes and the children's teeth are set on edge.'[1] The proverb was a protest, and a protest against the prophetic message. For all the prophets had been saying, 'Israel has sinned against Jehovah from the days of Joshua until now; therefore Jehovah is bringing disaster upon her.' The people now replied, in effect, 'This isn't fair; we ought not to suffer because our fathers have sinned; the people who sin are the people who ought to suffer and not their descendants.' This means—to use the language of to-day—that individualism was now an element in Hebrew thought. Israel, once upon a time, had 'thought in families,' or 'tribes' or 'nations.' At that stage it seemed quite right that a man's children should suffer, as for instance, Achan's children did, for his wrong-doing. But now men began to protest against this idea. There is a trace of this in Deuteronomy and in the Books of Kings.[2] So the proverb arose.

Now, of course, there is truth in the protest so made, for there is a doctrine of individual responsibility as well as of corporate experience. Many problems ensue when the two are taken together. Jeremiah did not solve, or even face, all of them. Indeed, they have not all been solved to this day. But Jeremiah did declare that every man should be

[1] Jer. xxxi. 29.

[2] Deut. xxiv. 16; 2 Kings xiv. 6. The coming of the individualistic way of thinking of men was a slow process. I have traced it in *The Bible Doctrine of Society*.

judged for his own sins, and not for his father's.[1] The sinfulness of the men of his own day was quite enough, in practice, to justify this retort. The prophet could say that his hearers themselves were so thoroughly sinful that they deserved captivity.

He faced also another and deeper problem. The prophets had been demanding for long generations that the Hebrew people should be righteous because their God was righteous. But righteousness is fundamentally an individual quality. However much a man may be helped or hindered by his ancestry or environment, at bottom he is good or bad by his own choice. It is a man's use of his own will that makes his character. The root of sin is the individual's bad will. Jeremiah saw this clearly. The failure of Josiah's reform thrust it upon him. For Josiah had tried, like all law-givers, to make men good, so to speak, 'from the outside.' He had touched all that law can touch—the outward actions of men, but he made no attempt to change their hearts. Law may prohibit theft, and even keep men from stealing, but it cannot keep men from wanting to steal, and that is the root of the evil. What a bad man needs, for ultimate cure, is a change of heart.

We associate this teaching with Jesus and Paul, but Jeremiah anticipated it in his great doctrine of the New Covenant.[2] 'Behold, the days come, saith Jehovah, when I will make a new covenant with the house of Israel and with the house of Judah. I will put my law in their inward parts, and in their heart will I write it; and (so) I will be their God, and they shall be my people.' It is deliberately said that this new covenant is to supersede the old covenant of Sinai.[3]

It is no wonder that our Lord Himself recalled this passage at the Last Supper, or that the writer of the Epistle to the Hebrews quoted it when he was explaining why Christianity was needed in place of Judaism. Though the words are not there, the doctrines of 'conscience,' and

[1] Jer. xxxi. 30. [2] Jer. xxxi. 31ff. [3] Ver. 32.

'conversion,' and 'the in-dwelling of the Spirit' are all anticipated in this prophecy. In some ways it is the greatest passage in the Old Testament. And the key to it is Jeremiah's own individual experience of God. What was the explanation of his own love of righteousness and hatred of iniquity? Not the heredity of the corrupt priesthood from which he sprang, nor the environment of wicked Jerusalem, but his own intimate, spiritual fellowship with the righteous God who loveth righteousness.

'The fathers have eaten sour grapes and the children's teeth are set on edge,' said the shallower exponents of the new-found individualism. 'Not so,' replied Jeremiah, 'All of you are individually evil, and Jehovah's only way to save any single evil man, is to change his heart. And this He will do one day.' Jeremiah despaired of men, yet he is a prophet of hope, not of despair, for he believed in God. In his prophecy of 'the covenant of the heart' Jeremiah made his greatest contribution to the development of Old Testament religion.

We now pass to Ezekiel.[1] It will be remembered that Nebuchadnezzar twice besieged Jerusalem and twice carried away a great number of captives.[2] Ezekiel was one of the first group of exiles. He was, therefore, a younger contemporary of Jeremiah. His period falls approximately between 595 and 570 B.C. From his own writings we catch sight of the consternation that fell upon the earlier captives when in 586 B.C. the news reached them—'Jerusalem is fallen!'[3]

This prophet preaches the same ethical monotheism as the other prophets; yet, like the others, he preaches it 'with a difference.' He has his own distinctive contribution to make to the Hebrew faith. There is no need to expound fully the truths that he shares with the other

[1] Selected passages—before the fall of Jerusalem in 586 B.C.: chs. i.; xvi.; xviii. After the fall of Jerusalem: xxxvi. 16-36; chs. xxxvii.; xliii. 1-12; xlvii. 1-12.

[2] 597 and 586 B.C. See p. 50.

[3] Ezek. xxxiii. 21ff.; cf. xxiv. 15ff.

prophets. If possible, he emphasizes them more than his predecessors. For instance, while they had traced the apostasy of Israel only to the days that followed the invasion of Canaan, Ezekiel declares that Israel has been persistently false to its god even from the days of the Exodus.[1] Again, he depicts the two Hebrew kingdoms as the two wives of Jehovah, whose harlotries surpass all the harlotries of human life.[2] They are only to be compared to Sodom itself![3] He repeats, at much greater length, Jeremiah's message of individualism, quoting the same proverb.[4] He repeats also Jeremiah's great prophecy of a changed heart, adding here the word 'spirit'—'I will put a new spirit within you.'[5] He shares Jeremiah's belief that all Israel will survive captivity and return to her own land. Here falls the most famous of his oracles—the vision of the Valley of Dry Bones.[6] Its background is the experience of a man who has crossed a desert amid a plodding band of captives. Around them bones lie strewn! These are all that is left of earlier caravans! Can such bones live? To many a Hebrew captive in Babylon the restoration of his nation looked as preposterous a suggestion. But Ezekiel declares that there is to be a resurrection of captive Israel, for cannot Jehovah do anything? So in his vision the prophet sees bone leap to bone, flesh cover skeleton, breath enter body, and there is risen Israel—an exceeding great army. In such ways Ezekiel repeats, with a conviction that is more than repetition, the messages of the earlier prophets.

To understand, however, his distinctive contribution to the sum of prophetic thought, a beginning may be made, as with some other prophets, from his account of his Call.[7] As with much else in this prophet, it is described in great detail, and it is hard 'to see the wood for the trees.' Yet the

[1] Ezek. xvi. 20. [2] Ezek. xxiii. [3] Ezek. xvi. 46ff. [4] Ezek. xviii.
[5] Ezek. xxxvi. 26. This word is avoided in Jeremiah, perhaps because it was part of the lingo of the false prophets who swarmed in Jerusalem in his time. (*cf.* 1 Kings xxii. 24).
[6] Ezek. xxxvii. [7] Ezek. i. 1ff.

chief features are not obscure. To begin at the opposite end to the prophet, Ezekiel sees Jehovah as a dim and awful figure sitting upon a throne and half-hidden in fire. He sees 'the appearance of the likeness of the glory of Jehovah.'[1] The round-about phrase is meant to give the impression that the true God, unlike the idols in the temples of Babylon, is beyond the seeing of men. So to speak, between Him and the prophet there is first the 'glory,' and then 'the likeness' and then 'the appearance!' It is an effective way of symbolizing the distance and yet the nearness of the one awful, living God. He sits upon a 'firmament' or fiery dais, which itself is 'awful.' The 'firmament' itself rests upon a moving pedestal of wheels and wings and 'living creatures,' full of eyes. The whole is a moving throne that gleams with the sacred fire and runs over the world like lightning.

Ezekiel is a great symbolist. For him Jehovah is the living God, who sees everything, and who, when He wishes to be anywhere, is there in a flash. Just now He wishes to be by the River Chebar, where there is a prophet gathering round him a little flock of derelict Jews who would fain worship Him. Jeremiah had declared that Jehovah would be with the faithful remnant in captivity; it is there that Ezekiel meets Jehovah.

It will be seen that this was to practice, in a new way, the doctrine of monotheism. Of course, monotheism logically requires the omnipresence of God, but it is history, and not logic—or perhaps history and logic together—that reduces a great theory to practice. For it is one thing theoretically to believe something; it is another to build one's daily life upon it. Ezekiel and his companions by the Chebar[2] practised the omnipresence of Jehovah. Though they did not know it, they were beginning a practice that has lasted

[1] Ezek. i. 28.

[2] Probably, though not certainly, one of the streams that intersect the plain where the Euphrates and Tigris make their way past Babylon to the sea.

among the Jews to this day. They met together to meet God in the place where they happened to be, and they found Him there. This was, of course, to pass for ever from the notion of a merely localized god.[1]

Further, as it has often been put, Ezekiel was minister to a kind of church. He led the worship of a voluntary group of exiles. This has had anticipations in the godly followers of Isaiah and Jeremiah, and even of Elijah and Elisha, but with Ezekiel the process was complete. An important fact ensues. It was to this group, or to its leader, that Jehovah now revealed Himself. The people that remained in Canaan had so defiled His chosen land that He had left it. When the prophet depicts the new Temple in the purified Canaan of the future, Jehovah needs to return to it from the Chebar.[2] Ezekiel sees Him return in vision in just the same form as he had seen Him on the day of his Call.[3] In other words, Jehovah now offers His fellowship to those who are faithful to Him, wherever they are, and to no others. We have passed a great step further towards the purely spiritual enjoyment of religion.

Ezekiel made a second, and—at least for the history of Israel in the immediately succeeding centuries—a still more important contribution to the development of Hebrew religion. As has already been seen, he was a great symbolist. All the prophets used symbol in a way that would seem extreme to our modern western ways,—for instance, at one time Jeremiah walked about with an actual yoke upon his neck,[4]—but here Ezekiel surpassed them all. Almost every one of his oracles shows this.

[1] Ezekiel too seems to have carried the doctrine that one God rules all nations to its logical limit. Amos had extended the sway of Jehovah to the little nations that neighboured Israel; Isaiah and Jeremiah had taught that He controlled the great empires of Egypt, Assyria and Babylon; but, beyond their scope, in the dim world that ringed civilization, there were the hordes of barbarians. Ezekiel seems to include them under the phrase, 'Gog and Magog,' and he teaches that Jehovah is master of these outmost men. (Ezek. xxxviii.).

[2] Ezek. xliii. 1ff.

[3] Ezek. i. 4ff.; iii. 22-v. 17; xliii. 3.

[4] Jer. xxvii. 2; xxviii. 10.

Now, a great symbolist may easily be a great ritualist. Ezekiel was both. He was born, like Jeremiah, of a priestly stock; but, while Jeremiah here rebelled against his inheritance, Ezekiel gladly accepted it. So, at the end of his book, when he has denounced, with all the vigour of every prophet, the unclean, idolatrous worship of the later monarchy, he goes on to foretell that the Temple shall be restored, with a purified ritual and a loyal priesthood. He spends nine chapters in describing its ordered architecture and its renewed ritual. Jeremiah, like the prophets of the first writing group, denounced the uselessness of mere ritual.[1] This was merely a negative attitude. Ezekiel is not content with this; he looks for a restored Temple and a restored ritual. Here he was—as will be seen below—the father, or one of the fathers, of the next age. He is both priest and prophet.

This contribution to Hebrew faith was not all gain, as will appear below. Its dangers appear even in Ezekiel himself, for he does not always clearly distinguish between the ethical and the ritual elements in religion.[2] But he made a great attempt to unite the two elements. For men of his temper the characteristic word is 'holy.' The Hebrew term so translated was not a new one. In early times it seems to have denoted 'separated to god,' and it could be used with this meaning of a man, a place, a sacrifice, and so on; and it had, it seems, at first no

[1] Some scholars hold that these prophets repudiated ritual altogether. This is doubtful, for, though some passages, taken alone, suggest it (e.g. Amos v. 21-26; Hos. vi. 6; Mic. vi. 6-8; Isaiah i. 10-17; Jer. vii. 22), others seem to tell a different story. For instance, Hosea seems to depict the loss of ritual as a disaster (Hos. iii. 4f.; cf. v. 6); and Amos has an oracle in defence of the Sabbath (Amos viii. 5), and of course the Sabbath was a piece of ritual. (*Cf.* also Isai. vi. 1; Nah. i. 15; Hab. ii. 20; Jer. xxxiii. 11; xxxiv. 18-20). If it be true that these prophets desired to abolish ritual altogether, their message was so far incomplete; for, whatever may be said of individual worship, corporate worship demands some kind of ritual as the symbols of its common spiritual life. (*Cf. The Sacramental Society*, ch. ii.).

[2] e.g. Ezek. xviii. 6; xliii. 7f.

ethical content. The prophets before Ezekiel had rarely used it.[1] Ezekiel uses it fairly often. And with him its content united ethical and ritual elements, as it does to this day.[2] This was on the whole a gain; for in the practice of religion the ethical and ritual elements, while logically distinct, ought to be indissolubly blended, for only so can ritual serve its complete purpose.

Perhaps the best single passage to quote for Ezekiel's concepts here is the opening paragraph of his forty-third chapter. When his mysterious guide has shown him the new Temple, court by court and detail by detail, he leads him to the 'gate that looketh toward the east,' and 'behold the glory of the God of Israel came from the way of the east,[3] and his voice was like the sound of many waters: and the earth shined with His glory. . . . And the glory of Jehovah filled the house. . . . And I heard one speaking unto me out of the house; and a man stood by me. And he said unto me, Son of man, this is the place of my throne . . . where I will dwell in the midst of the house of Israel for ever, and the house of Israel shall no more defile my holy name.' In his earlier chapters Ezekiel serves himself heir to the old prophetic line; here he is the father of the age that was to come.[4]

About thirty years after the approximate close of Ezekiel's ministry, another prophet spoke. We do not

[1] The chief exception is in the Vision of Isaiah, in the great verse, 'Holy, holy, holy is the Lord of Hosts.' (Isa. vi. 3).

[2] For instance, when we call a day, or a church 'holy,' the meaning is ritualist; but when we speak of 'a holy man,' it is ethical.

[3] That is, as seen above (p. 174) from the land of the exile.

[4] Of course, the idea that Jehovah has a chosen shrine in a given land is logically inconsistent with the notion, named above (pp. 173f.), that Jehovah may be met with anywhere, but men do not live merely by logic. We ourselves hold the last conviction, yet there are particular places where we find it easy to worship because of their associations—this, indeed, is one reason why we go to church. And there are few Christians to whom a place like Bethlehem or Nazareth is not especially dear. The problem involved does not fall for discussion here, but we must not trust Ezekiel upon a dilemma that we decline for ourselves.

know his name, but, as his prophecies are included in our book of Isaiah, he is usually called Deutero-Isaiah[1] for convenience.[2] He appears, like Ezekiel, to have ministered to a group of faithful exiled Jews. The occasion of his preaching was the rise and conquests of Cyrus, whom he does not hesitate to call Jehovah's 'anointed' or 'Messiah.'[3] As the power of Cyrus waxed and waxed, the death-blow of the Babylonian realm grew more and more imminent. This prophet foresees Cyrus' conquest of that hated enemy of Israel; he foresees too that Cyrus will permit the Jews to return to their own land. And so it came to pass.

Here, again, the prophet shares the general message of his predecessors, but makes his own contribution to the development of the Hebrew creed. He is a champion of ethical monotheism, and he carries this creed to its utmost limit. As we have seen, monolatry began to break into monotheism when the prophets declared that Jehovah, the righteous God, was master of other nations beside Israel. We have seen, too, that with Ezekiel this belief reached its climax in the prophecies about the barbarians that ringed civilization. But is Jehovah master of nature as well as of men? Can He do as He will with things as well as with peoples? Is He lord of mountains, and rivers, and sun, and rain, and harvest, and drought? It would be easy to show that earlier prophets, and Deuteronomists as well, had believed that God gave or withheld harvest as He would; easy too to show that even in such early stories as the crossing of the Red Sea, or the victory of Barak, Jehovah is lord of nature. But no one had yet said clearly that Jehovah was the *creator* of the world; that He is not only its master but its maker.

[1] i.e. Second Isaiah (chs. xl.-lv.). Isa. xiii. 1-xiv. 23; xxxiv.; xxxv. seem to belong to the same period.

[2] Selected passages: chs. xl.; xliv.; xlix.; and 'The Servant Songs' (i.e. xlii. 1-7; xlix. 1-6; l. 4-9; lii. 13-liii. 12).

[3] Isa. xlv. 1.

It seems natural to us to begin with this idea of creation when we talk of monotheism; but this was not the first idea historically.[1] In Hebrew religion this concept comes last, not first. Deutero-Isaiah was the first prophet unmistakeably to enunciate it. For him it is a postulate. 'Who hath measured the waters in the hollow of his hand, and meted out heaven with the span, and comprehended the dust of the earth in a measure, and weighed the mountains in scales and the hills in a balance?'[2] 'Thus saith Jehovah, thy redeemer, and he that formed thee from the womb: I am Jehovah, that maketh all things; that alone stretcheth forth the heavens; that spreadeth abroad the earth; who is with me?'[3] There are quite a number of such passages. This prophet preached to a derelict group of captives, clinging together in the midst of an alien and triumphant empire, with its majestic temples and bejewelled idols. Yet it never occurs to him that his God is not master of it all. When he looks at an idol, god of great Babylon though it is, he breaks out into ironical laughter. Fancy, here is a god that a carpenter has made![4] The question whether Jehovah is to be worshipped in the form of an image is at last settled in laughter! And the doctrine of omnipotence is complete at the same time.

In the use of this concept we see this prophet's special message. The earlier prophets had preached chiefly the judgement of Jehovah on wicked Israel. They had said something, but comparatively little, about His power to bless Israel, if only she were obedient. With Deutero-Isaiah it is just the other way. He says hardly anything about Jehovah's judgement on Israel, for he was preaching to a faithful and obedient remnant; his chief message is of hope, and restoration, and blessing. The word 'salvation' is common on his lips, for it is now Jehovah's will to save.

[1] We shall find that Genesis i. belongs to the next period.
[2] Isa. xl. 12.
[3] Isa. xliv. 24.
[4] Isa. xl. 18ff.; xliv. 9ff.

It is this message that gives his book its peculiar sweetness. 'Comfort ye, comfort ye my people, saith your God. Speak ye to the heart of Jerusalem, and cry unto her that her time of service is accomplished, that her iniquity is pardoned; that she hath received of Jehovah's hand double for all her sins;'[1] 'Ye shall go out with joy, and be led forth with peace: the mountains and the hills shall break forth before you into singing, and all the trees of the field shall clap their hands,'[2]—this is his message. Here again there are many more such passages. The earlier prophets had preached of darkness; this prophet testifies of dawn.

What of other nations? What of the Gentiles? Against them, as well as against Israel, the earlier prophets had launched many an oracle of doom, for to them all nations were sinful together. A prophet of this time thundered in this old way against Babylon.[3] If we put ourselves in the place of the exiled Jews, or if we read Psalm cxxxvii, we see how natural such oracles would be. But there is no such commination in Deutero-Isaiah. Instead he has two oracles of hope for the Gentiles:—'It is too light a thing that thou shouldest be my Servant to raise up the tribes of Jacob, and to restore the preserved of Israel; I will also give thee for a light to the Gentiles, that thou mayest be my salvation unto the end of the earth.'[4] The more the historical background of this prophecy is studied, the more wonderful this appears. There had been no such teaching since Isaiah himself.[5] The 'sure and certain hope' of this prophet is world-wide. He was one of those who love their enemies. Is this the New Testament or the Old?

The last quotation made comes from a group of passages called 'The Songs of the Servant of Jehovah.'[6] They are often studied apart from the rest of this prophet's oracles, both because of their poetic form and because of their

[1] Isa. xl. 1f.
[2] Isa. lv. 12.
[3] Isa. xiii. 1-xiv. 23.
[4] Isa. xlix. 6; *cf.* xlii. 6.
[5] See pp. 137, 141. As there seen, many writers assign the three passages there quoted to this period.
[6] See footnote on p. 177.

teaching. The last of them needs special study, but before we turn to it, we need to remember a little more of the historic situation. No doubt there were many exiled Hebrews who betook themselves to the ways of their heathen neighbours and were lost in the mass of the Babylonian empire. Some of them perhaps prospered. At any rate, the question now asked itself, 'Why do the righteous suffer and the wicked flourish?' For Babylon was wicked and the prophet's little group of hearers were righteous.

We shall find that this problem recurred often in Israel. It had emerged with Jeremiah[1] but it was now clamant. Earlier teachers had steadily declared that Jehovah punished the wicked and blessed the righteous, and it was now plain that there were at least exceptions to this. What was to be said? Deutero-Isaiah was the first Hebrew thinker to face this issue, and he came nearer a solution than any that followed him. For he discovered the great truth that men may be saved by the vicarious sufferings of others. To-day many people dislike the term 'vicarious'; but it only means that men may do some things for each other, and surely this is obvious! This prophet declares that one of the things that men can do for each other is to suffer, and that such suffering saves.

It is not certain whom he means by the 'Servant of Jehovah.' Outside the four Songs he seems clearly to apply the term to the people Israel.[2] But this hardly suits the Songs themselves. In them the Servant is either the faithful remnant of Israel, or some single Israelite. Perhaps the former account is the more likely. Under the term, 'The Servant of Jehovah,' the prophet then means 'faithful, suffering Israel.' If this be so, then the people whom the sufferers save may either be the rest of Israel, or the Gentiles, or both. Perhaps the last is the most likely interpretation.

[1] Jer. xii. 11. [2] e.g. Isa. xli. 8f.

Whoever the Servant was, and whomsoever his suffering saved, the general line of thought in the last and greatest 'Servant Song' is plain.[1] The poem falls into five paragraphs.[2] The first tells us that we are to hear of the 'prosperity,' or success, of the Servant; and that this success is a thing to astonish the world. The second tells us that the Servant is so dire a sufferer that men turn their faces from this 'man of sorrows' as from a loathsome leper. The third tells that none the less he is bearing the terrible results of other men's sins; the onlookers cry, '*He* was wounded for *our* transgressions; *he* was bruised for *our* iniquities.' In the fourth paragraph they exclaim, 'And see, he does not even writhe; other men's sins are killing him, and he does not even writhe.' The fifth returns to the message of the first, 'And this is the way of his success; this is why Jehovah has so smitten him.'

For the writer the application of his great discovery of vicarious suffering was to the undeserved suffering of loyal Israel. But the principle has many other applications. The first Christians unerringly made the greatest application of all. They called Jesus, the Crucified Jesus, 'the Servant.'[3] And they were right. He, as no other, was righteous; He, as no other, was obedient; He, as no other, suffered to save; for Him, as for no other, suffering was the one way of success. Here is the supreme instance in literature of the enunciation of a principle that is greater, far greater, than the writer knows.

The writing prophets from Amos to Deutero-Isaiah are the glory of the Old Testament. Before them there were, indeed, the first hints of Israel's unique achievement, but only the first hints. Before them we can see the one acorn, among the many that bestrewed the world of religion, begin to take root and grow; but it is in these prophets that it becomes an oak. After them something further ensued

[1] Isa. lii. 13—liii. 12. Our division of chapters here is peculiarly unhappy.
[2] As in the Revised Version.
[3] e.g. Acts iv. 27; viii. 32ff.

in the way of development, as we shall see. Yet in the next period it is problems that meet us, rather than solutions. In it, again, we shall find that even ethical monotheism is not the last word in religion. Yet to have so listened to God as to discover it, is the unique achievement of the line of men that stretch from Amos to Deutero-Isaiah. It passed on from them to Christianity, and through Christianity it is becoming the creed of all men.

To us it may seem an obvious truth. Many things that look easy and obvious to us took centuries and even millenniums to discover. We have a phrase 'As easy as ABC'—but men groped for ages before the alphabet was wrought out for common use. We think the figures 1, 2, 3, and so on, simple; but the easy use of Arabic digits for enumeration depends upon the discovery of the use of the figure 0 to make 2 into 20, 3 into 30, and so on—and to discover this was the work of an unknown genius. It is easy to-day to go to America. Let a man cross a plank, eat and sleep, eat and sleep, for a few days, cross another plank, and he is there! None the less—rather, all the more—Columbus was a great man. So for us the great sum of truths about God that is gathered in the phrase 'ethical monotheism,' seems obvious enough. But it was wrought out by the prophets of Israel; and they wrought it out because they had 'ears to hear' God when He spoke to their hearts. There is one God; He is personal; He is righteous; He is omnipotent—no race except Israel found the way to this set of truths. And they are the foundation of true life.

## Chapter XIII

# THE BOOKS OF THE FOUR CENTURIES AFTER THE EXILE

It will perhaps have been noticed that so far we have dealt with no more than three kinds of books—law, history (told with a religious purpose), and prophecy. No doubt there were other kinds of literature in Israel before the Exile, but we have not needed to say much about them. After the Exile there is much more variety in Hebrew books. This is natural, for the Jews were now plunged into the general stream of civilization, and, as civilization develops, there is a growing variety in literature. For instance, there were many more kinds of books in the England of the nineteenth century than in Anglo-Saxon times. In an elementary study like this one it is not possible to trace separately the teaching of each kind of book. In consequence it will be found that in the following chapters a variety of books is quoted to illustrate the several tendencies of the times. It will be an advantage, therefore, to classify here the post-Exilic literature under its various forms. The books are dated in this period in accordance with the general opinion of scholars.

As might be expected, it is not possible to bring every book rigidly within the classes named, for living literature always defies exact classification. Some books belong partly to one class and partly to another. We shall find in the next chapter that in this epoch the old literature of Israel was gathered, edited and arranged. Here we shall keep, in the main, to books that were written, in all probability, in this period. Many are included that are ascribed to historic names, as David, Solomon and Daniel. In the next chapter it will be found that it was one of the literary conventions of the period to write in this way. This is technically called 'pseudepigraphy.' The classification requires seven divisions.

1. *History*. It will be remembered that the period lasted for some four hundred years (538-160 B.C.), and that it falls into two almost equal parts—the Persian period (538-331 B.C.) and the Greek period (331-160 B.C.). It is remarkable how little the Jews of the time cared to record their own history. This, indeed, is symptomatic of their own opinion of the period, as we shall see.

The only historical books we have are the books of Ezra and Nehemiah, and the Books of Chronicles.[1] The Books of Chronicles tell the story of Israel before the Exile, and end therefore before our period begins. The Books of Ezra and Nehemiah, which are one book in the Hebrew Canon, tell of two brief bits of history. They begin with the few years that immediately succeeded the Exile[2]; then leaping at least sixty years in silence, they tell of the few years when Ezra and Nehemiah led the little people that clung around Jerusalem.[3] After this—that is, for at least two hundred and twenty years—we have no Jewish history. This means that we know nothing of it from our Bible.[4]

2. *Law*. We have seen that, before the Exile, we are able to trace four collections of Hebrew law,—the Decalogue, the Book of the Covenant,[5] the collection that fills a large part of the thirty-fourth chapter of Exodus, and the Book

[1] Some would add the little Book of Ruth.

[2] Ezra i.-vi.

[3] The story of Ezra fills chs. vii.-x. in his book, that of Nehemiah covers the book that bears his name. Both are partly autobiographical. As the two stories stand in our Bibles, Ezra preceded Nehemiah; many scholars think, however, that in reality he followed him; the reasons will be found in the commentaries.

[4] A book in the Apocrypha, First Maccabees, is a good history of the Maccabean struggle.

[5] Exod. xxi.-xxiii.

of Deuteronomy. In the period that we have now reached we have two more, one of them being embedded in the other.

Probably these later collections began to be made in the Exile; indeed the shorter of them was perhaps completed then. It is called 'The Code of Holiness,' because it uses the term 'holy' so frequently. It occupies a large part of the Book of Leviticus.[1] There is no need to say much about it here, for in part it carries on the tradition of the Deuteronomic school, and in part it falls in with the later Priestly document in which it is embedded. It repeats not a few of the edicts of the Book of the Covenant and Deuteronomy, sometimes developing them to meet the changed circumstances of a later day. It also exhibits the old 'humanitarian' temper of Hebrew law; for instance, it is in this document that we first meet with the great command, 'Thou shalt love thy neighbour as thyself.'[2]

The other collection of laws is called 'Priestly,' and it is very largely concerned with the right regulation of ritual. Comparatively little is said of this in the earlier codes, but in this period, when the priests were dominant in Judæa, and the characteristic national act was worship at the Temple, it absorbs attention. This priestly collection of laws fills the rest of Leviticus and a great part of Exodus.[3] In Exodus the ostensible description is of the ancient Tabernacle; in reality, it depicts rather the uses of the Second Temple. No doubt many of them went back to early times.

Here there appears, however, one of the 'cross divisions' named above. The Priestly document includes also a great many of the narratives of Genesis, Exodus, and Joshua,—that is to say, it includes history as well as law, though it is history from the 'Priestly' point of view. Here, however,

[1] Lev. xvii.-xxvi.
[2] Lev. xix. 18.
[3] Exod. xxv.-xxxi.; xxxv.-xl.; with other fragments.

the writers of the document were busy rather with redaction[1] than with original work, and what more needs to be said about it will be found in the next chapter. The Priestly collections of law, in the strict sense, are one of the chief products of post-Exilic Judaism.

3. *Prophecy.* Prophecy, on the other hand, was a spent and diminishing force. Five prophets are assigned to this period, and they might be called 'the third group of writing prophets,' though they have not the same unity of message as the first two groups.

First there is the group of prophecies that closes our Book of Isaiah.[2] As we do not know who wrote them, it is convenient to call their author or authors 'Trito-Isaiah.'[3] In many ways these prophecies repeat and recall the message of Deutero-Isaiah, though sometimes, as will appear later, they fail to maintain his lofty spirit. As the Temple seems in some passages to be still in ruins,[4] and sometimes to be rebuilt,[5] some scholars think that some of these oracles[6] were written between the Return and the Re-building of the Temple (i.e. between 538 and 520 B.C.), and some after the Re-building.

Two other prophets, Haggai and Zechariah,[7] spend themselves in urging the Jews to rebuild their ancient shrine, and therefore date themselves about 520 B.C.[8]

There remain two other prophecies, Malachi[9] and Obadiah, which probably belong to the fifth century before Christ.[10]

[1] That is, the process by which editors reduce earlier works to a unified digest.

[2] Isa. lvi.-lxvi.

[3] i.e. Third Isaiah. Selected passages: chs. lx.; lxv.

[4] e.g. Isa. lxiv. 11.

[5] e.g. Isa. lxvi. 6.

[6] Which do not all come first in the present collection, however.

[7] Selected passages: Hag. i.; Zech. iii.; viii.

[8] Only the first eight chapters, however, of our Book of Zechariah are assigned to this prophet; for the other chapters see p. 192.

[9] Selected passage: ch. iii. 7-iv. 6.

[10] The other books usually reckoned as prophecies will be found elsewhere in this classification.

It will be seen that these writings, while they have their own importance, do not rank with those of the great prophetic period. The fact is that the prophet spoke a word that he had just received from an active God; and the tendency of this period, as will appear, was to look for the working of God to the past and the future, rather than to the present.

If any unity is to be sought in this group of prophets, it is in their intense nationalism. Three of them centre their thoughts in the national shrine, Haggai and Zechariah advocating its rebuilding, and Malachi denouncing the neglect of its worship. Of the other two, one, Obadiah, spends himself in the denunciation of Edom, a people that was Israel's typical foe at this time, while the other, Trito-Isaiah, looks forward to a day when Israel shall dominate the world, and Jerusalem shall be its capital. Yet it should be added that this dominance centres in the world's worship of the one, true God, Jehovah, and that this prophet has other and better ideas than Israelite despotism.

4. *Poetry*. Here we have four books—the Book of Lamentations, the Song of Songs, the Book of Job,[1] and the Book of Psalms.[2] The first two of these are short books, each with a single subject. Lamentations is a series of acrostic poems on the destruction of Jerusalem in 586 B.C.[3] Part of it was probably written in the Exile, and the rest soon after.

The Song of Songs is a wedding-song, or collection of wedding songs. It sometimes transgresses the limits of

[1] Selected passages: chs. i. xxix.-xxxi.; xxxviii.; xlii.

[2] Hebrew poetry followed Semitic forms, which are not the same as those of Aryan languages, and are not quite so clearly distinguishable from elevated prose.

[3] It will be noticed that four of its five chapters have each twenty-two verses, and that the other one has three times twenty-two. There are twenty-two letters in the Hebrew alphabet, and the letters, taken in the usual order, begin the verses, or sets of three verses, in the several chapters. There are other acrostic poems in the Old Testament, notably Psalm cxix., where each letter in turn begins a set of eight verses.

reticence now observed in the West, but its subject is the bliss of true love and true marriage. By implication monogomy is here preferred to polygamy. Both for this reason, and because 'marriage is an honourable estate instituted to God,' it is well that the book is in the Bible. It bears witness that God made sex.

The Book of Job, while it has a prose frame-work, is a sustained piece of poetry on the single theme, 'Why do the righteous suffer?' It ranks high in the poetic literature of the world. In subject, however, as distinct from form, it belongs to the kind of writing called 'wisdom literature,' while in another way it falls under the division called 'fiction' below. Here, again, therefore, we find that technical classification fails us.

The Book of Psalms is now often called 'the hymn-book of the Second Temple.' Like other good hymn-books, it contains hymns on very various subjects, of very various tone, and of very various dates. As a collection it clearly belongs to this period, for such a psalm as the 137th could not have been written before the Exile. Hebrew specialists, judging by vocabulary, style and range of ideas, tell us that very many other psalms were probably composed in the four centuries now in question. At the same time, it is quite possible, and indeed likely, that some psalms come from the time of the Monarchy. In Israel, as among other early peoples, song was one of the earliest forms of literature.[1] It is, however, often very difficult to date a hymn, as any one will see who takes a modern hymn-book and tries to assign the hymns, whose dates he does not already know, to their proper centuries. Happily the spiritual value of a hymn does not depend on its date.[2]

[1] e.g. Judges v.; 2 Sam. i. 17ff.

[2] The meaning and value of the notes prefixed to many of the psalms is much disputed. Some of them refer to the music of the Temple. This may be so with the phrase translated 'A psalm of David,' for it is an unusual phrase and may mean 'a psalm to be sung in the manner called Davidic. At the same time there is no doubt that David was a poet. *Cf.* 2 Sam. i. 17ff; iii. 33f.

A hint of the methods of the specialists may be given, since it is one that an English reader can readily understand. Any psalm that refers to a contemporary Hebrew king must either be earlier than 586 B.C. or later than 153 (or even 105) B.C., for between these dates there was no king of Israel.

5. *Wisdom Literature.* Three books fall under this term,—the Book of Job (as already seen), the Book of Proverbs, and the Book of Ecclesiastes (or, to use its Hebrew name, Koheleth). The meaning of the term 'Wisdom Literature' will appear if the Book of Proverbs be studied. The greater part of this book consists of what we should usually call 'proverbs.'[1] And these proverbs, like those of other nations, are pieces of prudential advice, their one subject being 'How to get on in life.' In other words, they are the product of a certain kind of 'wise man,' the man of practical sagacity.

It is rarely possible either to ascribe a proverb to a particular author, or to discover its date. The Book of Proverbs, however, in its present form—considered as a collection of proverbial material of varying dates—almost certainly belongs to the post-exilic period.[2] As to the collection of brief sayings that fills most of the book, the distinction of the Hebrew collection is not that it inculcates 'practical shrewdness,' for here it is like all other sets of proverbs, but that it makes religion basal to the practice of every-day life. Its watchword is 'The fear of the Lord is the beginning of wisdom.' No

[1] There are several collections of these: x. 1-xxii. 16; xxii. 17-xxiv. 22; xxiv. 23-34; xxv.-xxix.; xxx.; xxxi. 1-9. The last passage in the book, xxxi. 10-31, is a continuous description of the ideal woman of Hebrew thought, but it is in the vein of 'the wise men.' Chs. i.-ix. are named below. A recently discovered Egyptian work, the *Teaching of Amen-em-ope*, has so close a literary likeness to Proverbs xxii. 17-24, that one of the two writers must be assumed to have read the other's work. Probably the Hebrew author is the borrower, but this is not certain.

[2] For instance, the first part of it (chs. i.-ix.) shows signs of the influence of Greek thought.

other collection of proverbs says this with anything like the same persistence and clearness. Very few English proverbs, for instance, name religion at all. In this realm, as in others, Israel is *the* religious race.

This idea reaches its culmination in the first nine chapters.[1] They come at the beginning of the book, but they were probably written last. While they contain short, pithy sayings of the usual proverbial sort, they are a continuous piece of writing in praise of 'Wisdom.' Here 'Wisdom' is personified. Over against her there is set another personification, 'Folly.' 'Wisdom' pleads with the sons of men to listen to her. She personifies a quality in God, for He is pictured as using her as 'a master craftsman,' or 'artisan,' when He made the universe. She is also depicted as a quality in good men. She is the divinely appointed guide of life. To use modern phrases, we here learn that a good conscience in man has its exemplar in God. The concept of 'wisdom' has here passed far beyond that of mere 'practical sagacity'; it is the principle of the good life in all its reach. As it is both a divine and a human quality it exemplifies what the Old Testament means when it says that man is made 'in the image of God.'

The other piece of 'wisdom literature' is the Book of Ecclesiastes.[2] It is the work of a pessimist, and it has as little logical consistency as the work of most pessimists. Its recurrent 'tag' is 'Vanity of vanities, all is vanity.' Like the first part of Proverbs, it seems to betray the influence of Greek thought. Many have wondered that it should be in the Bible at all; and, as we shall see, there was long hesitation before it was admitted. But we must remember that, after the Return from Exile, the Jews were a forlorn and disillusioned race, and that,

[1] Selected passage: ch. viii.

[2] This is its Greek name, and means 'preacher,' as does the Hebrew name 'Koheleth'; yet the author is by no means an orthodox 'church preacher,' as the term 'ecclesiastes' suggests. Selected passage: ch. viii. 16—ix. 16.

for an able man, who was not prepared to abandon honesty, there were 'no prospects' either in the Persian or the Greek period. The men who 'got on' at the little governor's court in Jerusalem, were the men who were not too fastidious in conduct. It was an ill time for gifted integrity. The writer was a man of this character. Most such men, living in such a time, would altogether abandon religious faith. As one reads this book, one is aware by the 'feel' of it rather than by definite statement, that Koheleth, with all his disillusion and all his pessimism, is just managing to hold on to some sort of a belief in God. At the time it was no mean achievement, and it is well that the pessimist has his corner in a book of optimism like the Bible.

6. *Fiction*. Here there are two books and a large part of a third—the Books of Esther and Jonah, and the earlier part of Daniel.[1] The Book of Job might also be taken here, because of its narrative frame-work. Some may think that fiction ought to have no place in the Bible; but, with *The Pilgrim's Progress*, for instance, in our hands, it is impossible to assert that fiction may not teach religion.

All the books named have the post-exilic background. In it Israel looked a very feeble folk. This is so whether we think of the little fragment of the race that clustered round Jerusalem, or the scattered remnants of the Dispersion. Israel was not only feeble, she was despised. And she was not only despised, she was persecuted. Probably there were sporadic persecutions in the Persian period; certainly there were persecutions in the Greek period, culminating in the great persecution of Antiochus Epiphanes.

The fiction of the period, like the fiction of any people in any period, unlocks the mind of the race at the time. Job sitting on his dunghill typifies poor little pitiful Israel; Mordecai, crouching at the king's gate, is another symbol

[1] Or, more exactly, chs. i. and iii.-vi., i.e. the stories of 'Daniel in the Lion's Den' and 'The Three Hebrew Children.'

of the same sorry plight; Jonah, flung into the sea, stands for Judaism, primarily in exile, but also throughout the period; Daniel in the lions' den, and Shadrach, Meshach and Abednego in the 'burning, fiery furnace,' depict Israel in the utter perils of fierce persecution.

The one message of all these books, each in its distinctive way, is the truth that, whatever befall, Jehovah is standing by His people and He will inevitably deliver them. It is quite likely that some, at least, of the stories are 'founded on fact,' and that they may therefore be called 'historical romance.' Their message was just the gospel that the times needed,—'When thou walkest through the fire, I will be with thee, and the floods, they shall not overflow thee.' The survival of Israel in these centuries is one of the wonders of the world. There is such a thing as 'inspired fiction.'

7. *Apocalyptic Literature.* Here there are four books,—the Book of Joel, a part of the Book of Isaiah,[1] the latter part of the Book of Zechariah,[2] and a large part of the Book of Daniel.[3] Once again the historical situation explains the prevalence of this kind of literature, a kind that seems strange, and sometimes even grotesque, to-day.

As we have seen, Israel had fallen on evil times, yet she still believed in Jehovah, and she believed that He was the one God of the whole earth. This, however, seemed in sharp contrast with fact; for if Israel's God was the God of the whole earth, why, did He leave her to pine and to suffer? The answer of the Apocalyptists is that He is in charge of history, of all the doings of all the nations, of Babylon, Media, Persia and Alexander's empire in turn; that, in His own mysterious ways He is all the while doing as He will with them all; and that in His own time He will

[1] Chs. xxiv.-xxvii.

[2] Chs. ix.-xiv.; the writer is sometimes called, for convenience, Deutero-Zechariah.

[3] Chs. ii., vii.-xii.: Daniel, therefore, cannot be assigned strictly to any one of our seven classes of literature, for the rest of it falls under 'fiction.'

break in upon the world in a great catastrophe, a 'Day of Jehovah,' when he will judge all nations and set up His own righteous kingdom, with Israel in glory as its triumphant and splendid head. In other words, these are books of hope.

They have many points of likeness to the prophecies; indeed they have till recent times been counted as prophecies. For the prophets, too, had taught that Jehovah is master of the world, and that He would one day vindicate His power and restore Israel. Yet there are differences along with points of likeness. The typical prophet wrestles with a sinful Israel; the Apocalyptists assume that Israel is righteous and other nations wicked. The typical prophet preaches doom to Israel, though he may go on to foretell her ultimate purification and triumph; the Apocalyptists, assuming that she is now 'under the harrow,' exhaust themselves in depicting her coming splendour. The prophets are chiefly interested in what Jehovah is doing now, though they have some thought about the future too; with the Apocalyptists the centre of interest, on the contrary, is in what Jehovah is going to do in the near future. While the prophets use many symbols, both in speech and act, many of their messages are given in plain words; the Apocalyptists love symbol to the point where it seems to us artificial. It is best, therefore, to treat Apocalyptic as a distinct form of literature, though it is impossible to say exactly where prophecy ends and Apocalyptic begins. The one merges into the other.

It is clear that, when any crisis in world history seemed to be approaching, it was likely to provoke this kind of writing. A devastating plague of locusts, which so beggared the land that even the offerings in the Temple were intermitted, lies behind the Book of Joel.[1] And there were two crises of history that would readily suit this kind of book—the sudden collapse of the old Persian empire before the

[1] Selected passage: Joel ii. 28—iii. 21.

onrush of Alexander, and the obstinate attempt of Antiochus Epiphanes to extirpate the worship of Jehovah. To others the second may have seemed a local struggle, but to the Jews the 'end of all things' seemed to threaten. Many students ascribe the Apocalypses that are found in the Books of Isaiah and Zechariah to the first of these epochal events.[1] There is an almost unanimous opinion that the Book of Daniel belongs to the second.[2]

It ought perhaps to be added that several of these seven kinds of literature are represented in the collection of books that we call 'the Apocrypha.' For instance, the First Book of Maccabees is history; the Song of the Three Holy Children[3] is poetry; the books of Ecclesiasticus (or Sirach) and Wisdom fall under 'wisdom literature'; Tobit, Judith, the History of Susanna and 'Bel and the Dragon' are a kind of fiction; and the Second Book of Esdras is Apocalyptic. Some of the other books are of mixed types.

[1] Selected passages: Isa. xxiv. 21—xxv. 8; Zech. ix. 8-17; xiv.

[2] Selected passages: chs. vii.; ix.; xii. 1-4.

[3] Found in the Prayer Book under the name 'the Benedicite.'

## Chapter XIV

## THE GROWTH OF THE CANON

The literature of the Old Testament is of a certain type. It is a great literature, at least in large parts of it, when considered from a purely literary point of view. It contains, again, much valuable history. It includes also classical instances of particular kinds of writing—prophecy, apocalyptic, law, hymns, and so on. But none of these things is the ultimate secret of its power.

It belongs to the kind of literature technically called 'canonical'; that is, it is a literature that great numbers of people regard as religiously authoritative. There are many other examples of this kind of literature—for instance, in the Koran and the writings of Mrs. Eddy. Such books lay down a standard or 'canon' of conduct for the people who believe that they are authoritative in religion. The Old Testament is the whole 'canon' of the Jew and a part of the 'canon' of the Christian. It is here that its ultimate importance grounds.

We are so used to thinking of the Bible as the book of the supreme religion, that many of us find it difficult to think of a religion that has no authoritative book. Yet primitive religions have none.

The leading examples of religions with 'canons' or authoritative 'scriptures,' on the other hand, are found among the faiths that look back to some great teacher as their founder. So the Muhammedan has a 'canon,' for he believes that the founder of his religion gave it to his followers as a rule of life.

In other instances religions look back, not to one man,

but to a number of men, as giving authoritative guidance in religion. The Jews fall into this class, and so, though not in the same way, do the Christians. The Jew thinks of Moses and Isaiah and Jeremiah and so on as men who spoke authentic words from God which are authoritative for life. The Christian thinks of these men as in some degree authoritative. But he subordinates their authority to the supreme authority of Jesus Christ, who alone, in his conviction, spoke perfectly, and therefore finally, of God and His ways with men.

Yet, when the idea of an authoritative book is examined, it is found that it is not by itself sufficient to cover all the facts. For the *writer* or *writers* of the book or books must be authoritative in religion. Before there can be an inspired book there must be inspired men. Sometimes, indeed, the writer of the books only reports the words of another—as for instance, the writers of the Four Gospels did,—but then the man whose words they report must have authority in religion. Where does this authority come from? The disciples of any religion answer, 'From God.'

It appears, therefore, that there is another way of learning God's will beside the way of reading it in a book. In this way God speaks directly to the conscience of some man, and he hands on the message to others. So the prophet declared, 'Thus saith Jehovah'; so our Lord spoke 'with authority' of the will of the Father. Ultimately all those who believe in 'revelation' at all—who believe that God makes His will known to men—must, in one way or other, hold that God has at some time made known His will to particular men. The concept of an authoritative book, taken alone, is incomplete.

This subject lends itself to much further discussion, but we must ask now how it applies to the Old Testament in particular. It is clear that, at least through a great part of the story of the Hebrews, the idea that God gives authoritative guidance for life in a book, and the idea that He gives such guidance through living men, were found together.

For instance, in the days of Josiah there was an authoritative book, for Hilkiah found it in the Temple; there was also an authoritative man, named Jeremiah, as a few of his contemporaries believed and as ultimately all Jews came to believe.

It is clear, too, that it is possible that one of these ideas of 'revelation' might be dominant at one time and the other idea at another. The finding of the experts is that in the earlier period of the Old Testament the concept that God spoke through direct 'revelation' to particular men was dominant, but that gradually the idea arose that His revelation was contained in a particular book, and that ultimately this idea became dominant and superseded the other.

The first idea has been abundantly illustrated above. We need now to look a little at the history of the second idea. We need to trace the story of the Hebrew 'canon.' At this point we shall again give the findings of the experts without asking how they reach them.

Moses was the founder of the Hebrew religion. This means that he himself believed, and that the 'children of Israel' believed, that he 'spake from God.' It is likely that some of the things that he said were written down; for, though the number of people in his day who could read and write were few, yet the art of writing was already very old. What words of his were written down? We do not know. It is possible, but far from certain, that he wrote down the Ten Commandments as later tradition affirmed. It is possible that some other things in the Books from Exodus to Deuteronomy go back to him; but we do not know which they are, or even whether there are any. It is true that very much in these books is ascribed to Moses, but in the history of other ancient religions, such as the Buddhist, the Zoroastrian, and the Jain, we find that a large number of later laws gather gradually round the name of the founder, yet that many of them were not written by him or taken down in writing from his lips.

In these instances the growth of a canon is far more like the growth of a tree than it is like the writing of modern books. The founder of the religion planted a seed; the canon is the tree that has grown from the seed. Modern study says the same about the 'Law of Moses.' It may be called his in some such way as St. Wilfrid might be called the 'builder' of Ripon Minster. The work of later centuries is there, yet his spirit dominates the whole. To begin a movement that lasts and lives and develops century by century is a greater thing than to write a great book. Of course a man may do both, but students do not confidently say this of Moses. He belongs to the large number of great men to whom we cannot certainly ascribe any particular piece of writing. To revert to the former figure, we can see the oak that he planted, but we cannot identify the acorn that he sowed.

When we pass to the first centuries after Joshua, the chief way of learning the will of Jehovah seems to have been to appeal to some recognized 'man of God' and not to a book. Saul and David, for instance, asked a priest for an oracle when they wished to know the will of Jehovah. Every prophet claimed to know and to tell his will. It is likely, however, that there was already a body of Hebrew customs that was regarded as an embodiment of the will of Jehovah, and that this was handed on partly by memorizing and partly by writing. It has been seen above that at this time there were certain great shrines in which the cultus of Jehovah centred.[1] There is some evidence that the priests at these shrines kept 'holy books' in which they wrote out the traditional records of revelation. It may be that, as oracles were given from time to time, some of these were written down and added to the book. The collection of laws in Exod. xxxiv. and the 'Book of the Covenant'[2] are perhaps the oldest of these collections that have come down as distinct collections to us.

There is a good deal of evidence to suggest that, by

[1] p. 98. [2] Exod. xxi.-xxiii.

somewhere about 800 B.C., there was quite a considerable 'holy book' in Judah, which included stories as well as laws, and another in the North.[1] If these records existed, it seems antecedently likely that there would be such a book at Jerusalem; also, that when the Northern kingdom perished in 722 B.C., its holy book or books would be carried there, for how else did they survive? At any rate, we read that when Josiah restored the Temple about 621 B.C., the priest Hilkiah 'found the book of the law of Jehovah' in it and brought it to the king. As we have seen above, it is likely that this contained a large part of what we call Deuteronomy.[2] We do not know how old it was, nor whether the collection of laws that it contains had been slowly growing. This seems likely, for it often repeats laws of the two earlier codes of law named above with amplifications. On the other hand, there are parts of it[3] that read as though they were the product of a single author at a particular time. The publication of this law by King Josiah as the authoritative law of Jehovah marks a great stage in the process by which a 'holy book' began to take precedence of oracle and prophecy in the religion of Israel.[4] It is clear, however, that this precedence was not finally won for further centuries; for so long as Israel had prophets, the idea that Jehovah made known His will directly and authoritatively to particular men survived.

It not only survived, but in the two centuries that preceded and followed the reign of Josiah, it reached its zenith. For this is the period of the great prophets. When Amos or Isaiah or Jeremiah or Deutero-Isaiah spoke there was no question of quoting from a book, but

[1] The first of these is called technically document J, because from its beginning in Gen. ii. 4, it uses the name 'Jehovah' for the god of Israel, while the second is called 'E' because it treats this name as new in Exod. iii. 14 (*cf.* vi. 2—from document P, see below), using 'Elohim,' or 'god,' for the god of Israel, until it reaches that point.

[2] The Deuteronomic documents are called 'D.'

[3] Such as chs. vi. and xxviii.

[4] *Cf.* pp. 159ff.

of 'Thus saith Jehovah.' This is true even though some of the prophets do occasionally refer to the 'law' of Jehovah.[1]

Yet the idea of a written record developed here too. For how were the words of a prophet to be remembered? Unless someone, we do not know who, had written down the oracles of Amos, for instance, how could they have come down to us? Here is another sign that the holy books of the North passed to the South when the North perished, for Amos and Hosea preached in the North. We begin to have direct evidence in the Book of Isaiah,[2] and there is a famous story of the way in which Jeremiah himself arranged for some, at least, of his prophecies to be written down, in order that there might be a permanent record of them.[3] Yet, of course, these prophetic records would only be counted authoritative by those who followed these prophets—by Isaiah's 'disciples' or by Jeremiah's faithful acolyte Baruch. But it will be obvious that here we have the beginnings of a second kind of holy book—prophecy taking a place alongside law.

A moment's thought will show that the Exile would be a likely time for the collecting and writing of holy books. For the faithful Jew expected to return from Exile and to worship again at the Temple in the old way. Meanwhile the nation needed to carry on its life in an altogether alien environment. Clearly, to collect the old traditions and the old stories would help. Indeed, if we may judge by the example of the later Synagogues, it would largely be for the purpose of feeding their faith on such records that the Jews gathered together on the recurrent Sabbaths in Exile. Yet the Bible itself gives us no direct evidence of this.[4] In itself, however, the thing is likely.

In particular, it would be natural now to write down in detail an account of the ritual of the Temple. So long as there is regular worship at any shrine, the mere repetition

[1] e.g. Hos. iv. 6; Ezek. vii. 26. [2] Isa. viii. 16. [3] Jer. xxxvi.
[4] Unless Psalm cxxxvii. 2 means that, when they gathered, they sang their old songs.

of the ritual gives an authoritative account of what it ought to be, even though, at the same time, it allows for a gradual and almost imperceptible process of change. But, when the Jew was in Exile, the ritual ceased. How was it to be remembered against the day when it should be restored? It is probable that at this time the practice began of writing down its details.

Again, in the period that followed the Exile, as we have seen, prophecy gradually died away, and the life of Israel centred in Law and Temple.[1] The natural counterpart of this would be the gathering of sacred records into authoritative forms. Scholars assign to this period the final form of a fourth document in our Pentateuch,—a document called 'Priestly' because of its intense interest in the Temple and its ritual, and because, therefore, its probable authors were priests.[2]

With the period of Ezra and Nehemiah we reach the time when the idea that the religion of Jehovah centred in the holy book, became finally dominant in Israel. Prophecy had died away, and Apocalyptic had not yet come. Or, at least, if there were still prophets[3] they were not reckoned of much account; and if there was already Apocalyptic, it was not yet counted revelation. On the other hand, Israel's 'covenant' with Jehovah, definitely based upon an authoritative book, was now the master idea. The story of the eighth and ninth chapters of Nehemiah displays this. In it the whole people assemble to listen to the reading of a written 'law,'[4] and bind themselves to keep it. The era of the Canon had fully come.

What was this 'law'? The answer of scholars is that in the immediately preceding generations the 'scribes'[5]

[1] Ch. xiii.

[2] Technically this is called document 'P,' from the first letter of 'Priestly.'

[3] Neh. vi. 7, 14.

[4] The Hebrew word means 'teaching' and is wider than the English word 'law.'

[5] That is, literally, 'writers.'

of Israel had patiently taken the four collections named above—the 'Jahvist' and 'Elohist' documents of somewhere about 800 B.C., the 'Deuteronomist' document of about 600 B.C., and the 'Priestly' document of about 500 B.C.—and had pieced and dove-tailed them together, until they had taken the form in which we know them in the first books of our Bible.[1] In other words, in the days of Ezra and Nehemiah the Pentateuch was the Bible of Israel. Its characteristic name was 'Torah,'—that is, 'Teaching'—or, in the broadest sense, 'Law.' This is the first part of the Hebrew Canon, as of the Christian; and for a long time it was the only Hebrew Canon. To this day it takes precedence of all other scriptures[2] with the orthodox Jews.

As the line of prophets dwindled and ceased, the books that recorded the words of the old prophets were more and more valued. Besides, there were other records, records that we should call 'history,' that told of the dealings of Jehovah with His people in old times. There were the stories of Joshua and the Judges, of Samuel and David, of the later kings and of Elijah and Elisha. Was there not in them many a message from Jehovah? Had He not been active in all the story? Probably the books that tell of these times began to be collected long before the period we have now reached. We find that some of these books quote earlier records—two early collections of songs, for instance[3]—and the 'books of the chronicles' of the kings of Israel and Judah. The many instances of this last phrase show that the authors of our books did not quote all that they found in these 'chronicles.' They selected, and it seems clear that they selected those parts of the earlier books that seemed to teach the ways of Jehovah with His people. It is not

[1] It may be, however, that Ezra's canon was P and that our Pentateuch dates a century later.
[2] That is, 'writings.'
[3] e.g. 2 Sam. i. 18; Nums. xxi. 14.

meant that every single statement made in our books exhibits this characteristic, but that the selection was made chiefly on this method. There is a great illustration in the inclusion of the famous stories about Elijah and Elisha. It is unlikely that these formed part of the royal 'chronicles,' and indeed the chapters about these two prophets have a distinct literary quality. We do not know who compiled our present books, but we do know that the Book of Kings, at least, did not reach its present form until the Exile, for it mentions an event that belongs to that period.[1] It ought to be mentioned that there are some signs that the four books of which we now speak—Joshua, Judges, Samuel, Kings[2]—passed through the hands of men of the Deuteronomic school, for here and there are passages that have its distinctive vocabulary, style and spirit.[3] But now we come to a remarkable fact. When these books were included in the Jewish Canon, they were not called 'histories' but 'prophets'! This shows how the Jews thought of them—as books of religious teaching, rather than as mere records of the past. And with these four 'prophetic' books they put four others—Isaiah, Jeremiah, Ezekiel, and 'the Twelve.'[4] 'The Twelve' included the writings that we call, in some instances undeservedly, 'the minor prophets.' So far as scholars can judge, this second part was added to the Hebrew Canon somewhere about 200 B.C. That Canon, therefore, might now be called 'the Law and the Prophets.'

This brings us to a certain question. It has been seen above that there are many passages in the prophets, especially in the Book of Isaiah, which modern scholars do not ascribe to the prophets under whose name they appear in the Hebrew Canon; for instance, chapters xi.-lv. in the Book of Isaiah are ascribed to an unknown prophet of the Exile. How then do they come to be put under

[1] 2 Kings xxv. 27ff.
[2] Samuel and Kings formed each one book in the Hebrew Canon.
[3] See Appendix B.
[4] Not Daniel—see below.

these names in the Hebrew Canon? To understand the answer, we must ask ourselves how men knew that such-and-such a man wrote such-and-such a book. To-day we say 'Why, we turn to the title-page, and there it is!' But the device of putting the name of a book, the name of the author, the name of the publisher, and the date of a book, on a 'title-page' is comparatively recent. If the books of to-day had no title-page, how should we know who wrote them? There might be an old tradition that so-and-so wrote a given book, or there might be a passage in the book itself that implied that so-and-so wrote it, or some other book might refer to it as so-and-so's book, or it might be written in so-and-so's characteristic style, and so on. In the days when the unknown men to whom we owe the collection of the second part of the Hebrew Canon, were at work, there were no title-pages, and they would be guided by such reasons as those just given. We have no reason for supposing that their ascriptions of the many oracles that lay before them, to particular authors, was always accurate. Indeed, in the case of Jeremiah, the Septuagint[1] editors omitted quite a number of oracles that the Hebrew editors included. Besides, these men seem to have had before them a large number of oracles of uncertain authorship. They did their best with the information at their disposal, but there is no reason to suppose that they were inerrant. It is quite possible that the concentrated study of the experts of to-day, with the advantages of centuries of Bible study, and centuries of the practice of literary criticism, behind them, reaches better results.

It is to be remembered that the religious value of a book does not depend upon its author. Would the plays of Shakespeare be any less great if it turned out after all that Bacon wrote them? Or is the Te Deum any less a great Christian song because the old tradition that Ambrose and Augustine were its authors, seems at least doubtful?

[1] See p. 206.

At any rate, we find a second Canon of eight volumes—Joshua, Judges, Samuel, Kings, Isaiah, Jeremiah, Ezekiel, 'the Twelve'—being added to the first Canon of five. In the Synagogues of to-day, and for many centuries past, while the whole Law is read every year, a given section being read—in the same way as our 'First Lesson'—Sabbath by Sabbath, certain selected parts of the Prophets are also read—in some such way as our 'Second Lesson.'

Yet the Hebrew Canon was not yet complete. There were certain other books, of very various kinds, that gradually came to be counted holy. For instance, there was the Book of Psalms—probably, as already seen, the 'hymn-book of the Second Temple.' There were five books called 'Rolls'—the Song of Songs, Ruth, Lamentations, Koheleth, Esther—that seem somehow to have been connected with the great Feasts of the Hebrew Year. There was the book Ezra-Nehemiah[1] that told the story of the final restoration of Israel's confidence in her destiny. Were these to be included in the Canon?

Ultimately a third collection of books was added. This was a miscellaneous collection, and its final name was just 'Writings.' Its books occur in different orders in the oldest lists. In the order that prevails to-day among the Jews the collection falls into three parts. First, there are three books of poetry and Wisdom literature (Psalms, Job, Proverbs); next come the five small books called 'Rolls' named just above; and last, there are three other books (Daniel, Ezra-Nehemiah, Chronicles).[2] There is interesting evidence[3] that the Book of Chronicles[4] came last in our Lord's own day, for it is in that book that we read of the martyrdom of Zechariah.[5]

[1] One book in the Hebrew.

[2] It will be seen that the Apocalyptic books, other than Daniel, were reckoned as 'Prophets'; it has been remarked above (p. 193) that it is very hard to draw a line between the two.

[3] In Matt. xxiii. 35.

[4] One book in the Hebrew.

[5] 2 Chron. xxiv. 20-23.

The Jews took time in deciding the contents of their Canon, as the account here given shows. In particular, it is interesting to note that, while the third part of the Canon was perhaps closed by 100 B.C., even in the days of Jesus Himself, there was still discussion whether certain books—Esther, Koheleth, Song of Songs, Chronicles—*ought* to be included in it. It is interesting to think that men of the same class as the Scribes with whom both Jesus and Paul contended, were at the same time vindicating a Canon that was to be the Christian Canon as well as the Jewish. And the ultimate name of the Hebrew Canon—'The Law, the Prophets, and the Writings'—does not seem yet to have been reached. The nearest thing to it in the New Testament is the phrase 'The Law, the Prophets and the Psalms.'[1]

It ought to be mentioned here that somewhere about 250 B.C. the Jews in Egypt began to translate their Scriptures into Greek. This translation is called the 'Septuagint' (lxx), from the Latin word for 'seventy,' as there was a story that the translation was made by seventy scribes. Now, there are a number of books, usually called 'The Apocrypha,' which the Septuagint includes but the Hebrew Canon excludes. And the Greek editors not only included these additional books; they arranged the Canon differently. They put histories first, then poetical and Wisdom books, then prophecies. This is the arrangement of the Christian Canon of the Old Testament—the histories extending from Genesis to Second Chronicles, the poetical and Wisdom books from Job to the Song of Songs, and the prophetic books from Isaiah to Malachi.[2] The Greek and Roman churches accept the Septuagint selection of books and include the Apocrypha. The Protestant churches did not at first all treat the Apocrypha alike, but to-day, for the most part, they accept the Hebrew

[1] Luke xxiv. 44. The Psalms formed the first book in the third volume of the Canon.

[2] Here Daniel is counted among the prophets.

selection of books, and exclude the Apocrypha.[1] To this day, therefore, the Christian Church is not agreed about the contents of the Old Testament Canon. Soon after it reached completion, there came another prophet, John the Baptist, and after him a greater prophet still, and, as Christians think, the way was open for the addition of the last and culminant part of the Canon, the New Testament.

[1] The Anglican Church takes a middle course, gathering together the Apocrypha in a separate collection, and allowing them some degree of value—Article vi. in the Thirty-nine Articles.

## Chapter XV

# A 'LIGHT IN A DARK PLACE'

Until recently the period after the Exile was treated as unimportant. To-day it is recognized that it played a great part in the story of Hebrew religion. It is significant in two ways—first, in what it did; second, in what it failed to do. A chapter is given to these two subjects in turn.

It has been seen that the great prophets had reached the creed known as 'ethical monotheism' and that this is unique in the history of nations. In the four centuries that followed the Exile, the Jews maintained, and to some extent developed, this doctrine. This was a very great achievement, for several reasons. The chief may be named.

First, the Jew held fast by 'monotheism.' It was the age-long custom of men to judge gods by their prowess. If a god worked mightily for his people, he was a great god. There is obvious common sense in this opinion. It had once prevailed in Israel, as in other ancient peoples. For instance, Jehovah's deliverance of Israel from Sennacherib was proof positive to the Hebrew that Jehovah was mighty. But now He seemed to be either unable or unwilling to do anything for His helpless and derelict people. Generation after generation, century after century, the Jews remained a subject and insignificant race. World-empire followed world-empire, but it made no difference to Israel. Alike amid the vast Persian empire and the vaster Greek empire she seemed like a cork on the waters. Yet Israel never hesitated in the conviction that her God was the master of the universe.[1] All the facts seemed to contradict this belief, but she defied the 'facts.'

Mention should be made of two particular aspects of this achievement. To-day it seems natural to distinguish between what we call 'church' and 'state,' but the distinction was never clearly drawn until the Seventeenth Christian Century. The old, old convictions of men knew no such distinction. In the Assyrian inscriptions, for instance, the national god or gods, the king and his empire, and the national worship, formed just one complex idea. Indeed, to an Assyrian the idea did not seem complex but simple, in something of the way in which a tree, say, did not 'of old time' seem a complex thing but a single, simple thing. And the Israelite had here the same thoughts as the Assyrian. Jehovah and His worship, the king and his kingdom, the people in its everyday life—all these 'went together' in Hebrew thought. But with the Exile Israel ceased to be a state. Her political liberty—for a while, even her political existence—was gone. The gods of other conquered races succumbed before such a catastrophe, or at the least shrunk into the little local deities of a paltry priesthood. But Israel's belief in her God and in His world-wide sway refused to be so frustrate. It is often said that at this time Israel ceased to be a state and became a church. It is easy to read the words and miss their meaning. It was a new thing in the earth, a kind of miracle.

[1] This does not mean that there were no Jews at all who lost heart, or that none of them fell before the old temptation to polytheism. On the contrary, it is likely that many took over the ways of their masters and lapsed into heathenism. Again, one of the most interesting of archæological discoveries—that of a bundle of *papyri* belonging to a settlement of Jews at the First Cataract of the Nile—shows us a community that worshipped both Jehovah and other gods. This community dated from before 529 B.C., and the *papyri* date between 500 and 400 B.C. The place in question is called Yeb in the *papyri*; the Greeks called it Elephantine, and it is now called Aswan. What is meant above is that there was a large mass of Jews who held by their old faith—probably the great majority of the Jews, indeed,—and that these were the people who treasured monotheism for the ultimate benefit of the world.

Under this aspect of the survival of monotheism we turn to the old, old axioms of the life of the past. Under another we look at a phenomenon that was new, yet widespread and persistent. It is a very complicated phenomenon. It might be summed up under two phrases—first, there was a general disintegration of the old national religions; second, men's indestructible hunger after religion none the less persisted.

The disintegration of national religions probably began with the rise of the first of the world-empires of Old Testament times, the Assyrian; for, as has already been seen, when such a people as Aram or Moab was conquered, the cult of her gods would tend to cease. But this tendency seems to have grown very strong under the Persian sway. For now it seemed inevitable that there would be a world-empire of some sort, in which national religions would be swallowed up like national states. From this period we find that even such religions as the Babylonian dwindled to death. And the tendency, once under way, grew in volume century after century. In the end it reached the old religions of the conquering states themselves. It is not certain what fate befell the old Persian faith,[1] but the old Greek polytheism began to lose its hold upon the Greeks; and a little later the old Roman faith began to disintegrate too.

This did not mean that the cult of Babylonian or Greek or Roman gods ceased, but that the religions of these peoples ceased to be the core of the national life and shrank into a kind of appendix. Some men, no doubt, became 'indifferent' and ceased to worship at all; others persisted in the old *cultus* because it was ancient, or interesting, or customary. All the priesthoods, of course, would do their utmost for their cults because they lived by them. And the other factor named above played a growingly important part—man's ineradicable need for worship. The more

[1] The story of Zoroastrianism falls here, and it is still obscure.

religiously minded men, robbed of their old gods, sought new ones. And they sought them wherever there seemed to be any sort of living god—in distant and ancient shrines, where worship still went on; or in the worship of a strange god, merely because he was strange, and had not been 'found out' in his powerlessness like the national gods; or in the cult of some mysterious deity whom few knew. It was an era of the decay of old religion, of the sway of superstition and the search after new gods. One of the chief consequences, ultimately, was the spread of the 'Mystery religions' that covered so much of the world in the first Christian centuries. Amid all this seething chaos a single people stood, generation after generation, by its old faith. Israel still held by Jehovah, and by Jehovah alone.

But what was the attitude of the various conquering powers to these phenomena? It is not quite certain, but it is very probable that the first of them, Assyria and Babylon, demanded that the conquered peoples should worship their conquerors' god. This would not be difficult for polytheists, for they could easily add another god to their pantheon, and even put him first. In Judah itself, for example, Manasseh seems to have submerged the worship of Jehovah under the worship of Assyrian deities. But the disintegration of religions passed to the cults of the conquerors themselves. This is certainly true of the Greek and the Roman, and may be true of the Persian too. What then were the conquerors to say to the conquered about religion? They might say either of two things. They might say that, as religion had ceased to count for much in national life, as no one was now likely to rebel in the name of his god, the conquered could worship as they liked. This means that the conquerors would be tolerant of all faiths. The Persian seems to have gone furthest in this direction. The most famous instance is the edict of Cyrus that permitted the Jews, not only to return to Palestine, but to set up their own Temple in Jerusalem again and to worship what god they liked there.[1] This tolerant attitude prevailed as a rule with the Greek conquerors too.

But another attitude was possible. The conqueror might hold that his religion, however little faith he himself now had in it, was still a part of his politics, and that willingness to adopt it was a test of the loyalty of the conquered. He might require, for purely political reasons, that all whom he ruled, should worship his gods. He might say that the refusal to do this was tantamount to treason. In other words, religion might be treated as altogether a part of state-craft. Under this idea a ruler would dictate his subjects' religion just as he would dictate their taxes or their laws. This was the attitude of one, at least, of the Greek rulers, Antiochus Epiphanes, and it accounts for the passionate outburst of Hebrew resistance under the Maccabees. Israel was the one people successfully to resist the widespread disintegration of religion ; it was the one race effectively to use the opportunity of Persian tolerance ; it was the one race that fought for its faith and prevailed. Flung into the sea, like Jonah, it did not perish ; like the Three Hebrew Children, it walked in fire and did not die.

These difficulties pressed upon Israel because she was monotheistic. They were intensified because she believed in ethical monotheism, because she believed that Jehovah was righteous. For whether the general state of the world was considered, or the particular plight of the Jew, alike in the Dispersion and in Judæa, it seemed obvious that, if there were indeed but one God, He did not care for righteousness at all.

For a little while the Jew might rejoice in the triumph of Persia over Babylon, but the rule of the Persian in the two

[1] Indeed, it may be that the Persians went further and held that, when all was said and done, all the gods were the same gods, under varying names. This would account for the use of such a phrase as 'the god of heaven' for Jehovah in a Persian letter (Ezra i. 2), a phrase that recurs in the Yeb *papyri*. (See footnote on p. 209).

centuries of his power, while it was probably better than that of Assyria or Babylon, was still the oppression of an Eastern despotism. And, as usual in Eastern despotism, the oppression waxed as the empire's period lengthened. At the capital Shushan it would be a wonder if a righteous Mordecai prevailed over an astute and unscrupulous Haman, or a Daniel emerged triumphant from the machinations of satraps and counsellors. Usually the battle would fall to the 'unrighteous' alien, not to the 'righteous' Jew. The very fact that he was 'righteous' would handicap him; for the level of conduct demanded by the Hebrew law would be far higher than that of any Eastern realm.

At the little court of the Persian governor at Jerusalem the evils of Shushan would multiply, for the little governor would surpass his lord in carelessness of justice, in cruelty and in 'graft.' This is why Koheleth cries out so bitterly against the odds of life. He had tried to be both righteous and successful, and he knew how impossible it was. Again, this is why, in so many of the Psalms of the time, good men cry out to Jehovah with an exceeding bitter cry—'Why do the wicked flourish and the righteous suffer?' And this is why the writer of Job posits the problem that he does so little to solve. Job, crouching ragged and leprous on his dung-hill, is an epitome of the plight of the righteous.

It was the same if the wider world were examined. Israel might be sinful in the eyes of Jehovah—her best minds knew well that she was—but she was easily the best people in the world. Compared with Persia, and still more perhaps, compared with the corrupt Greek world of Alexander's empire, she was righteous indeed. Yet it was not she that prospered, but they!

In spite of all, however, Israel stood by the conviction that there was but one God, that He ruled the universe and that He was righteous. She found relief, indeed, as we shall see, in searching the future and finding there His vindication of righteousness in the judgement of the nations —yet this was faith, not sight. It is the superb achievement of Israel that through these dismal centuries she held undimmed the prophets' belief in an ethical monotheism. This faith she has kept, against 'fearful odds,' to this day. Christians have learnt the habit from her. But the initial achievement is hers and hers alone.

If now it is asked how this little people did this great thing, the Psalms give the ultimate answer. In them we find clear and abundant evidence that many and many a Hebrew, most of them of unknown name, was intimate with the one God. In other words, Israel had now fought its way finally to the centre of all true religion, the fellowship of man with God.

Three elements in religion were distinguished above—the spiritual, the ethical, and the ritual. Of these the first is fundamental. It underlies all living religion everywhere, though men have always been slow to dig down to this foundation. Even Israel only slowly did so. But now she had reached rock. And now conscious fellowship with God was not confined to a Jeremiah or two. It was the treasure of many ordinary men.

This appears in other literature of the period—for instance, in the brief prayers interjected in the memoirs of Nehemiah—but its clearest witness is the iterated evidence of psalm after psalm. The true Jew was able to hold fast by ethical monotheism, in spite of all contradictions, because he knew the one, holy, righteous God—not only knew about Him, but knew Him as persons know one another.

It is not possible to do much more to illustrate this truth. The reader may be left to add further illustrations for himself. But, especially when one is speaking of a community, the spiritual always shows itself outwardly, usually in institutions that embody and symbolize the spiritual experience. This was so in Israel in the days after the Exile.

When we ask what the institutions were, we come upon the other two elements in religion, the ethical and ritual.

For the two institutions that Israel loved in these centuries with an exceeding depth of love, were the Law and the Temple. It is hard for us to do justice to this love, for two reasons. It is very difficult for any one to do justice to any ritual that is not the natural expression of his own spiritual life,—in which his own soul has not habitually been immersed. To us any system that centres in sacrifice, in the killing of animals, seems repulsive. We find it hard therefore, to sympathize with the worship of the Temple; and the ordering of the Temple worship fills a great part of the Law documents of this period. Again, Christians are used to thinking of the failures and shortcomings of the Jewish Law and Temple worship. This is natural, for it is their shortcomings that are emphasized in the New Testament; something will be said of them in the next chapter. But we need first to recognize, and to try to understand, the passionate love of the Jews, even of the best of the Jews, for just these two institutions. There is no doubt about the fact. To the Jew in Jerusalem the rising of the smoke of 'the morning and evening sacrifice' from the Temple court is comparable with the 'morning' and 'evening prayer' of Christendom. When, under Antiochus Epiphanes, it ceased to rise for three years, the Jew's heart flamed out in horror, and he betook himself to the desperate sword. Similarly, when the Jew of the Dispersion came on pilgrimage to the holy city, his heart swelled with rapture. Some of the later Psalms tell us with what intense rapture.

Nor is it true that for the better kind of Jew the ritual was mere ritual. He had not forgotten the lesson of the prophets that mere ritual is useless. No doubt there were Jews, as there are Christians, who did not keep the line between the spiritual and the ritual always clear, nor the line between the ritual and the ethical. But at least the best of the Jews knew these distinctions well enough. It is impossible to read such Psalms as the eighth, the fortieth, and the fifty-first, and to say that those who wrote them, or those who sang them, thought of Jehovah merely as a

God who demanded correct ritual. By now, at least the better Jew had learnt how to distinguish the three elements in religion, and he related them rightly to each other. He knew that the fundamental thing is to know God; that if a man knows God, this will manifest itself in righteousness of life; and that it will express itself in ritual. And he loved both the Law, which enshrined the finest ethic then in the world, and the Temple, whose ritual 'appealed' to him as it never can to us.

So far as the Law is concerned, there is proof enough in the fact that during many centuries it has held the 'Dispersion' together. Unable to worship day by day, or week by week, at the Temple, the Jews of the Dispersion at this time found a substitute in the Synagogues. They built these everywhere in the civilized world. They were the focus of Hebrew life in the scattered communities of Jews in the world-empires. No one was forced to attend them. Men worshipped at the Synagogue because they loved to worship there. And the whole worship gathered round the reading and exposition of the Law. Of this love for the Law, again, there are great examples in the Psalms. The longest of all, for instance, the 119th, mentions the Law, under one name or another, in all but one of its hundred and seventy-six verses. 'Oh, how I love thy law'—this is the passionate expression of Israel's joy in its great ethic and ritual.

It has been said above that the Hebrews of this period not only preserved the prophetic doctrine of ethical monotheism, but in some ways extended it. A few particular passages may be used to illustrate this, some of them illustrating the word 'ethical' and some the word 'monotheism.'

*a.* The first example may be taken from the Temple ritual. In the days before the Exile the kind of offerings called 'the sin-offering' and 'the guilt offering' are quite in the background. As has been seen,[1] the prominent

[1] Pp. 102f. 156.

sacrifices then were the 'whole burnt-offering' and the so-called 'peace-offering,' and in these the dominant concepts were gift and fellowship. After the Exile the 'sin-offering' and 'guilt-offering' come to the front. This was because the Hebrew's consciousness of sin was now much deeper.

At first sight this may seem to contradict the statement made above that the Jews were now the most righteous people in the world, but it only illustrates the familiar paradox that the greatest saints are the most conscious of sin. The Jews knew what the righteousness was that Jehovah demanded from men, and they knew, as none other, that they did not meet His demand. In the Temple they now sang such psalms as the fifty-first, 'Behold, I was shapen in iniquity, and in sin did my mother conceive me.' 'Create in me a clean heart, O God, and renew a right spirit within me.'

In the same Temple one of the great days of the year was now the Day of Atonement.[1] Its ritual is described in the sixteenth chapter of Leviticus.[2] The people gathered in the vast open-air court, facing the great open-air altar of sacrifice. The High Priest came out to them, not clothed, as usual, in splendid garments, not wearing his jewelled breast-plate, but clad in white robes of penitence. He slew a bullock as sin-offering for the priesthood and passed alone through the Holy Place into the Holy of Holies to sprinkle its blood in that secret shrine. Then he slew a goat as the people's 'sin-offering' and sprinkled its blood in the Holy of

[1] It is often said, on the basis of Num. xv. 30 and Lev. iv. and v., that the Jewish sin-offerings were only for 'unwitting sins,' but this does not apply to the companion class of guilt-offerings, for such sins as those named in Lev. vi. 1-7 and xix. 20-22, could not all be 'unwitting,' yet there was 'atonement' for these. In the case of the Day of Atonement too, I, at least, find it impossible to believe that Israel kept its solemnities year after year and century after century, the worshippers all the while coming and going with the consciousness that it had nothing to do with their known sins.

[2] It will help the reader of this chapter if he notes that the ritual is described twice,—once, more summarily, in verses 1-10, and then more in detail in the verses that follow.

Holies. It was on this one day in the whole year that any one dared to enter there. Having shrunk within its awful gloom and shrunk out again, the High Priest confessed the sins of Israel over the head of a second goat. This was then sent into the wilderness, carrying away the sins 'to Azazel,' a weird demon of ill. Then, and not till then, the High Priest donned again his glorious robes and offered the burnt-offerings, one for himself and one for the people. In these offerings Israel felt itself again one with Jehovah. They were the renewal of the daily burnt-offerings of the year.

It is possible, of course, to interpret all this—like so much other ritual—as 'mere superstition.' But it is also possible to interpret it as a series of great symbols of the awful righteousness of the holy God, of the separation that sin makes between Him and men, and of the need that this barrier should be done away if there is to be fellowship between God and men.

A great shortcoming in the ritual will be named below, but this does not mean that it was utter failure. It did bear witness to the Jews' conviction that God is holy, with the purity of utter righteousness, and that man is sinful indeed. On the Day of Atonement a devout Jew said in symbol what he said in words when he moaned the fifty-first Psalm. In this period the better part of Israel at least came to believe in 'the exceeding sinfulness of sin.'

*b*. We may turn next to two passages near the beginning of Genesis. The experts tell us that in the story of the Flood two documents have been combined, and that one of them belongs to a time long before the Exile and the other to the centuries that followed.[1] They also tell us that the story that 'once upon a time' the world was overwhelmed by water, is very widespread; and, in particular that it occurs in early Babylonian mythology. It is quite probable that there was once a great flood, or series of floods, in Mesopotamia.

[1] *Cf*. pp. 202, 239.

So far we have in Genesis merely a Hebrew variant of a legend founded upon fact. But the Hebrew account ascribes the Flood to a single God, Jehovah, and declares that the calamity befell the world because of the universal sin of men. Only righteous Noah and his family escape. In other words, when the Hebrews came slowly to mould their own account of the story, they left upon it indubitable marks of 'ethical monotheism.' Even their legends betray their great creed, or rather, as an expert in legends would say, *of course* their legends betray their great creed.

*c.* Again, the experts tell us that there are two accounts of creation at the beginning of Genesis, the point of division being at the fourth verse of the second chapter. Of the two the account that comes second in our Bible is ascribed to the pre-Exilic period, and the one that comes first[1] to the post-Exilic. This latter passage is rightly famous both in literature and religion.

In some ways, indeed, it bears the marks of its period. The idea that the world was made in a week, for instance, contradicts the findings of modern science. It may have Babylonian origins, though here the evidence as yet is scanty.

Again, clearly the author thought of the earth as a large flat area, of the sky as a solid blue dome that over-arches it and of sun and moon as moving repeatedly across the dome, and as finding their way somehow under the flat earth so as always to begin their journeys across the dome at the same side. Clearly, too, the author thought that above the dome there was water; probably he thought that, when it rained, some of this water was coming through the dome, 'the windows of heaven'[2] being opened. All this belongs to ancient 'cosmology.' If any one will rid his mind of the pre-suppositions of modern science, he will see that this is just what the world does, in fact, look like.

So far the author is just a 'child of his age.' But his

[1] Gen. i. 1-ii. 3. The division of chapters is here very unfortunate.
[2] Gen. viii. 2.

account of creation unerringly inculcates three great religious truths—that the one God made the universe; that everything that the one God does is 'good'; that man is made 'in the image of God.'[1] It is clear that there are here great doctrines of God and man. Without them there could be no Christianity. And the doctrines are so well taught that the children of many ages have inevitably learnt them as they have read the simple and stately paragraphs. They would not have learnt them either as certainly or as well if they had been cast in the philosophical or scientific language of to-day or of any other time. This is one of the greatest examples of the way in which God, working through the ways and ideas of men, has yet taught men His own great truths.

Some notes may be added. First, it goes without saying that a belief in monotheism underlies the passage. Second, at first sight it may seem as though the emphasis on the 'goodness' of God's handiwork teaches ethics, but the word 'good' is here used in a wider sense; 'light,' for instance, is not ethically 'good.' The place to begin on the ethical side is with the concept that man is in some ways 'like' God. In the context[2] the point of likeness is called 'dominion.' The author had noted that, in a limited but real way, man, like God, uses 'nature' for his own ends. We ourselves do this, as a matter of course, whenever we cut down a tree to make boxes, or kill an animal for food, or use wireless to carry news. The writer declares that this habit of man is part of the purpose of God. Yet to reach the full Old Testament doctrine of the nature of man, we must go beyond this passage. Its key is the reiterated claim of the Old Testament that man ought to be 'righteous' because God is 'righteous.' This idea is the true core of the belief

[1] As every one of these truths was a culmination,—i.e. each completed a long process of earlier Hebrew thought. For instance, Deutero-Isaiah had taught the first (*cf.* pp. 177f.).

[2] As in Ps. viii.

that man is 'made in the image of God.' So, here too, we reach the doctrine of 'ethical monotheism,' and we find it not as an otiose tenet, but as a living power.[1]

*d.* The doctrine of 'ethical monotheism,' if it is taken practically and seriously, involves a doctrine about the future as well as about the past and the present. The one righteous God must ultimately vindicate both His power and His righteousness; He must, in the end, set up a 'kingdom of God' upon earth. As we have seen, this was an element in the teaching of the prophets.[2] It is frequent also in post-Exilic literature; but there it takes, more habitually than with the prophets, an Apocalyptic form. Indeed, this might be called the dominant theme of Apocalyptic.[3]

One or two illustrations may be given. The future was still sometimes conceived as a Messianic realm, ruled by a scion of David. This particular concept is not now very common in the documents, but it has one great example in a passage that our Lord Himself selected when on 'Palm Sunday' He determined publicly to claim that He was Messiah.[4] In the apocalypse of Joel, again, there is an assertion of deep insight—that God's final realm can only come if every one of His servants is 'filled with' His Spirit.[5] This, of course, began to be 'fulfilled,' as Peter saw, at Pentecost.

[1] I have not enlarged upon the importance of the belief that nature is 'good,' but its practical issues go very far. For instance, since Hinduism teaches that nature is 'evil,' India, through all her millenniums, has never troubled much to examine it; it is in Christendom, with the first chapter of Genesis in its hand, that men have set themselves enthusiastically to explore the innumerable secrets of nature, never doubting the postulate that all those secrets are 'good.' The results of their explorations we call 'science.'

[2] P. 193.

[3] *Cf.* pp. 192f.

[4] Zech. ix. 9.

[5] Joel iii. 28f. This had an anticipation in Num. xi. 29. Jeremiah's prophecy of the New Covenant, and Ezekiel's repetition of the same idea (Jer. xxxi. 31ff.; Ezek. xxxvi. 26f.) had also, in effect, required it. In all these passages, however, it is Israel that is in view, not all mankind, as in Christianity.

Again, there is a very significant use of the phrase 'son of man' in one of the visions of Daniel.[1] It gives a good example of Apocalyptic. In the earlier part of the vision the four world-empires of Babylon, Media, Persia and Greece, are typified under the symbols of 'wild beasts'—a lion, a bear, a leopard, and a ten-horned monster. All these were under the sway of Jehovah, and served His purposes, though they did not know it. But no wild beast could be the symbol of the final world-empire. This must be human, not animal or beast-like. There is to come a last world-empire, and its symbol is 'one like unto a son of man.' It is to him that God gives 'an everlasting kingdom.'[2]

There is no passage in the Old Testament that thinks more nobly of man, or tells more nobly of the future. There is no need to say that Jesus' chosen name for Himself was 'Son of Man.' While He gave the phrase His own stamp, and while there are other passages in Jewish literature, both within and outside the Canon, that use the phrase, it is very likely that our Lord borrowed it from this vision. He was the one perfectly human being who has ever lived, and this is one of the two reasons why He 'shall reign' over all men 'for ever and ever.' The other reason is that He is God.

*e.* Another point should just be named, though, as it raised a problem that the Old Testament for the most part left unsolved, it belongs more properly to the next chapter. We have seen that, under the leadership of the great prophets, Israel began to learn what we call 'the value of the individual.'[3] This concept now became one of the axioms of ordinary Hebrew thought.[4] It clearly raises a problem for believers in 'ethical monotheism.' For, if the two concepts in the phrase be taken together, it

[1] Dan. vii. 13.
[2] For further details see such commentaries as Driver's in the Cambridge Bible series.
[3] Pp. 169ff. 192.
[4] This is shown in detail in *The Bible Doctrine of Society*, ch. iv

follows that the righteous God must do justice, not only to the world of men, nor only to nations, but to every single man. In His universe it is clearly wrong that even one wicked man should finally prosper, or even one good man finally suffer.

It was possible to point to many instances where God did justice to individual men during this life, but this did not cover all the facts. In particular, it did not cover the case of a good man who *died* in misery. The only possible answer to this problem was to claim that God would in his case vindicate His own righteousness in the Hereafter. It will be seen below that at this time Israel first began to feel after a belief in resurrection. So far as it did, it came within sight of a further development of the doctrine of 'ethical monotheism.'

## Chapter XVI

# THE INCOMPLETENESS OF THE OLD TESTAMENT

We now turn to the things that the post-Exilic Jew failed to do. The doctrine of 'ethical monotheism,' as he held it, asked certain questions, or started certain problems, that he was unable to answer and solve. All of them grew out of the great doctrine itself. The form that they assumed, however, and the insufficient answers that were given to them, took colour from the historical situation of Israel in the centuries that followed the Exile. Of these problems four were principal. Something will be said of each in turn, and some hint given of the way in which the New Testament faces them.

The first difficulty sprang directly out of the concept of monotheism. So long as men were able to believe in many gods it was possible to think of them as living, and marrying, and feasting, and behaving in general much as men do—in a more delightful way, no doubt, yet still in a very similar way. And it seemed possible for men to be on fairly familiar terms with such gods.

But whenever men reached the idea that there is only one God, it began to seem difficult to get to know Him and to live in close touch with Him. This is true in one way if the one God is thought of in a pantheistic fashion as immanent in the universe, and in another way if He is thought of as separate from the world of men. Under the pantheism of India, for example, the One Supreme, who is all and in all, ceased to be personal—and it is very hard to enter into living fellowship with the Impersonal. Popular Hinduism, therefore, retained a belief in a vast number of personal gods. If, on the other hand, the one God is not identified with His world, there is always a tendency to what is called Deism. The one God seems so great that men find it hard to believe that He will trouble Himself with such poor, little things as themselves. And the vaster the concept of the universe, the more difficult it is to believe this. It was this difficulty that beset Israel. She had come to believe in one almighty, personal God, who had made the universe and was sovereign within it. How was any mere man to hope that such a God would enter into fellowship with him? If even a mortal monarch is too great to bother with ordinary people, what about the Immortal beyond the stars? Yet all the time the essence of religion, as we have already more than once seen, is intimate fellowship between men and God.

How did the Jews of the four centuries before Christ meet this difficulty? It is true that there were Jews who, in spite of the difficulty, did 'know God' personally. Some of the Psalms show this[1] and there is evidence too in the earliest of the Rabbinic writings. None the less, the difficulty was there, however unconsciously or subconsciously it was felt. 'What is man that Thou art mindful of him? Or the son of man that Thou visitest him?' A great psalm posits the question, but it does not wholly answer it. Yet the representative Jew of the time had his own way at once of admitting the great gulf that seemed to be fixed between God and man and of seeking to fill it. He developed the idea that there are intermediaries between God and men. These intermediaries were not human, for the merely human would not serve the need; nor were they in the full sense divine, for this would mean that there was more than one God. They were superhuman beings with more or less of the divine about them.

For instance, there was a great development of the doctrine of angels. In the earliest Hebrew documents the 'angel of Jehovah' plays a considerable part, but in the

[1] P. 214.

times of the great prophets of the Monarchy angels do not much appear. With Ezekiel, however—that is, just when the doctrine of 'ethical monotheism' was becoming part of the mental 'make-up' of the ordinary Jew—angels again begin to become prominent, and the tendency strengthened. Here the Jew may have borrowed from the Persian, for in the Persian faith there is a large place given to such super-human beings, but if Israel borrowed just this from the Persian faith, it was because she seemed to need just this. There are examples both in the Old Testament[1] and outside it.[2] Yet, as soon as one thinks of the intimacy of worship, an angel seems a sorry go-between! He will understand fully neither man nor God.

Another attempt to bridge the gulf between them was made by the development of the doctrine of the Divine Spirit. This too was the revival of an old idea. The revival began here also with Ezekiel,[3] who once more shows himself as the father of the post-Exilic age. Yet this particular concept rather died away than developed as the period between the Exile and the Advent lengthened. It was only Christianity that at last did it justice. To discover the reasons is difficult, and would hardly be in place here, but there is no doubt of the two facts, that the doctrine of the Spirit dwindled in Judaism, and sprang to new life in Christianity.

There were yet other ways of conceiving an intermediary between God and men; but while some of them started from Old Testament passages, their development falls in Jewish books outside the Canon. There is, for instance, the concept of 'the Shekinah,' which began from the strange fire that was the symbol of Jehovah in several of the early records; there was the concept 'Wisdom,' which

[1] e.g. Zech. i. 9, etc. Dan. xii. 1. The doctrine of 'evil spirits' reached its Old Testament climax at the same time—e.g. Zech. iii. 1, Job i. 6.

[2] e.g. Tobit iii. 17; Bel and Dragon, verse 36.

[3] P. 172.

found a starting-point in the eighth of Proverbs[1]; there was the concept of the Logos or Word, which was, at least in part, of Greek origin, but which was linked to the Old Testament by such texts as 'The world was framed by the word of God.'

All these beings were more or less vague. None of them was human, but it was hard to say how far they were Divine. Apart from the angels, none was personal. They all point to the defect in monotheism named above. What was needed was someone who was Himself God,—for no one but God can enter into adequate fellowship with God; and who was himself Man,—for no one but man can enter into complete fellowship with men. The answer to this need is the Incarnation. 'No one knoweth the Son save the Father, neither doth any know the Father save the Son, and he to whom the Son willeth to reveal Him.' 'Come unto Me, all ye that are weary.' Man is weary till he finds God. Of himself he cannot reach the unreachable. But the unreachable can reach him—just in one way, by becoming man. The Jew had hints and surmises that he ought to be able to call the Almighty his 'father,' but the name only fell readily from Christian lips.

The gulf here spoken of reaches its final expression in the gulf between the creator and the creature. The philosophers of all ages, who have believed in a creator, agree in this finding. For the creature to seek to reach the creator is as futile as if a man, crying out for light, were to seek to leap to the sun. He cannot leap ninety-five millions of miles! But sunlight passes the gulf.[2] The eye cannot reach the sun, so the sun comes to the eye. Man cannot reach God, so God comes to him. 'He that hath seen Me, hath seen the Father.' 'This is life eternal, that they should know Thee, the only true God, and Jesus Christ whom Thou has sent.'

[1] See p. 190 above.

[2] The comparison with light underlies more than one of the great New Testament passages about Christ,—e.g. Heb. i. 3; John i. 8f.

But we are speaking, not only of monotheism, but of *ethical* monotheism; and this means that there is a second great gulf between God and men, deeper perhaps and wider than that between the creator and the creature. It is the gulf between the holy,—in the austere, ethical sense of that term,—and the sinful. Here, again, some of the Psalms, in particular, show that the best of the Jews were aware of the gulf. How should they not be with the centuries of the prophets behind them?

When John the Baptist came, he cried out that the gulf was there. And Jesus did not contradict him. Rather, He emphasized the gulf. Any careful reader of the Sermon on the Mount knows this. In it Jesus does not lessen the demands that the holy God makes of men; He enlarges and deepens them. He demands that men shall not be guilty of so much as a selfish motive or an unclean thought! And He did not set out in this teaching merely to display a great but impossible ideal. When we come to the end of the Sermon we read, 'Every one that heareth these sayings of Mine and doeth them not, shall be likened unto a foolish man. . . .'!

In the face of this great gulf the typical Jew of the period turned to the two great institutions of which we spoke in the last section—the Law and the Temple. Under the first of these he claimed that God did not demand too much of men after all; it was enough if he kept the six hundred commands of the Law. This is Pharisaism. And its deeper hypocrisy is that in it man refuses to face God's demands. He turns away from the demand for a 'clean heart' and a 'right spirit,' and, at first consciously, but ultimately sub-consciously or even unconsciously, he thinks that 'a decent, moral life' is all that God asks.

There was a Pharisee, however, who could not persuade himself of this. He has written an account of his agony as he faced the holy demand of God in the seventh of Romans. And, as he writhes before the inevitable demand, he cries, 'I cannot! I cannot!' In the eighth of Romans he cries, 'I can! I can!' The difference has come through the Death and Resurrection of our Lord Jesus Christ and the gift of the Holy Spirit. In the New Testament these three go together. In their own fashion the men of to-day repeat the error of the Pharisee; they do not live as though God cannot tolerate the least fleck of inward evil. They do not practise the belief that God is holy.

Other Jews of Christ's day turned to the Temple. We have already seen how the characteristic sacrifice of this period was the sin-offering of the Day of Atonement. We have seen how it epitomized the sense of sin in Israel and of the way in which sin severs men from the holy God. It failed, however, when it tried to show how to close the gulf. There were Jews who felt this; the writer of the Epistle to the Hebrews was one of these. Yet he loved the old symbolism too much to say that there was nothing in it, He said that it was an earthly 'shadow' and symbol of something real and heavenly. It was the 'shadow' of the Atonement! This is not the place to explore the deep mysteries that gather about the word. But, as Jesus bridges the first great gulf between God and man, so He bridges the second. When a man 'abides in Him,' inward sin shrinks and shrinks; and, as it shrinks, man steals closer and closer and closer to the holy God. This is the minimum of meaning for creeping Christians; the writer to the Hebrews, passing straight to the maximum, says that the Christian comes 'with boldness to the throne of grace.' 'In Christ' the gulf is gone.

The third great problem that ethical monotheism posed for the Jew was the problem of the Gentiles. The Hebrew had believed for many generations that Jehovah was the God of Israel. He still believed this. But he also believed now that Jehovah was the one God. It was impossible to hold that He had nothing to do with any nation except Israel. In some way or other, He must have to do with the Gentile as well as the Jew. How was he related to the Gentile millions?

In the period after the Exile there were several ways of dealing with this question. First, it was possible to leave the question on one side, and to concentrate on the belief that God loved Israel and would see to her weal. This is the way of such books as Ezra and Nehemiah. Second, it was possible to hold that all the Gentiles were wicked people, whom God would judge and punish. This was the attitude of such books as Esther and Deutero-Zechariah.[1] The name Particularism is given to these two attitudes. Next, it was possible to hold that God would set His one loved people at the head of the world-empire, and would set other nations to serve it. This means that Israel was to rule all nations as Assyria, and Babylon, and Persia had done. Some added that the nations would serve Israel's God. This is the attitude, for instance, of Trito-Isaiah.[2] It is a better kind of Particularism.

Lastly, it was possible to hold that, while Israel was indeed a 'peculiar people,' a people whom God had blessed above all nations, yet that He had given it its privileges so that it might share them with other nations. In other words, it was possible to hold that Israel was a trustee of the knowledge of the true God for the benefit of the world. The name Universalism is given to this idea. It is a very high belief, and it is one that Israel found it very difficult to accept. Has any nation ever found it easy to believe that its privilege, whatever it is, has been given it in order that it may give it away? But there were those in post-Exilic Israel who rose to this high creed. It was clearly taught, indeed, in the Exile itself by Deutero-Isaiah, for he spoke of the servant of Jehovah as a 'light to the Gentiles.'[3] The idea occurs too in Malachi, at least in one verse.[4] But its great expositon is the Book of Jonah. In this inspired allegory Jonah stands for Israel. He is bidden to evangelize Nineveh, the capital of his cruel foe, Assyria. He flees from the duty. The episode of the 'great fish'

[1] e.g. Zech. xiv. [2] e.g. Isa. lx. 10-16. [3] P. 179. [4] Mal. i. 11.

symbolizes the Exile.[1] Israel in Exile was like a man flung into the sea! It is not too violent a figure. Yet even in the sea God took care of 'His own'; He had 'prepared a great fish'! And Jonah is so sure of safety that he praises God while he is in the fish! After the Return from Exile Israel is bidden again to evangelize the Gentiles—Jonah is sent to Nineveh a second time. Now he does undertake the duty, but reluctantly. And he is disappointed by the success of his own preaching Then follows the 'gourd.' This is the final symbol of Israel's privilege. So long as it flourishes, Jonah is content; as soon as God takes it away, Jonah is 'very angry.' It is a masterly picture of the privileged man cuddling his privilege, careless of what befalls the rest of men. So the books show us two things,—that there were Jews in the days before Christ who were Universalist indeed, yet that the prevailing temper of Israel was Particularist.

To use the New Testament term, we here come to the problem of the Proselyte. The Jew's attitude to him was paradoxical; he 'compassed sea and land to make one proselyte,' yet there were Rabbis who called the Proselytes 'the leprosy of Israel.' And, of course, the Jew required the convert to keep the Jewish Law in all its details. We know how differently Christianity treated this problem. Our Lord's teaching, like the teaching of the prophets, is naturally universal. It makes demands, offers promises, opens 'eternal life,' to all men. We knew how Paul drew out the inevitable consequence that the Jewish Law, so far as it was merely ritual, could not bind a Gentile convert. We know how the Apostle contended for this faith against Jews without the Church and Judaisers within. Here, again, the New Testament solves a problem that baffled the Old. The evangel of Jonah was 'fulfilled' at last.[2]

The fourth unsolved problem was the problem of the Future. Here it is necessary to remember that there can be no proof of any doctrine about the future, of the same

[1] *Cf.* Jer. li. 34, 44. [2] Matt. v. 17.

kind as about the past. This difference affects all religions and all philosophies. It follows that, even when the New Testament doctrine is considered, it still can be called 'only a hope,' and it still leaves some questions unanswered. None the less, as will appear below, it does advance in a very definite way upon the Old Testament doctrine, and it has its own firm basis.

In considering the Old Testament doctrine, the ancient belief about the universe must be recalled, the belief that the earth is a sort of great flat plate, over-arched by a solid blue dome.[1] This concept, with variations, persisted till long after New Testament times. It must now be supplemented. The common ancient belief, among many nations —including the Hebrew, Greek, and the Roman—was that under the earth, or rather, in the midst of the 'stuff' of which the earth was made, there is a huge hollow, and that all the dead, good and bad alike, pass into this great hollow when they die. The Hebrew name for the hollow was Sheol and the Greek name Hades. In Old Testament times there was no idea that it was a place 'of rewards and punishments' or that it was divided into parts, one for the good and one for the bad. These developments began after Old Testament times, and for a long time they did not take any one fixed and accepted form among the Jews. In older Hebrew thought, as in other ancient thought, the dead or 'shades' carried on a vain, shadowy existence in the underworld in much the same way as men do on earth,—only, so to say, it was an existence 'with all the juice taken out of it.'[2] The best Old Testament example is the picture in Isaiah of the older kings and kingdoms of the world sarcastically welcoming Babylon and its king as they join the dead—'Art thou also become as one of us? How art thou fallen from heaven, O Day-

[1] Pp. 219f.

[2] There was also the idea that death was a kind of sleep, exemplified in the phrase 'he slept with his fathers,' but we know of no attempt to harmonize the two concepts. Few people to-day take the trouble to harmonize all their beliefs about the Future.

Star, son of the morning?'[1] The underworld wearily and emptily repeated this world as a shadow repeats it substance. Of course, under this concept the state of the living was better than that of the dead. The dead were all miserable together!

It is clear that this belief is not consonant with ethical monotheism. It is clear that it raised, in a culminant instance, the problem of the sufferings of the righteous.[2] If 'righteous' men died in their misery, what was to be said either of the power or of the ethics of the One God? And there were such men. The answer, on the basis of the ideas of the universe set out above—and the only answer—was that a good man would return from the underworld to the brighter and happier earth. The Old Testament began to give this answer. In at least two passages,[3] and perhaps in more,[4] it declared that the dead, or at least some of them, would rise again,—that is, would return here. In one passage, at least, this is asserted of 'many men,' good and bad, the good rising to 'everlasting life' and the bad to 'shame and everlasting contempt.'[5] But these passages are few; for the most part the Old Testament left the problem unanswered.

In the New Testament the Resurrection of Jesus changes everything. On its basis the confident creed arose that every Christian, like his Lord, would escape from Hades and live for ever. Sometimes his future life was conceived in an Apocalyptic way as life on a purified and renewed earth; sometimes in a more spiritual fashion as 'eternal life.' But in either case the Christian is to be like his Lord and with his Lord,—'So shall we be for ever with the Lord.' And the essence of this future was to be fellowship with God in Christ. 'This is life eternal, that they should know Thee, the only true God, and Jesus Christ whom Thou hast sent.' The future was to be the fruition and

[1] Isa. xiv. 9ff. [2] See pp. 222f. [3] Isa. xxvi. 19; Dan. xii. 2.
[4] Isa. liii. 9ff.; Job xix. 25ff.; Ps. xvi. 10f.
[5] Dan. xii. 2.

perfecting, that is, of a fellowship that begins here. When the good man begins this bliss, will he make any question of his sufferings here?

There was, however, another side to the problem of the Future. This world is clearly a very imperfect place. Was the good man who had died, to return to an imperfect universe? And, still more urgently, can the one good God leave this world as it is? Must He not vindicate His own righteousness by perfecting His world? Here the Old Testament had given a far more confident answer. As we have seen,[1] the prophets preached that God would one day establish goodness, peace and prosperity in the earth. And here the Apocalyptists had repeated the prophets' message in their own symbolic way.'[2]

Yet the New Testament made its own characteristic and revolutionary addition. Starting from the Resurrection of Jesus, it taught that our Lord is both master of the process by which the Kingdom of God is to come, and Head of it when it comes. It would be possible to quote most of such books as the Epistle to the Hebrews and the Apocalypse of John to illustrate this. Indeed, the belief permeates the New Testament.

But there is something more. Jesus Christ is master of the process of the world and its King at last because He suffered for the sins of men. In the Epistle to the Hebrews it is the great High Priest who shed His blood for His 'brethren,' who is 'seated on the right hand of God.' For the Apocalypse, 'in the midst of the throne,' there is 'a Lamb as it had been slain.' As has been seen,[3] the writer of the fifty-third of Isaiah had discerned the truth that prosperity comes by suffering for other men. Jesus brought this deep truth to its perfect climax. The Future is His, for He died for others. And good men—if any other is to be called good when we speak of Him!—will not complain, but rejoice, if they suffer with Him in

[1] Chs. x. and xii. [2] Pp. 192ff. [3] Pp. 180f.

this kind of redemption. So the problem of the suffering of the righteous is transfigured into triumph. And so Jesus Christ, the Suffering Servant of Jehovah, is the final vindication of ethical monotheism. 'He shall reign for ever and ever.'

It is now plain, perhaps, that the Old Testament is incomplete without the New. But it is also true that the New Testament is incomplete without the Old. 'Think not that I came to destroy the Old Testament; I came not to destroy but to complete.' There was one nation that, however falteringly, followed the lead of God until it reached the truth that there is but one God, and that He is omnipotent, merciful and righteous. This is Israel's unique achievement. It is on this foundation that Jesus builds the new Israel. Without it Christianity would be a house without a foundation. Or, to change the figure, it would be like a flower that had not grown on a plant. God does not make such flowers. When Israel had both found its way to its great, true doctrine of God, and had exhibited the incompleteness of that doctrine, then, at last, 'the fulness of the time' had come, and 'God sent forth His Son.'

# APPENDIX

## A.—TABLE OF DATES.

An attempt is here made to give the minimum number of dates needed for the understanding of the Old Testament. Nine are printed in italics; if any one will memorize these, he will probably find that they are pegs on which he will gradually be able to hang the rest of the Old Testament chronology. It is also of great value to remember the 'periods' named, for they not only relate the story of Israel to that of the world, but they give the key to much of the development of Hebrew religion.

The letters '*ca*' are an abbreviation for a Latin word '*circa*,' which means 'about.' Many of the dates are only approximate, and some of those given for the shorter books are by no means certain. For further details the volumes in Appendix C may be consulted. The findings of the experts for the historical books are summarized at the end of Appendix B.

| | Politics. | Religion. |
|---|---|---|
| | I. PERIOD WITHOUT ANY DOMINANT EMPIRE | |
| B.C. | | |
| between 1600 and 1220. | The Exodus. | Moses. |
| ca. 1000. | *David*. | Samuel.<br>Nathan. |
| | Solomon. | Building of Temple. |
| ca. 930. | Division of Hebrew Kingdoms. | |
| a. 890-840. | House of Omri in North.<br>*Ahab*, (*ca*. 850). | Elijah. |

2. ASSYRIAN PERIOD

| | | |
|---|---|---|
| | | Elisha. |
| | | Jehoiada. |
| ca. 840-740. | House of Jehu in North. | Amos. |
| | Hezekiah. | Hosea. |
| 722. | *End of Northern Kingdom.* | |
| 701 or 681. | Sennacherib fails to take Jerusalem. | Isaiah. |
| | | Micah. |
| ca. 620. | Josiah. | Zephaniah. |
| | | Nahum. |
| | | Habakkuk. |
| | | Jeremiah. |
| | | Hilkiah. |

3. BABYLONIAN PERIOD

| | | |
|---|---|---|
| 586. | *End of Southern Kingdom.* | Lamentations. |
| | | Ezekiel. |
| | | Deutero-Isaiah. |

4. PERSIAN PERIOD

| | | |
|---|---|---|
| 536. | *Return from Exile.* | Haggai. |
| | | Zechariah. |
| | | Trito-Isaiah. |
| | | Malachi. |
| ca. 440 or 400. | *Nehemiah.* | Completion of Canon of 'Law.' |
| | | Obadiah. |
| | | Job. |

5. GRECIAN PERIOD

| | | |
|---|---|---|
| 331. | *Alexander in Palestine.* | Joel. |
| | | Deutero-Zechariah. |
| | | Isaiah xxiv.-xxvii. |
| | | Jonah. |
| ca. 300-200. | Palestine under the Ptolemies. | Greek translation of Old Testament begun. |
| | | Completion of Canon of 'Prophets.' |
| ca. 200-150. | Palestine under the Seleucids of Antioch. | Ecclesiastes. |
| 165. | *Rededication of Temple by Judas Maccabæus.* | Daniel. |
| | Maccabæan Rule. | Completion of Canon of 'Writings.' |
| 63. | *Romans capture Jerusalem.* | |

## B.—THE DATES OF THE DOCUMENTS IN THE HISTORICAL BOOKS. (GENESIS TO NEHEMIAH).

It has been seen above (ch. xiv.) that the experts tell us that these books are not the work of single authors, but are the outcome of the work of many generations of Hebrew writers, and that to a very great extent they are the products of schools of writers, each school having its own religious point of view. Each of these schools used material that was already old, but it did not hesitate to use it in the way that suited its own religious purposes. This meant that it selected its materials. Sometimes, too, it threw the materials into a new form. There seems to have been no such idea as appears in Greek and modern historians—the idea that history should be written for its own sake, and should therefore be as 'objective' as possible. The Hebrew schools all wrote for a religious purpose. It will be remembered too that in the books that we call 'historical' there are large collections of 'laws'; and that for the Hebrews history was of value because it could be treated as the vehicle of 'teaching,' that is, of 'law' in the wide Hebrew sense (p. 201).

The sets of documents that form the present historical books may be assigned conveniently to four periods, as shewn below. Something may be said about each of these.

No one knows how old some of the documents are that fall under Section I. Some of them—for instance, the Song of Deborah, and the story of David's reign—were probably written down very soon after the events that they record. The list includes the chief passages in the Hexateuch (that is, the first six books in the Bible), that belong to the collections of writings that go under the letters 'J' and 'E' (see p. 199). No attempt is here made to give a complete list of passages assigned to them; for these the reader must refer to the commentaries; but those named here are, apart from unimportant editorial additions, assigned to this early period.

The second period (II) runs approximately from 740 to 550 B.C., and its spirit is Deuteronomic 'D' (see p. 199). It includes Deuteronomy itself and additions made by Deuteronomists to other records. It ought perhaps to be mentioned that the Book of Judges has a 'Deuteronomic framework,' within which the old stories are held in a unity. For instance, the references to the length of time that each hero 'judged' belongs to this framework. The traces of Deuteronomic interest are slightest in the Books of Kings (Solomon's Prayer in 1 Kings, viii, being an exception, as well as 2 Kings, xvii. 7-14). The Deuteronomic style is easy to trace, even in English.

The third period (III) runs from about 570 to about 450 B.C. It overlaps period II because the 'Priestly' school that produced the documents called 'P,' (see p. 201) began its work before the Deuteronomic school died away. Here too even an English reader may often readily discern a distinctive style and interest. It is to this school that we owe the Hexateuch in its present form. In drawing it up the Priestly editors used material both from documents J, E. and D, adding from still other sources as well. Some famous stories,—e.g. that of the Flood,—do not appear below because they are composite; that is, they include materials from documents of varying dates.

The Priestly school continued its work in later generations still, and we have further books from its industry in Chronicles, Ezra and Nehemiah (period IV). Here again the school used older material. Some used in Chronicles is probably very old indeed, but it is all thrown into the Priestly style.

## I.

### DOCUMENTS WRITTEN BEFORE 750 B.C.

| *Book.* | *Principal Passages.* |
| --- | --- |
| Genesis. | ii. 5-iv. 26 ; xii. i.-xiii. 18 ; xv. ; xvi. ; xviii.-xxii. ; xxiv.-xxvii. ; xxviii. 10-xxxiii, 20 ; xxxvii.-xlv. ; xlvii, 13-31 ; xlviii. 8-xlix. 27 ; l. 14-26. |
| Exodus. | i. 8-ii. 22 ; iii. 1-vi. 1 ; ix. 13-xi. 8 ; xii. 29-39 ; xiii. 3-22 ; xv. ; xvii. 2-xix. 25 ; xxi-xxiv. ; xxxii. 1-xxxiv. 28. |
| Numbers. | x. 29-xii. 16 ; xiii. 17-33 ; xiv. 11-25 ; xxi. 1-xxv. 5 ; xxxii. 1-27. |
| Joshua. | ii. ; iii. 10-iv. 20 ; v. 13-viii. 29 ; ix. 3-x. 27 ; xxiv. |
| Judges. | All except passages under ii. and iii. |
| 1 Samuel. | All except the Psalms and passages under ii. |
| 2 Samuel. | All except the Psalms and passage under ii. |

## II.

### DOCUMENTS WRITTEN BETWEEN 740 AND 550 B.C.

| | |
| --- | --- |
| Deuteronomy. | All. |
| Joshua. | i. ; viii. 30-ix. 2 ; x. 28-43 ; xi. 10-xiii. 14 ; xxi. 43-xxii. 8 ; xxiii. |
| Judges. | ii. 11-23 ; iii. 4-15 ; vi. 7-10 ; viii. 33-35 ; x. 6-18. |
| Ruth. | Some place this book here and some under iii. |
| 1 Samuel. | ii. 27-36 ; vii. 2-viii. 22 ; x. 17-27 ; xi. 14-xii. 25 ; xv. |
| 2 Samuel | vii. |
| 1 and 2 Kings. | All. |

## III.

### DOCUMENTS WRITTEN BETWEEN 570 AND 450 B.C.

| | |
| --- | --- |
| Genesis. | i. 1-ii. 3 ; ix. 1-17 ; xvii. ; xxiii. ; xxvii. 46-xxviii. 9 ; xxxv. 22-xxxvi. 43 ; xlvi. 6-27 ; xlix. 28-33. |
| Exodus. | vi. 2-vii. 13 ; viii. 16-19 ; ix. 8-12 ; xi. 9-xii. 20 ; xvi. 1-24, 31-36 ; xxv.-xxxi. ; xxxiv. 29-xl. 38. |

| | |
|---|---|
| Leviticus. | All, chaps. xvii.-xxvi. being earlier than the rest. |
| Numbers. | All except passages under I. |
| Joshua. | xiii. 15-xiv. 5 ; xv. 20-62 ; xviii. 11-xxi. 42 ; xxii. 9-34. |
| Judges. | xx. and xxi. |

IV.

DOCUMENTS WRITTEN ABOUT 300 B.C.

| | |
|---|---|
| 1 and 2 Chronicles. | All. |
| Ezra. | All. |
| Nehemiah. | All. |

N.B.—There is still much difference of opinion about the date of Genesis xiv. and of the Decalogue (Exodus xx. and Deuteronomy v.).

## C. BOOKS FOR FURTHER READING

THERE is an excellent sixpenny pamphlet entitled *A Scripture Bibliography* (Nisbet) which gives full information about books on all subjects connected with the Bible. The suggestions given below are meant to be an answer to the question, 'What should a reader of this book read next ?' The list is therefore quite short. Any bookseller will give information about the prices.

GENERAL. Both Sanders' *History of the Hebrews* (Scribners) and Sarson and Phillips' *History of the People of Israel* (Longmans) cover the same ground as this book in greater detail. For permanent use the *Clarendon Bible* is to be recommended. It is to consist of six volumes ; of these four have been issued (1933),—*from Moses to Elisha, The Decline and Fall of the Hebrew Kingdoms, Israel after the Exile,* and *Judaism in the Greek Period* (Oxford Press). *The People and the Book,* edited by Peake (Oxford Press), is a valuable survey of the present findings of Old Testament experts on all the important subjects.

For constant help in Old Testament study the one volume *Abingdon Commentary* (Epworth Press) and

Hastings' one volume *Bible Dictionary* (T. & T. Clark) are the best books. Their prices may seem high, but neither of them costs much more than a tennis racquet nor as much as a 'push-bike.'

TRANSLATIONS. The Revised Version should be used, in an edition that contains the marginal translations, as these are usually better renderings than those in the text. Most of the criticisms of the Revised Version have been levelled at its rendering of the New Testament, not of the Old. Moffatt's *New Translation of the Bible* (Hodder) is already famous. It is very illuminating, but in the Old Testament rearrangements and corrections of the Hebrew text are often silently made, while the rendering of 'JHVH' as 'the Eternal' is at least questionable. Modern translations of a number of separate books are mentioned in the 'Scripture Bibliography' named above.

HISTORY AND GEOGRAPHY. For the history Ottley's *Short History of the Hebrews* (Cambridge Press) is good, while Baynes' *Israel among the Nations* (S.C.M.) puts the story of the Hebrews into its proper international background. For the geography G. Adam Smith's *Historical Geography of the Holy Land* (Hodder) is *the* classic.

RELIGION. Oesterley and Robinson's *Hebrew Religion* (S.P.C.K.) is here the best book to read next.

ARCHÆOLOGY. Bedale's *Old Testament and Archæology* (Epworth Press) is a good introductory book. Barton's *Archæology and the Bible* (American Sunday School Union) gives all the relevant archæological information in a convenient form, apart from discoveries made since its publication.

CRITICAL INTRODUCTION. The findings of the Higher Critics are given in sufficient detail in G. Buchanan Gray's *Critical Introduction to the Old Testament* (Duckworth).

THE PROPHETS. It will have been seen that the prophets played a very great part in the development of Hebrew faith. Their books become fascinating when they are read in their historical context. In addition to the Commentaries named below, the following books may be mentioned. They are not 'commentaries' in their usual sense, but they present each prophet as a living man among living men. G. Adam Smith, *Isaiah* (Hodder, 2 vols.); J. Skinner, *Prophecy and Religion* (for Jeremiah; Cambridge Press); W. F. Lofthouse, *The Prophet of Reconstruction* (for Ezekiel; J. Clarke); G. Adam Smith, *The Books of the Twelve Prophets* (for the so-called 'minor' prophets; Hodder, 2 vols.).

COMMENTARIES ON PARTICULAR BOOKS. In the *Cambridge Bible* (Cambridge Press): the volumes on Genesis, Exodus, Leviticus, Numbers, Deuteronomy, Joshua, Judges and Ruth, Samuel, Chronicles, Isaiah, Daniel, Hosea, Joel and Amos, Obadiah and Jonah, Micah, Nahum and Habakkuk and Zephaniah, Haggai and Zechariah and Malachi.

In the *Century Bible* (T. C. & E. C. Jack): the volumes on Kings, Ezra and Nehemiah and Esther, Job, Psalms (2 vols.), Proverbs, Ecclesiastes and Song of Songs, Jeremiah and Lamentations (2 vols.), Ezekiel.

# INDEX OF NAMES AND SUBJECTS

# INDEX OF TEXTS

MALACHI



TOBIT



ECCLESIASTICUS



1 MACCABEES



BEL AND DRAGON



MATTHEW



MARK



LUKE



JOHN



ACTS.



ROMANS



1 CORINTHIANS



PHILIPPIANS



HEBREWS